SACRED SERVICE

in

CIVIC SPACE

SACRED SERVICE

in

CIVIC SPACE

Three Hundred Years
of Community
Ministry *in*
Unitarian Universalism

KATHLEEN R. PARKER

Meadville Lombard Press
Chicago, Illinois

Sacred Service in Civic Space: Three Hundred Years of Community Ministry in Unitarian Universalism.

Copyright © 2007 by Kathleen R. Parker

First Edition, 2007

Meadville Lombard Press
5701 S. Woodlawn Ave.
Chicago, IL 60637

ISBN: 0-9795589-0-5 (10)   978-0-9795589-0-0 (13)

LIBRARY OF CONGRESS CONTROL NUMBER: 2007929215

Cover design and interior design by Dan Doolin

Cover photos clockwise from top left: Benjamin Rush, Frances Ellen Watkins Harper, John Haynes Holmes, Olympia Brown, Sophia Lyon Fahs, Francis Greenwood Peabody, Carolyn Bartlett Crane, James Luther Adams, Joseph Tuckerman, Thomas E. Wise, Mary White Ovington, Clarence Russell Skinner, James Reeb, Mary Livermore, Adin Ballou, Frederick May Eliot.

Photos are courtesy of the *Dictionary of Unitarian Universalist Biography*, an on-line publication of the Unitarian Universalist Historical Society, with the exception of Francis Greenwood Peabody: courtesy of Andover-Harvard Theological Library, Harvard Divinity School; Sophia Lyon Fahs: courtesy of Union Theological Seminary Archives, The Burke Library at Union Theological Seminary, Columbia University Libraries; and James Reeb: courtesy of the Unitarian Universalist Association Archives.

Every effort has been made to secure permission to reproduce the images featured on the front cover of this book. Additional copyright holders are invited to contact the publisher so that proper credit can be given in future editions.

*For Grace
and Sam*

Contents

Foreword by Lee Barker   ix

Acknowledgments   xi

Introduction   1

Historical Theological Perspectives toward
    Community Ministry   5

PART I
The Pressing Rise of Liberal Religion

Chapter 1: Community Ministry in Early New England   15

Chapter 2: The Early Liberal Moralists   29

Chapter 3: The "New Religion": Authorship and Oratory
              as Public Ministry   45

Chapter 4: Community Ministers-at-Large in the West   59

PART II
Liberal Religion and Antebellum Reform

Chapter 5: Utopian Societies as Community Ministry   73

Chapter 6: Ordained Ministers as Reformers   81

Chapter 7: Reform Work as Lay Community Ministry   91

Chapter 8: Community Ministry in the Era of
              the Civil War   101

PART III
After the War: From "Gilded Age" to Social Gospel

Chapter 9: Mid-Century Continuities:
              The Theological Schools   117

Chapter 10: Suffrage Pioneers as Lay Community
            Ministers   123
Chapter 11: Ordained Women Move Ministry
            Beyond Congregations   133
Chapter 12: African Americans and Community Ministry 149
Chapter 13: The Social Gospel: Allies for Racial and
            Economic Justice   159

PART IV
20th-Century Challenges in Community Ministry

Chapter 14: The Politics of Peace Ministry.   173
Chapter 15: Ministries of Institutional Leadership   181
Chapter 16: Unitarians and Universalists at Mid-Century 197
Chapter 17: New Occasions Teach New Duties   205
Chapter 18: Engaging Social Change in the 1980s   219

PART V
Community Ministry Gains Formal Standing

Chapter 19: Founding the Society for the Larger Ministry. 241
Chapter 20: Community Ministry since 1991   251
Chapter 21: The Revival of Campus Ministry   271
Chapter 22: The Community Ministry Summit:
            A Framework for the Future   279
Conclusion   291
Notes   297
Index   345

Foreword

One needs to look no further than this seminary to see the change.

Less than a generation ago, Meadville Lombard Theological School served students who took up their studies with nearly a single-minded understanding of ministry. They arrived at the seminary door with the following assumptions: Ministry was carried out in congregations, and it was exclusively through congregations that the world would be reshaped in a vision of justice, equity, and compassion.

These days, students appear on our campus with a different, expanded understanding of the possibilities for ministry. These are the current assumptions: Congregational life is central to Unitarian Universalism, but ministry often calls one to be a "border crosser," one who moves beyond the center of the congregation in order to reshape the world with our common values.

This is the call to community ministry. It is carried out in prisons and halfway houses, in classrooms and homeless shelters, in every precinct where there is the demand for service and love.

There may be a movement-wide impression that this shift has taken place abruptly and recently. But there is a longer view to behold, and in this book, Kathleen Parker delivers it. In fact, the shift we are seeing today is one of many similar episodes that have occurred throughout the history of liberal religion.

Meadville Lombard is proud to publish this book. Not only does it add to the store of our Unitarian Universalist history, it also tells us about the life and pulse of our present day.

Drop into any one of our seminary classrooms, listen to ministry students passionately discuss their futures, and you will see there has been a change. *Sacred Service in Civic Space: Three Hundred Years of Community Ministry in Unitarian Universalism* tells us how and why.

— LEE BARKER
President and Professor of Ministry
Meadville Lombard Theological School
Chicago, Illinois
April 2007

Acknowledgments

T he process of researching and writing this history of community ministry has changed my life. For giving me this opportunity, I am indebted to the Rev. Dr. Dorothy Emerson. Dorothy obtained a grant from the Unitarian Universalist Funding Program to compile and edit a collected work of essays on community ministry. The Community Ministry Summit, held in Boston in 2003, endorsed the completion of this work as one of its goals, and it became my privilege to contribute a summary chapter of the history of community ministry. As often happens, the research soon took on a life of its own, and my intended thirty-five page historical chapter became a book-length manuscript, more suitable for publication in its own right. That work is what you hold before you now.

The individuals featured in this history of community ministry—known through print research and interview—are the people whose community ministries make this work everything that it is. Finding, organizing, and editing their stories would not have been possible without the assistance of many people. David Pettee generously shared the notes from his course in community ministry at Starr King School for the Ministry, which provided a blueprint from which to begin. Barbara Child provided an account of the founding of the Society for the Larger Ministry. Dorothy Emerson gave assistance with contacts and content advice. Both she and Charles Howe were essential to the editorial process, all three of us confirming with each other points of clarity, chronology, and interpretation. Neil Gerdes at Meadville Lombard Theological School gave advice in the beginning and supplied substantial additional direction in the final editorial stages of reassessing content and filling gaps. Mark Harris read a late version and offered important critical insights, most of which made their way in some form into the final document. Many others read and reviewed portions of the manuscript and offered helpful suggestions and encouragement.

I am grateful to all who so willingly agreed to be interviewed. Among them, my thanks go especially to Neil Shadle, Steve Shick, Leslie Westbrook, David Pettee, Deborah Pope-Lance, Tom Chulak, Maddie Sifantus, Mark Morrison-Reed, Carolyn McDade, Robert Rafford, David Arksey, Michelle Bentley, Cheng Imm Tan, and Orloff Miller. Their unique and compelling stories of ministry inspired me, as they will you, and their offerings of insight helped to clarify the direction of this book in important and meaningful ways. The others I do not mention were also vital to this work. My primary regret is that there are so many more with whom I did not speak at all. To all who have authored useful books or articles, you may find that your prior work has, thankfully, found its way into the pages of this volume. Responsibility for any errors of fact or omission falls to me alone.

I wish also to thank the members of the community ministry editorial committee—Anita Farber-Robertson, Mary McKinnon Ganz, Deborah Holder, Charles Howe, Maddie Sifantus, and Dorothy Emerson—for their gift of process and for their encouragement ultimately to let this volume stand on its own. A more concise version of this history will appear in the collected work of essays, still in process under the editorial direction of Rev. Dr. Farber-Robertson. In addition, I want to thank the Unitarian Universalist Funding Program for its generous financial assistance toward the writing and publishing of this work, Laura Horton-Ludwig for her scrupulous proofreading, and Dan Doolin for his very fine and creative typesetting skills.

Finally, I owe a very special thank you to particular members of my family—Alecia Parker, my daughter, and John Jewitt, her husband; Tom Parker, my son; Judith VanderWilt, my sister; and Marlin VanderWilt, my brother-in-law. They have sustained me with their love, encouragement, patience, and helpful suggestions. Lastly, I could not have written this book without the support and companionship of my friends at the First Unitarian Church of Pittsburgh, including Jennifer Halperin, our Director of Religious Education and the Rev. Dr. David Herndon, our minister. They have journeyed with me a long way. Today they celebrate, with everyone who has had a stake in this project, that this history of community ministry will at last be shared with all of you.

—KATHLEEN PARKER
May 2007

There is, I submit, a certain spirit which appears within and among us . . . in which we seek, in relationship, to enhance and enlarge the whole being and the whole community. . . . Community ministers have vital experience with this invisible church, this implicit congregation of All Souls, with its graceful persistence. . . . Any organized effort to respond to this spirit, to say yes to it, to encourage it, to embody it in the structures and institutions of the world, is the ministry of the true church of democracy. Rejecting all idolatries, it is committed to nothing but the deep purposes of a whole, democratic earth for all its creatures.

— NEIL SHADLE, "Community Ministry
and the True Church of Democracy,"
James Reeb Memorial Lecture, 1994

Introduction

Let brotherly [and sisterly] love continue.
Do not neglect to show hospitality to strangers....
Remember those who are in prison, as though in prison
with them; and those who are ill-treated,
since you also are in the body...

—HEBREWS 13:1–3

To minister is to serve. It is an act that takes place in the presence of a community of two or more people. In whatever form, it presumes a kind of engagement that is intentional, meaningful, and loving. In Unitarian Universalism, our parish ministers articulate the meanings of faith that call us as a church family to search out our best inner selves and to look for the same in others. They provide leadership to promote congregational coherence and to cultivate a faithful sense of mission. Beyond our congregations, community ministers bring the practical meanings of faith into a more expansive and amorphous arena of care. Their ministries attend to human needs in settings that often demand specialized expertise or connect with people in the most extreme exigencies of life.

This book is a celebration of community ministry in Unitarian Universalism. The stories collected here are about Unitarians,

Universalists, and Unitarian Universalists who have ministered to communities of people beyond the parish setting. In their time, they may have been known as ministers-at-large, social reformers, extra-parochial clergy, specialized ministers, and community-focused ministers. Much of the time, community ministers have been separate from parish ministers, but not in all cases and not in any defined sense. Often parish ministers have reached beyond their congregations, or have left them, to embrace the needs of the larger community. In other cases, parish ministers and community ministers have collaborated to incorporate forms of community ministry into the mission of the church. The intermingling of parish and community minister roles has been a common feature of ministry in community, as will be seen in the pages that follow.

This work also considers Unitarian and Universalist lay ministers. For reasons that are probably both personal and historical, such people did not enter ordained ministry, or if they did, they entered it after giving many years to lay ministerial work. The lay ministers in this book brought lifetime commitments based on intentional religious dedication to the work of improving society. They are included here because they offer critical "holy models," a phrase used by Frederick Eliot to describe lay persons living lives of religious vocation.[1] James Luther Adams described the "radical laity" as people who serve both as priests and as prophets. As priests they are "concerned with the interpersonal fellowship of the family"; as prophets they "share in the analysis, criticism, and transformation of institutions."[2] The lay "priests" and "prophets" described in this history of community ministry help us all the more to recognize and value the breadth of our Unitarian and Universalist commitment to wholeness in human experience and in society. Awareness of the full range of community ministry in our history gives added weight to our sense of religious purpose as Unitarian Universalists today. It also enlarges the place from which we may envision the continuation of community ministry into the future.

This book organizes the stories of community ministry by time period and/or category of service. These distinctions are not intended to be arbitrary or inflexible; there are cases, for instance, in which a ministry of reform, seen in the life of Theodore Parker, could also qualify as a ministry of authorship and oratory, and vice versa. The resulting structure appears like a compendium of individual ministers and their work, and in this sense the result may function well as a reference work for students of ministry and history. Care has been taken, however, to also contextualize these individual accounts in a narrative of relevant American social history, showing that the work being done by individual ministers reflects the economic and political conditions bearing upon life in each case. Out of this narrative emerges the primary thesis of this work: The human need that inspires ministerial insight and care is relative to time and circumstance, a premise that is fundamental to the range and shape of all ministerial work. In this way it is both incidental and central that a history of ministry traces an evolution in religious response to a changing world.

Secondly, it will be seen that Unitarian and Universalist ministers, engaged in the larger community, have often been at the forefront of needed social and political change, willing to challenge tradition when changes in law or institutional behavior promised greater wholeness in life. In this way, for example, Lydia Maria Child wrote to condemn slavery, Thomas Wentworth Higginson personally battled the Fugitive Slave Law, Ralph Waldo Emerson and Mary Livermore lectured to the country, Francis Greenwood Peabody laid the groundwork for the Social Gospel Movement, John Haynes Holmes proclaimed socialism as the religion of Jesus, Emily Greene Balch worked for international peace, Sophia Lyon Fahs fashioned a progressive religious education curriculum drawing on new historical biblical scholarship, James Reeb and others journeyed to Selma for the right of African Americans to vote, Neil Shadle and Michelle Bentley brought human renewal into places of urban blight, and Orloff Miller ministered to victims of AIDS. There are many more whose names appear in the pages that follow. Inspired by deep religious imperatives, they reckoned with brokenness as they found it and brought into being creative visions of healing and change.

Thirdly, this book recognizes that at the core of community ministry is a liberal theology, transcending any one construct of an afterlife, individual prophet, national identity, geographical attachment, patriarchy, or other exclusive and divisive mythology concerning the ultimate meaning of human existence. What is sacred in community ministry is the act of giving human care and connection out of a place deeper than any need for personal or political identification. What is sacred in community ministry is that quiet place of knowing, beyond all boundaries of belonging, that we are indeed all "in the body."

Historical Theological Perspectives toward Community Ministry

It is spiritually exhilarating to realize that in our small efforts, we are part of a great living stream of reformers, a great cloud of witnesses who seek to create the Beloved Community on Earth, who seek to place the stubborn ounces of our weight on the side of justice.

— RICHARD S. GILBERT, *The Prophetic Imperative: Social Gospel in Theory and Practice*

In *The Challenge of a Liberal Faith*, George Marshall relates the story of a Jesuit medical doctor who was on the faculty at Fordham University. He recalled that while he was in medical school at Harvard, a surgery professor who was a Unitarian would pause with his students over each cadaver and remind them that "this corpse was once the temple of the Holy Spirit." Marshall reflects that "the religious liberal is always cognizant that no matter the circumstance, the sense of the divine image, the innate human dignity, is never lacking." The liberal sees this as the "underlying issue: reverence for humanity, a proper sense of human dignity."[3] In this recognition, we see that liberal religion may free us from the constraints of doctrine and creed, but it does not free us from an imperative to live for the deepest, most worthwhile achievement of being human. Indeed, liberal religion calls us to that imperative.

In his classic foundational work, *On Being Human Religiously,* James Luther Adams put the need for liberal religion in historical perspective, which provides an appropriate framing for this book. Liberalism, Adams reminds us, emanates from a principle of liberation of the individual from "the idolatries of creedalism, of church and political authoritarianism, or nationalistic, racial, or sexual chauvinism."[4] It was out of the impulse to free individuals from the tyranny of state and church authority in the early modern world that a classic liberal philosophic and economic mode of governance was born. In the beginning, *laissez-faire* free market capitalism seemed like a good thing for all. Unfortunately, this "specialized" form of liberalism, as Adams names it, has produced "a possessive individualism that eschews responsibility for the social consequences of economic power" and is "virtually unaccountable to the general public." These "structures of domination" have "frustrated both equality and justice."[5]

Roger Betsworth, author of *Social Ethics: An Examination of American Moral Traditions,* similarly refers to this phenomenon of our times. He cites Alan Trachtenberg's *The Incorporation of America,* wherein is described the emergence of a changed, more tightly structured society with vast new hierarchies of control."[6] We know that this vast behemoth of power, directed by "a dogma of political nonintervention," has proven its potential to produce alienation of spirit and inequalities in material well-being.[7] The odds that liberal religion can have a significant ameliorative impact seem small. So also were the odds against young David in his mythic battle against the mighty Goliath, yet he rejected the heavy armor and sword of tradition in favor of approaching his adversary with "five smooth stones."(1 Samuel 17:38–40) With this analogy in mind, James Luther Adams proposes a theology by which religious liberals might approach the magnitude of suffering in the world, delineating five major principles as the "Five Smooth Stones of Liberalism."[8]

The First Stone lays out the premise that revelation is continuous, dependent always on creativity and processes not ultimately of our own making. Whatever the destiny of the planet or of individual life, "a sustaining meaning is discernible and commanding in the here and now." Theists and humanists alike, says Adams, can appreciate that God—or "that which ultimately concerns humanity"—enters our understanding here and now in ways that are about living in the world at hand. The Second Stone maintains that relations between persons ought ideally to rest on "mutual, free consent and not coercion." Thus, all persons by nature "potentially share in the deepest meanings of existence, all have the capacity for discovering or responding to 'saving truth' and all are responsible for selecting and putting into action the right means and ends of cooperation for the fulfillment of human destiny." The Third Stone affirms the moral obligation to direct one's efforts toward "the establishment of a just and loving community." This is what makes "the role of the prophet central and indispensable in liberalism," argues Adams. He describes the prophet as "one who stands on the edge of the community's experience and tradition, under the Great Taskmaster's eye, viewing human life from a piercing perspective and bringing an imperative sense of the perennial and inescapable struggle of good against evil, justice against injustice. . . . With fear and trembling, the prophet announces the crisis and demands an ethical decision in the here and now."[9]

With the Fourth Stone, Adams argues that the faith of the liberal must express itself in societal forms: in education, in economic and social organizations, and in political organization. Without these, freedom and justice in community are impossible. Injustice in community is a form of power, states Adams; the creation of justice in community requires the active organization of power by those not oblivious to the injustices of domestic, economic and political orders. With the Fifth Stone, Adams offers the hope-filled view that the resources available to us to create meaningful change should encourage our attitude of ultimate optimism. There is something in the genuine liberal perspective that, while recognizing the tragic nature of the human condition, "we continue to live with a dynamic hope." All good prophets sense that "at the depths of human nature and at the boundaries of what we are, there are potential resources that can prevent a retreat to nihilism."

These five principles provide theological grounding that is less about an individual's relationship to God than about individuals living among and for each other. Ministers in community, says Adams, are consciously open to the revelation of meaning in every day life. They approach ministry with an attitude of mutuality in relations. They undertake the often dangerous role of prophet in pointing out injustice. They actively respond to hurt and injustice, understanding that an organized effort is the best way to have an impact on organized structures of inequality, ignorance, poverty, and emotional alienation. Finally, they continually live in the hope that fulfillment of their vision is worth pursuing, keeping in mind the condition of humanity that makes each person precious and redeemable.

The sacred narratives of human history speak to these same principles. In the pivotal story of the Exodus, Yahweh is credited with freeing the Hebrew people from their enslavement in Egypt. This becomes the basis for an episodic narrative in which the people of Israel are exhorted to remember this saving act and to accord similar compassion to the poor and the outcast among them. Of this material, Arthur Simon writes, "There are no categories of people so low or so distant that respect for them is unnecessary."[10]

Among the Hebrew prophets, justice was to be the measure of fairness and wholeness in relationships, such that families and communities and entire nations would experience well-being. The prophet Isaiah is an important source for this message. "Seek justice, correct oppression; defend the fatherless, plead for the widow" (1:17), and again, "Behold my servant . . . he will bring forth justice to the nations . . . a bruised reed he will not break, and a dimly burning wick he will not quench; he will faithfully bring forth justice" (42:1–3). Writing from the eighth century B.C.E., Amos sees the gross inequities between rich and poor, and condemns the idle rich. "Hear this word, you cows of Bashan . . . who oppress the poor, who crush the needy. . . . The Lord God has sworn by his holiness that, behold, the days are coming upon you, when they shall take you away with hooks, even the last of you with fish-hooks"(4:1). For religious liberals, this ancient concept of God is disturbingly vengeful. It is well to remember, however, that such prophetic perceptions of divine wrath arose from a deep sense of human anger over cruelty and injustice in society. With their dire warnings, prophets were ministering to the most degraded members of their communities by calling upon those with means to bring about mercy and justice.

The early Christian scriptures brought forward a message of liberation and compassion that extended to an audience beyond the Jewish community. Early Unitarians relied on these writings as a revelation of what they called Pure Christianity, unadulterated by later doctrinal formulations. Jesus said "I was hungry and you gave me food, I was thirsty and you gave me drink, I was a stranger and you welcomed me, I was naked and you clothed me, I was sick and you visited me, I was in prison and you came to me" (Matthew 25:35–41). Here is a call for larger ministry to the most vulnerable members of the world family.

There are also stories of Jesus feeding large crowds of people with a very little food, yet there was miraculously enough for all to eat and some left over (Matthew 14:15–21; Mark 6:41–44; Matthew 15:32–38). In these accounts, Jesus had "compassion on the crowd." The food was distributed irrespective of people's status: "they sat down in groups, by hundreds and by fifties" (Mark 6:40). Further, the people were fed with what was at hand. An important lesson here is that small acts of ministry may have an impact far greater than one might imagine.

George Marshall characterizes the Hebrew prophets and Jesus as individuals who rose up against the power structures of their day. "The prophets spoke forth out of an outraged sense of moral indignation . . . Jesus of Nazareth condemned the scribes and Pharisees as 'blind guides; you pay the tithe of mint and anise and cumin, and have omitted the weightier matters of the law: justice, mercy, and faith!'" [11] Marshall also cites Gautama of India, who broke from his father's wish that he live a life of comfort. Having escaped the palace, finally, he witnessed Four Passing Sights: poverty, disease, old age, and death. From these experiences he gained the religious principles of mindfulness and the transformative power of the "non-self."[12] By this he would become Buddha to millions.

Mohammed confronted the acquisitive greed by which the Quraysh tribe dominated Mecca. Their earliest leader, Qusayy, had purposely placed idols for all the regional deities into the Ka'ba, thus requiring that pilgrims come to Mecca to honor and worship their gods. Caravans made the deep descent into the barren valley where Mecca lay and paid required fees to Qusayy and his successors. In this process, Mecca became a lucrative trading center that made the Quraysh tribe very rich. Mohammad came to understand that the only way to bring about social and economic reform in Mecca was "to overturn the religio-economic system on which the city was built." His prophesy that "there is no god but God" was an attack on the right of the Quraysh to turn religious practice toward its own financial gain. Mohammad's teachings admonish followers to seek inner peace and perform kind deeds in service to Allah.[13]

Humanism is based on faith in the possibility that we can achieve the best possible good for humankind through reason, scientific study, and compassionate attention to societal problems. Since the mid-1970s, *Humanist Manifesto II* acknowledges the full range of human capacities for women and for men, including the experiences of emotion and spiritual insight.[14] In real-life experience, Humanism affirms the commitment of liberalism to a world of human connection, justice, and healing.

Forrest Church holds before us an image of the "Cathedral of the World." The windows in the cathedral are of varying shapes, sizes, and colors, yet each is illuminated by the same source of light. We derive fresh power from this image as we reflect on the multiple religious forms in which humankind has conceived of the saving liberal commitment to justice, fairness, and wholeness in the world.[15]

Richard S. Gilbert integrates the practical and theoretical aspects of the Unitarian Universalist sense of purpose in ministry to the larger world.[16] Like Adams, he sees the prophetic imperative as "our impulse of conscience" emanating from our outrage over the indignities and inequities of our times. Just as historic extremes in poverty, wage exploitation, racial oppression, and unfair gender prescriptions have sparked us out of our complacency, we are called today, in the midst of our ultra-conservative materialist times, "to intervene in human history for the sake of social justice."[17] Gilbert is understandably somewhat cautionary, warning against the "too easy optimism of the early Social Gospel period" that has been chastened by the brutalities, wars, deprivations, and extreme conservatism of the twentieth century. He points out that in the new millennium, "we will need to do some serious soul searching and world repairing." He adds, "the two go hand in hand."

Liberal religion offers an expansive vision of the church writ large in the community. Gilbert's "Beloved Community" is also Adams' "community of justice and love" and Shadle's "parish as community"—the "true church of democracy." For Adams, the "holy thing in life is the participation in those processes that give body and form to universal justice." Whether one serves as priest, or prophet, or teacher, or healer, the call to community ministry is centered in this belief: that the Beloved Community of justice and love must be made real. Here is a theology that transcends traditional theological formulations of an afterlife, a supernatural plan for salvation, nationalist goals, exclusive categories, patriarchy, or collective creeds. Community ministers bring sacred service to civic space, in the great profound hope that from our ministry in the common places of life will arise the gift of grace, for ourselves and for others: a dynamic of restoration that does not "fix things," but "opens us up, giving us ears to hear and eyes to see; not by saving us out of this world, but by showing us this real world in which our salvation lies and must be worked out."[18]

PART I

The Pressing Rise of Liberal Religion

These opening chapters explore the emergence of liberal religious thinking in eighteenth-century New England and argue for its connection to community ministry. Central to the rising liberal religious message were the complementary ideas of God as a benevolent force and human beings as potentially righteous. From this message was derived a religious impulse driven by moral action on earth rather than fear of damnation after death. Ministry in community extended to Native Americans, soldiers in the Continental Army, the Boston poor, isolated western settlements, divinity school classrooms, and anti-slavery audiences.

CHAPTER ONE

Community Ministry in Early New England

T he New England Puritan structure of ministry has a bearing on our Unitarian Universalist concept of community ministry today. In colonial New England, the minister and the congregation participated in a covenantal relationship.[19] The minister's position was made official through a service of ordination and installation, by which the congregation (along with the help of ministers attached to other congregations) acknowledged his divine call and charged him to fulfill it. In keeping with this expectation, the Cambridge Platform of 1648 read, "There ought to be no ordination of a minister at large. He would be a pastor without a people."[20] The very liberal Brattle Street Church of Boston further enhanced the relationship of the individual congregation to the minister when, in the eighteenth century, it adopted a policy that allowed persons to "be established in pastoral office without the approbation of neighboring churches or elders."[21]

Some ministers were expected to balance what might be competing claims on their insight and leadership. Prior to 1650, a parish hired two ministers: one as pastor, and one as teacher. For example, in the early years, Rev. John Cotton was officially styled "the teacher" at Boston's First Church, while Rev. John Norton was the minister.[22] After 1650, these separate functions became the responsibility of one person. Implicit in this example is the Puritan recognition of the varied duties that any one minister would perform within the parish community. The Rev. Neil Shadle, Professor Emeritus at Meadville Lombard Theological School, reminds us that in colonial New England, "the 'parish' was the whole of the town. Most everyone belonged to the church by virtue of residency, though voting was reserved for the converted and the propertied."[23] In this way, parish ministry was one with community ministry, a fact of leadership and obligation that served to maintain theological integrity and social order in the community at large.

As we know, however, maintaining the ideal of community as parish became problematic in reality, as a theology of conformity was used to empower a politics of exclusion and abuse. The Puritans did want cohesive community; they did want economic fairness, even limiting profit by law to five percent. But the cruel banishment of early dissenters is evidence of the rigidity of their orthodoxy. David Robinson joins Conrad Wright in arguing that the indigenous origins of our liberal religious grounding are found in early models of religious dissent, beginning with the antinomians, who argued that revelation was personal and ongoing.[24] Such an impulse would prove contrary to the weighted Calvinist formulation of depravity and election. Perhaps it is from this place, where theology became a moral question rather than a doctrine of judgment, that we derive our impulse for community ministry.

Early in the tradition, Rev. John Eliot ministered to the Native people destined to endure the intrusion of English/European settlement and undergo near virtual extinction. Eliot had composed a written alphabet in the Algonquian language and then produced a translated version of the Bible.[25] Appointed as "apostle to the Indians" in 1646, he led the movement of regional Indians into "praying towns." This was in part a fulfillment of a plan articulated in the 1629 Massachusetts Charter aimed at "winning and inciting the Natives of the country to the knowledge and obedience of the only true God and Savior." [26] Indeed support for evangelizing the Native Americans came from London. In 1650, the English Parliament passed an act to "propagate the Gospel of Jesus Christ in New England." Money was collected from all parishes in England and Wales, with the result that by 1674, there were sixteen Indian "praying towns" inhabited by nearly a quarter of the Indian population of southeastern New England. Further, the president of Harvard College, Henry Dunster, generously joined in these efforts by purchasing lands for Indians to "live in an orderly way" and voted that Eliot be paid a gratuity for his continued work. [27]

Fulfilling this goal of the Massachusetts Charter, it turned out, was a conflicted process, as good intentions got mixed with rationalization, presumption, avarice, and ultimately violence. The program of praying towns had, for example, taken on greater appeal among Native peoples as a refuge in the aftermath of the brutal Puritan slaughter of the Pequot tribe in 1638. Four decades of continued English encroachment bred hatred and ultimately sparked the 1675 coordinated Indian assaults known collectively to the English as King Philip's War. These attacks constituted a war of terrible proportions in which 4000 Indians and 2000 Puritans lost their lives. Metacom, chief of the Wampanoag and leader of the assault, was taken captive and beheaded. When his family and hundreds of other Indians were sold into slavery in the West Indies—surely a death sentence—John Eliot protested, drawing on biblical texts to argue that enslavement of the Indians was immoral. We are told that "Eliot's pleas fell on deaf ears and much of his work lay in shambles." [28] Eliot could not have supported the actions taken by Metacom and his followers, but he also could not condone the repercussions exacted on the Indians by the English. The Native people had become his parish community.

An evangelical Congregational minister, the Rev. Eleazar Wheelock, had been attempting since 1754 to educate and Christianize Indians at his Moor's Indian Charity School in eastern Connecticut. He had begun this school out of his work with individual Mohegan Indians, whereupon he came to envision a plan for educating and converting Indians by removing them from their native environment and bringing them to his school. Moor's School met with mixed results, as some Indian students sickened and died in these strange surroundings. Nonetheless Wheelock determined to enlarge his educational program via a new college, obtaining in 1769 a [Royal] charter from the governor "for the education and instruction of Youth of the Indian Tribes in this Land in reading, writing and all parts of Learning." From this effort came Dartmouth College in Hanover, New Hampshire.[29] One successful student of Moor's School was Joseph Brant, a Mohawk who negotiated with the English Crown on behalf of the Iroquois Nations. Brant's children attended Dartmouth College.[30]

The eighteenth century ushered in multiple changes in thinking and circumstance, the signs of which appeared in incipient form in the hundred years or so prior to this time. Discoveries in science and medicine were evidence that the world held vast potential for investigation. Implicit in these developments was an optimistic view that people had the capacity to reason and to improve themselves and their circumstances in life. In the matter of religion, Sir Isaac Newton's proofs of gravity held out the promise of "an ordered, benevolent Universe, the product of a rational and benevolent God."[31] Certain liberal New England ministers found in these ideas the basis for a re-orientation in their view of revelation and religious purpose. In his Dudleian lectures of 1759, Ebenezer Gay spoke of external nature as a source of "natural religion" with emphasis on its moral implications. Religion mattered only to the extent that it could be practiced. The "pull of gravity," he said, "symbolizes the automatic inclination of the soul" to seek the will of God in "acts of human kindness and divine worship."[32]

They called it "Supernatural Rationalism." At the forefront of this thinking were three liberal Congregational ministers in eastern Massachusetts—Ebenezer Gay, Charles Chauncy, and Jonathan Mayhew—who saw divine revelation in nature, but insisted that it be complemented by reliance on biblical revelation as well. The latter, notes Robinson, is what separated this movement from the Deists, who thought it was enough to rely on natural revelation alone. The thrust of their thinking was to attack Calvinist doctrines of original sin and election to salvation, which they believed under-mined human inclination toward moral action. Jonathan Mayhew's *Seven Sermons* of 1748 wrote of private judgment as the necessary arbiter of religious opinion—certainly an affirmation of the ongo-ing process of revelation—seeing in religious experience "the cen-tral truth of a moral law written on our hearts."[33]

Here is where the seeds of a liberal religious idea known as Arminianism began to take root in colonial New England. Armin-ian thinking held that humans are born with the capacity for sin and for righteousness, and emphasized developing the "potential for goodness in human nature."[34] The doctrines of total depravity, predestination, and election were necessarily incompatible with the Arminian view. Robinson reflects on these developments and concludes, with Conrad Wright, that liberal theology in America acquired staying power in the eighteenth century due to this growing disaffection from Calvinism. As Robinson phrases it, an indigenous liberal religious movement "took root in the rich soil of Calvinist decay."[35]

Charles Chauncy, the scholarly minister of the First Church of Boston, brought the Arminian view to bear against George Whitefield, the itinerant revivalist from England who was preaching in the colonies in the revival style that marked the Great Awakening. In his *Enthusiasm Described and Cautioned Against* (1742), Chauncy claimed that the passions of the revivalists were not an "inspiration by the spirit of God" but rather the "influence of an over-heated imagination." Indeed he regarded revivalist enthusiasm as unchar-itable and exclusionary—which therefore made it immoral.[36] This view signaled the indigenous seeds of American Unitarianism, well before Joseph Priestley arrived from England. It was formulated on "a commitment to the moral, as opposed to the theological, stan-dard of judgment, combined with Biblicism and rationalism."[37]

The rational anti-Calvinist views shared by Chauncy and other Arminians stood in contrast to both the emotional Calvinism of the "New Light" revivalists and the formal Calvinism of the "Old Light" orthodox. The extent to which the moral emphasis assumed by the Arminian view was different is perhaps better understood in light of the following example. Colonial involvement in King George's War (1746–1748) left Boston with a sizeable population of widows and orphans. Boston's leaders responded by constructing a two-story workhouse where the able-bodied poor would be expected to live and engage in productive pursuits such as "spinning flax, weaving linen, and picking oakum." It was understood to be a hopeful thing, of benefit both to the poor and to the larger public. Chauncy argued that because of this effort, "some hundreds of Women and Children have been kept at Work, whereby they have done a great deal towards supplying themselves with Bread, to the easing the Town of its Burthen in providing for the poor."[38] Chauncy's tone is noticeably more generous than that of the highly orthodox Cotton Mather, who had written, "for those that Indulge themselves in Idleness, the Express Command of God unto us, is That you should let them Starve."[39] Ultimately, the workhouse did not succeed and the building was sold to the British as a barracks in 1768. The poor widows for whom it was created refused to leave their own dwellings to live and work outside the rhythms of their daily routines. This story is a reminder that liberal religion must be mindful of its own suppositions, and be open to the enlightenment of revelation in daily life.

Chauncy's more optimistic view of human nature led him to compose in 1784 a work suggesting the eventual salvation of all souls. He titled it *The Mystery Hid from Ages and Generations . . . or The Salvation of all Men.* He wrote, "As the First Cause of all things is infinitely benevolent, 'tis not easy to conceive that he should bring mankind into existence, unless he intended to make them finally happy."[40] Chauncy kept his authorship secret, fearing that it would link him too closely with John Murray and other detested Universalists. Murray had brought from England a Rellyan version of Universalist thinking, but as with the Arminians, an indigenous version had earlier sprouted among disaffected Baptists who found Calvinist doctrines of human depravity and election too harsh, particularly in the overheated environment of revivalism. As David Robinson observes, the "necessity of salvation" was "pulling against the question of election to grace."[41] Thus, when Thomas Potter welcomed John Murray at Good Luck Point in New Jersey, he was already sympathetic to Universalist belief. Another pre-Murray convert was Caleb Rich of Massachusetts. Rich had arrived at Universalism through a personal struggle in which the threat of Hell did not seem to him a worthy motivation for living a good life.

Universalists were condemned in both England and America. Rich had been a Baptist, but when he began preaching his idea of universal salvation to his fellow Baptists, he was denied fellowship in the Baptist church. Eventually he attracted followers in Warwick, Massachusetts, where he established in 1774 the first Universalist Society in America.[42] In England John Murray had been voted out of his Methodist society when he began preaching John Relly's version of Universalism. When he came to America in 1770, he met with new forms of resistance—from revivalist Baptists and orthodox Calvinists, as well as the more highly educated, Arminian-thinking liberal Congregationalists. In 1774, he was finally invited to preach to a group of Rellyan Universalists in Gloucester. Immediately members of established churches began expelling their members who attended Murray's services, which led him to establish an independent Universalist church.[43]

John Murray had come to America after the premature deaths of his wife and son, hoping to "bury himself in the wilderness."[44] In spite of the early opposition he encountered, he is said to have made friends "among every class of people, from the highest to the most humble," even gaining the friendship of some Anglican and Congregational ministers.[45] In late spring of 1775, Murray was invited by the officers of the Rhode Island Brigade, stationed with the army besieging Boston, to serve as their chaplain. At this point, we might say he assumed the role of a community minister. When George Washington arrived in Cambridge to take charge of the Revolutionary forces, Murray was with the Rhode Island Brigade paying their respects to the Commander in Chief. As a chaplain, Murray met with opposition from other chaplains who had sought his removal. Washington confronted this opposition by confirming Murray's appointment as chaplain with a commission. This was high civic affirmation of sacred service, an act which transcended theology. As it turned out, Murray's term as military chaplain lasted only seven months due to illness. He soon found an alternate way to minister, however. The war had interrupted commercial enterprise, which brought great hardship to many families. In response, Murray solicited funds from army officers to supply food and provisions to "upwards of a thousand individuals" in the winter of 1776.

Despite his work in service to the American cause, Murray came under investigation by the local Committee of Public Safety in Gloucester, perhaps because of his English birth, or perhaps because this is where he had experienced the most outspoken religious opposition. Indeed, Murray had been described by those who bore him ill will as "one of the most unprincipled of all men . . . a consummate hypocrite . . . and an unprincipled adventurer."[46] To counter the investigation, Major General Nathaniel Greene, the military strategist whose consummate leadership led to the defeat of Cornwallis in the South, submitted a letter attesting to Murray's good character. This probably helped clear him of political suspicion.[47] In spite of being called a "false and dangerous man" whose ideas were "heretical," Murray embraced opportunities for wartime community ministry, serving as a Universalist chaplain to the Continental Army and as administrator of aid to war-torn destitute civilians.

Other mission work was inspired by the trauma of the years after the war. With increased mobility, disputes over land claims, rising economic competition, and Federalist tax policies that favored eastern elites, common people in frontier towns felt economically oppressed by century's end. This was the context in which Universalist minister Paul Coffin made four annual trips along the Coos Road into west-central Maine from 1796 to 1800. Here he sought to resolve religious disputes between neighboring communities. Such religious disputes as Coffin found in the remote villages of Maine were a continuation of the earlier eighteenth-century story of religious ferment. On the frontier, citizens looked to their own resources to survive the extremity of their circumstances and embraced a more personal view of God, rooted in a re-intensified Calvinist understanding of sin and salvation. From among their ranks, however, there soon emerged others who found in that intensity reason to reject Calvinist doctrines altogether. Their message of Universal salvation spread rapidly in frontier communities through the likes of missionaries like Paul Coffin.

The eighteenth century in America was also a time of near-unrelenting warfare, accompanied by losses of life, economic instability, and social dislocation. In response, concerned individuals established relief institutions that attracted the support of churches and their ministers. In 1770 there were fifty charitable institutions in operation throughout New England; by 1820, it is estimated there were over 2000 such institutions. Among these early reformers, none were as dedicated as Philadelphia physician Benjamin Rush. Rush was a pioneer in promoting the general health of the population, establishing in 1786 the first free dispensary in the country. When Philadelphia was hit by a great yellow fever epidemic in 1793, Rush cared for those struck down by the dread disease, keeping meticulous records in the hope of determining a cure.

Significantly, Rush pioneered the idea that alcoholism was a disease rather than a sin. He published in 1784 *An Inquiry into the Effects of Spirituous Liquors on the Human Body and Mind*. Drunkenness, Rush argued, was a disease of the will that built up gradually over time. Having offered his diagnosis, Rush advocated a "sober house" where drunkards could get special treatment and appealed to "ministers of the gospel of every denomination" to help him "save our fellow men from being destroyed by the great destroyer of their lives and souls."[48] Rush's insistence on radical bloodletting as a general treatment, unfortunately, probably produced more harm than good. Nonetheless, he was widely admired as a physician and immensely popular as a professor, his lectures drawing crowds of students beyond the capacity of the classroom to hold them.

Benjamin Rush is important to this history of community ministry because his work was framed by a religious view that he called the "universality of atonement." In 1780, he abandoned his Calvinist upbringing, and later reported, "From that time on I have never doubted upon the subject of the salvation of all men." The strength of his Universalist convictions became increasingly evident in his dedication to humanitarian reform. Rush embraced humane approaches toward mental illness, advocating "kind treatment" along with the usual regrettable bleeding. His typology of insanity earned him the title "the father of American psychiatry." Over time, Rush would champion prison and judicial reform, the abolition of slavery, an end of the death penalty, the education of women, conservation of natural resources, proper diet, abstinence from the use of tobacco and strong drink, and the appointment of a "Secretary of Peace" to the federal cabinet. When Rush died, John Adams wrote of him, "I know of no Character living or dead, who has done more real good in America."[49]

In the eighteenth century, Arminian (later Unitarian) and Universalist beginnings cleared small spaces in the densely wooded landscape of orthodoxy to plant seeds of liberal religious thought and practice. They posed two emergent alternatives to the Calvinist status quo, each offering in its own way a more optimistic view of the human capacity for good. One was taken up by the more educated and economically well-situated; the other was embraced by people closer to the ordinary exigencies of life. In both cases, the possibility for being righteous was not precluded by the doctrine of election; in both cases, compassion and the capacity for righteousness took precedence over depravity as the lens through which to view humanity.

This chapter emphasizes the development of liberal religion in the eighteenth century as a necessary precondition for community ministry. The Arminian religious views articulated by Charles Chauncy, Jonathan Mayhew, and Ebenezer Gay constituted a significant shift in affirming a theology of human moral action and intelligence before God. In the same period, the emergence of a conviction of universal salvation, as voiced covertly by Charles Chauncy, and forthrightly by Universalist preachers Caleb Rich and John Murray, affirmed a theology of human possibility in the larger scheme of God's benevolent creation. By the last decades of the century, the Congregational churches of eastern Massachusetts found increasing signs of division among their parishioners. Conservative congregants remained tied officially to the Westminster Confession, affirming the doctrines of reformed (Calvinist) theology.[50] Within their ranks, however, large numbers of liberal congregants were now moving toward an Arian view, which questioned the doctrine of the Trinity. The presence of the two factions within the denomination culminated finally in a pronounced break into two religious sects with the election of the more liberal Henry Ware, Sr. as the Hollis Professor of Divinity at Harvard College. Because Ware stood in the tradition of eighteenth-century liberal Christianity, it is fitting to conclude this chapter with a brief account of his election to the post at Harvard. His position as Professor of Divinity is also important because it demonstrates an early form of community ministry, training ministers for spiritual leadership in Massachusetts congregational churches.

Ware had been able to attend Harvard through the financial support of his older brothers, their father having died when Henry was fifteen. He graduated with highest honors in 1785 and was invited to serve as minister to the First Parish of Hingham, Massachusetts, after completing two years of private study. Harvard had functioned since its founding in 1636 as a school for the classical training of ministers and magistrates for a godly commonwealth. The curriculum applied to ministers, lawyers, and merchants alike. All took general courses, and though Hebrew was available, there were no formal courses in theology for advanced students. Rather, training for ministers followed graduation and was accomplished through an apprenticeship with a settled clergyman, or through tutelage under a professor of theology.[51] Thus, Ware's years of private study after graduating were consistent with an ongoing expected pattern.

In relation to the Congregational factions, Ware was well known to be in the liberal camp. His views were representative more particularly of a version of the tradition of "Supernatural Rationalism," which had, since the time of Chauncy, been comprised of a doctrine of Natural Religion complemented by Christian revelation derived from the Bible.[52] He had further taken an Arian position, by which Christ was believed to be more than a mere man, but not one person of a triune God; he was not God, but was the son of God, a super-angelic being who existed from the beginning, whose role was to provide a pattern of perfect obedience to God's will.[53] Ware's election to the Hollis professorship was opposed by the more conservative Trinitarian faction who believed it was important to stay firm on "the proper divinity of Jesus Christ."[54] But in his anti-Calvinist and anti-Trinitarian views, Ware stood right about where most of his liberal contemporaries stood. He also represented where they did not stand: they were not Deists or free thinkers in that they still looked to the Bible to find God's purposes. They should also not be confused with Transcendentalists, who came later. Ware's generation based religion on external evidences rather than inner consciousness; and they did not think of Nature as a source of ecstasy but rather as a rational source of revelation.[55]

Ware's views are more fully accessed in the weekly lectures he was required to give as Hollis Professor of Divinity. The lectures ran on a four-year cycle, so they were repeated a number of times over the course of his tenure. They were collected in 1842 into a two-volume book entitled *Inquiry into the Foundation, Evidences, and Truths of Religion*. Ware's *Inquiry* reveals that he had moved from an Arian view of Christ to a Socinian view, whereby Christ was simply a man and had no existence before his birth into this world. This shift was typical of Ware's generation of American anti-Trinitarians, adopted a generation earlier in England. Ware predicated religion on the existence of God, who bestows many blessings, requires obedience, and holds out the promise of eternal life. Notably, Ware argued that "Religion consists not in our having right views either of truth or duty, but our being brought into that state of affections, and the subjection of the will to the will of God...." Thus, Wright observes, Ware's concept of religion focused "not on Christian evidences and Christian doctrine, but on the quality of the inner spiritual life."[56] His was a subdued piety, however, also typical of his generation. Objecting to emotional religious conversion, he wrote, "The most perfect character is formed by gradual increases from strength to strength ... religion is not a transient emotion, does not consist in a few acts, that flow from sudden impressions; but is a fixed character. . . ."[57] Younger contemporaries would soon demonstrate a warmer, more fluid style of religious expression, of special relevance perhaps to the era of reform they had the privilege to inherit. We will learn their story in the next chapter.

The proliferation of religious sects in the eighteenth century led to the end of the Standing Order, the arrangement by which states had provided financial support for the dominant church, in the event that church members were unable to do so. Murray's Universalist society in Gloucester was among the first in Massachusetts to resist paying a tax in support of the Congregational church. It won an exemption in 1786 after a three-year court battle. Baptists would accomplish a broader end in the same year in Virginia.[58] These changes enhanced the autonomy of emerging congregations and at the same time identified ministers by their attachment to a given denomination. As protector of the undifferentiated social order that supported it, the early Puritan church had long been in retreat. Ironically, it is in that Puritan covenantal model that we are able to locate the parish in the larger community, even in a heterogeneous secular state.[59] In the liberal theologies that broke with orthodox Calvinism and rejected innate depravity, we find a moral imperative alert to human need in the larger human family.

CHAPTER TWO

The Early Liberal Moralists

For the Congregationalists, the irony of Ware's election to the Hollis Professorship is that he did not get the post precisely because he was a liberal. It was in fact proposed that Ware be made the President of the College and a well-liked moderate Calvinist, Dr. Jesse Appleton, be given the professorship. This idea was rejected because one person in the Corporation, Eliphalet Pearson, had ambitions of his own to become the president; furthermore, Appleton was perceived to have "a dissonant and unpleasant voice." Ware, it was conceded, met the standards that Thomas Hollis had prescribed for his foundation: that the professor should hold the Bible as "the only and most perfect rule of faith and practice" interpreted "according to the best light God had given him." Hollis had avoided giving any narrower creedal instruction than that.[60]

Ware's election was perceived by the conservatives, led by Jedidiah Morse, as a revolution. They departed and founded Andover Theological Seminary in 1808. This left the liberals to build up a program of theological instruction that would serve a constituency in which "Calvinism no longer held a monopoly." As Professor of Divinity, Henry Ware, Sr. participated in the movement to provide "more systematic guidance of the students in theology."

He taught a critical interpretation of the Greek Testament and gave instruction in "positive and controversial Divinity, including evidences and principles of natural religion," as well as "the evidence, Doctrines and Duties of revealed Religion."[61] Ware provided a stabilizing presence as energy was directed toward the establishment in 1819 of a distinct Divinity Department with a "Faculty of Theology" under the leadership of a president, Rev. John Thornton Kirkland. Kirkland advocated that "every encouragement be given to the serious, impartial, and unbiased investigation of Christian truth; and that no assent to the peculiarities of any denomination of Christians be required of the Students or Instructors."[62] These early decades were directed toward institutionalizing support for the liberal view, which encountered little theological controversy during this period. The rising generation turned to the moral dimension of liberal theology, exemplified in the warm, almost evangelical piety of Joseph Stevens Buckminster, William Ellery Channing, Joseph Tuckerman, and Henry Ware, Jr. For Universalists, the moral emphasis in religious belief was evident in that same era in Hosea Ballou and Thomas Whittemore. We will see how the liberal moral view was important to community ministry.

The movement toward individual moral development had its earliest manifestation in the brilliant, tragically short-lived career of Joseph Stevens Buckminster. Serving as minister to the Brattle Street Church in Boston, he achieved nearly legendary status for his eloquence in the pulpit. He shared the elder Ware's sympathy for rational piety, but he also warned of the "lukewarmness of indifferent professors."[63] He was concerned that too much rationality encouraged apathy. He wrote, "If Christianity is to exist at all, let it exist with some vitality. If God is to be loved, he is to be loved supremely."[64]

Buckminster was also a writer, a literary critic, and the founder of *The Monthly Anthology and Boston Review*. Two of his co-editors on the *Review* were Channing and Tuckerman. Robinson writes that the liberals' emphasis on human moral capacity had "implications for other human abilities, including literature and fine arts."[65] The *Monthly Anthology* would last only eight years, but it established a legacy that would lead to the Boston Athenaeum, the recipient of Buckminster's library of some 3000 volumes after he died. Buckminster was an early model of the minister who is also a man of letters.

Buckminster is important also because he was an early leader in adopting the methods of the German higher criticism of the Bible. He was influential in promoting rational investigation of the Bible, insisting that the scriptures be read in their historical context. Buckminster believed that biblical texts should be scrutinized just as would be any account from antiquity. Robinson refers to Buckminster as a pivotal figure of American cultural history, whose qualities resonated with the age to come.[66] His early death in 1812 due to epilepsy, at age 28, was a personal tragedy for his intimates; it was also an incalculable loss for the developing movement of liberal Christians in New England.

The voice that would succeed Buckminster belonged to the third child of William and Lucy Ellery Channing, born in 1780, part of a distinguished and prosperous family in Newport, Rhode Island. Since Newport had been founded by Baptists on the principle of religious freedom, William Ellery Channing grew up in a community populated by a variety of religious adherents. Frank Carpenter reports that the Channing family slaves, Duchess Quamino and Newport Gardiner, leaders in Newport's African community, taught him that "integrity is the essence of religion."[67] So was nurtured the moral framework for Channing's religious belief, from which he would eventually condemn slavery. Years later, as a student at Harvard, he found support for his liberal perspective in the works of the Scottish philosopher Francis Hutcheson, who "asserted a universal capacity for unselfish benevolence."[68]

Channing's place in this study is vital. First, he was incomparably significant to the early nineteenth-century institutionalization and articulation of belief among his generation of liberals; second, he initiated the community outreach of the Federal Street Church, where he served as minister for nearly forty years and developed his own ministry of prophecy and social concern.

From 1813 to 1826, Channing was one of the Fellows of Harvard College. This made him a member of the small governing board known as the "Harvard Corporation." He was known in this role to be very attentive to the students' needs.[69] Early in his ministry, Channing accepted an appointment to serve on a committee that would "digest and report a plan of instruction and a course of exercises for the Theological Students at the University." This report was submitted in 1816. It laid the foundation for a curriculum that included Biblical Criticism, Ecclesiastical Polity, and History and Constitution of the Churches of New England. It also led to the creation of the Society for the Promotion of Theological Education, an auxiliary to raise funds for the further development of a theological school. On March 19, 1819, the Corporation accepted the report and for the first time spoke of a "Faculty of Theology," composed of a president and four professors.[70] Channing would play a further role of institutional significance when he agreed to deliver a sermon that synthesized the threads of liberal Unitarian thought for his generation. The occasion was the ordination of the Rev. Jared Sparks at the First Independent Church of Baltimore on May 5, 1819. In keeping with a preconceived plan, at a site 400 miles south of Boston, Channing powerfully affirmed for the liberals the meaning of *Unitarian Christianity*.

Channing's address first outlined the need to rely on biblical evidences as discovered through a reasoned historical interpretation of the scriptures. "We regard the Scriptures as the records of God's successive revelations to mankind," he began. For liberals the "Bible is a book written for men, in the language of men, and its meaning is to be sought in the same manner as other books."[71] To conservatives who criticized the use of reason in religion, he answered, "Say what we may, God has given us a rational nature, and will call us to account for it." Proceeding from this premise, Channing asserted the unity of God and objected to the Trinity as an irrational and unscriptural doctrine. "From the many passages that treat of God, we ask for one, one only, in which we are told, that he is a threefold being. . . . On the contrary, in the New Testament . . . God is declared to be one." To worship Jesus became a distraction from "a deep veneration of the moral perfections of God, which is the essence of piety." As for Jesus, his moral perfection as a human being was the basis for all humans to strive for moral perfection. Channing asserted the complete benevolence of God, a being who would not "render certain and infallible the total depravity of every human being." The mission of Jesus, he argued, was "to form us to a sublime and heavenly virtue." These arguments, in the end, led Channing to summarize the moral basis of the liberal Unitarian Christian position. "We conceive that the true love of God is a moral sentiment. . . . We esteem him a pious man who . . . shows his delight in God's benevolence by loving and serving his neighbor."

The classic Unitarian Christian position, evident in Channing's argument, was to accept that Jesus lived and was crucified for the salvation of men—that he embodied the perfect Love of God that was to be emulated by humankind, not for God's sake, but for the sake of human happiness and well-being. Jesus inhabited a status somewhere above humans but below God. With Channing's straightforward defense of the name Unitarian, the liberal faction of anti-Trinitarian Congregationalists finally accepted the designation that had, up until this date, been used by the orthodox opposition to describe what they saw as the most heinous aspect of liberal belief.[72] In the next year, Channing played a leading role in convening the Berry Street Conference that was the forerunner to the American Unitarian Association (AUA), formed in May 1825. The purposes of the AUA were the diffusion of pure Christianity, communication among Unitarian churches, and a missionary effort to aid in the founding of new churches.

Beyond his work on behalf of the early Unitarian denomination, Channing is known to have been active in social service work and in political reform. He cared about the poor, though mostly his concern was for their spiritual impoverishment, their education, and the behaviors that led them away from Christ. "The great calamity of the poor is not their poverty," he was careful to say, "but the tendency of their privations, and of their social rank, to degradation of the mind."[73] In the mid-1820s, he and his Wednesday

Evening Association convinced the trustees of the Federal Street Church to hire Joseph Tuckerman to serve the poor in Boston's maritime communities. This was the start of a valuable ministry-at-large that would continue and expand long after Tuckerman was gone, coordinating the commitment and resources of many Boston churches in service to the poor. More is said on Tuckerman's ministry in the story that follows. Channing also was an advocate of temperance, speaking against it publicly and signing petitions to state and local legislators to limit distribution of alcoholic beverages. Much of his advocacy was done from the sidelines, through his writing or preaching. He was not a group activist, which may have been due to his general shyness, or to his poor health.[74]

Ultimately "Channing's growing faith in human nature confronted one intractable fact in nineteenth-century America—slavery."[75] His initial revulsion over slavery took shape when, for health reasons, he spent the winter of 1831 on the island of St. Croix. There he witnessed slaves' villages from his piazza and wrote letters home that described the evils of slavery. Not surprisingly, he characterized slavery as a system that "not only degraded but morally deformed the slave."[76] Channing was urged to deepen his commitment to the anti-slavery cause through contacts with Samuel J. May and Lydia Maria Francis Child, both of whom had been influenced by William Lloyd Garrison, publisher of the *Liberator*. May and Child are discussed in upcoming chapters on reform. In 1835, he produced a book entitled *Slavery*, which was quite a sensation, coming from a man of such high standing as Channing. He offered a theological appeal: the great evil of slavery was that it denied the divine potential in humanity and corrupted the slave owner as well.[77] Thus, he condemned the sin of slavery, but not the sinner, the slave owner. Furthermore, he expressed criticism of the abolitionists who were too zealous. These attitudes had the effect of alienating him from abolitionists. However, in 1837 he gained a better reputation among them when he produced a letter and pamphlet directed to Henry Clay, denouncing the annexation of Texas for motives to advance slavery. In the same year, he spoke publicly to a capacity crowd of 5000, meeting at Faneuil Hall to protest the murder of abolitionist Elijah P. Lovejoy in Alton, Illinois. Channing had in fact helped secure the Hall on the basis of free speech after city officials denied an application for its use.[78]

Channing's work on behalf of the anti-slavery movement has been criticized by some as being lukewarm, especially since he was unwilling to condemn slave owners. Such criticism does not take into account the fact that abolitionists were few in number in the 1830s and were nearly universally hated as radicals. Indeed, in the aftermath of the publication of *Slavery,* we are told that the standing committee of the Federal Street Church no longer allowed abolitionists to speak from the pulpit. In addition, notices of anti-slavery meetings to be held elsewhere were kept from Channing so he could not announce them to the congregation.[79] When the church refused to host memorial services for Channing's abolitionist friend, Charles Follen, Channing's association with the church came to an end. Finally, many of his affluent friends outside the church stopped speaking to him and circulated rumors that his wife's fortune derived from the slave trade.[80] It is safe to assume that, had Channing lived into the 1850s and witnessed the Fugitive Slave Law (enacted in 1850, requiring northerners to aid in the capture of runaway slaves), he would have been aroused to a level of action easily matching the more widespread abolitionist sentiment sweeping the north in that decade. In light of his times, Channing's condemnation of slavery in the 1830s was in fact quite remarkable.

The War of 1812 and the unfolding stresses of a new market economy brought unprecedented opportunity for some and incalculable loss for others. Visible in many American cities were wildly fluctuating extremes in wealth and poverty. Among the ranks of the poor were incoming immigrants and native-born artisans displaced by factories. Sailors and dock workers in port cities ranked in the very lowest tiers of society. It is in this context of mobility and disparity that we view the work of Joseph Tuckerman, recognized among Unitarian Universalists today as the patron saint of community ministry.

Joseph Tuckerman was born in Boston in 1778, the son of Edward Tuckerman, a prominent landowner and builder. At the age of sixteen, he entered Harvard, where one of his roommates was William Ellery Channing. Tuckerman and Channing developed an enduring friendship based on their mutual liberal Christian devotion to ethical action in human relations. Michelle Walsh states, "In Tuckerman, Channing would come to believe he had found a man whose piety represented the highest example of liberal evangelical Christianity."[81] Tuckerman was not a serious student at Harvard; nonetheless he graduated in 1801 and, after some additional study, was invited to pastor the Congregational church in Chelsea, Massachusetts.[82] During his twenty-four years of work at the Chelsea congregation, Tuckerman exhibited an uncommon interest in the lives of his congregants, visiting fifteen or twenty families every day, conversing with them about their trades and acting as their counselor, benefactor, and physician. Occasionally he was known to give out medications at no charge. In time he became acutely aware of the plight of sailors living in Boston, which in 1812 led him to found the Society for the Religious and Moral Improvement of Seamen. This was perhaps the first reform organization to appear in an era that would be characterized by hundreds of such organizations in the years leading up to the Civil War.

Typical of the liberal Unitarian Christians of his time, Tuckerman derived inspiration from the Bible, which he studied daily as if it were a textbook. He would select a biblical text each morning before breakfast to guide his thoughts and actions for the day, aiming as he said, for "my own improvement as a Christian, husband, father, and minister of Jesus Christ."[83] After twenty-five years of integrating his parish and community ministries, Tuckerman was forced to step down from his parish post because aggravation to his throat made regular preaching impossible. At this juncture, Channing saw an opportunity to recommend his friend for a ministry of service to the poor of Boston, under the auspices of the Wednesday Evening Association at the Federal Street Church in Boston.[84] He hoped to gain sponsorship as well from other Unitarian churches through the AUA, which he had recently helped to organize. Circumspect over the prospects of such a venture, and having no money, the fledgling AUA was in fact unprepared to fund it. Instead, the AUA appealed to the women of Boston's Unitarian churches to raise the promised annual salary of $600.00, which they did for the next eight years. Tuckerman was moved to accept Channing's offer. Thus began, through a coordinated and creative ethical vision, Tuckerman's fifteen-year commitment to serving as an urban minister to the poor and unchurched in Boston's North Side. The scheme by which he was supported inaugurated the first official designation of "minister-at-large" in the Unitarian denomination.

Tuckerman visited the poor in the worst of situations, reporting an astonishing 2000 visits in his first year. His attitude toward poor relief was typical of middle-class thinking in his day: indiscriminate philanthropy as well as state support for the poor was to be avoided. These approaches were thought to foster a spirit of dependency.[85] The inspiration behind Tuckerman's ministry, however, transcended the prevailing undercurrent of prejudice: "It is the first object of the Ministry-at-Large never to be lost sight of . . . to extend its offices to the poor and to the poorest, to the low and to the lowest, to the most friendless and the most uncared for, the most miserable."[86] To accomplish these ends, he implemented the scientific approach being advocated among his peers. For him, this translated into taking hardened offenders and putting them to work in a "farm school." He helped organize Sunday Schools and established ten schools to prepare children for entry into the earliest of public schools. He also studied social problems and wrote up his findings. Pioneering where other Unitarians would follow, Tuckerman advocated prison and insane asylum reform.[87] On prison reform, he advocated educational programs for prison inmates. Significantly, while most reformers regarded poverty as the result of sin and kept their social distance, Tuckerman confessed to feeling overwhelmed by the sheer misery he encountered. Out of his liberal Unitarian Christian beliefs, he viewed each individual as worth saving. "There is no human being, however depraved, who is yet totally depraved, no one for whom moral efforts are not to be made as long as God shall uphold him in being."[88]

In 1828 Tuckerman made an appeal to the AUA for extended financial assistance. All that was needed for this work, he urged, was "a deep piety, a benevolent heart, and an earnest desire to do good."[89] Tuckerman's two marriages (he remarried after his first wife died) provided him with the means to be financially independent; nonetheless he advocated that an amount of $600 or $800 be permanently allocated by the AUA for the salary of a minister-at-large so this office would not be perceived as an inferior ministry. "The good to be done in the ministry-at-large is not to be exceeded in any other department of ministerial labor." Moreover, he argued, the "division of the expense for a minister-at-large would make the burden very light, when compared with the magnitude of the benefits that would result."[90] Tuckerman's vision for a ministry such as this, his tireless labor on behalf of the poor, and his strategy of building cooperation among many forces "anticipated the future course of poor relief in the United States."[91]

Having reached a point of exhaustion and ill health, Tuckerman took a year's leave of absence in England. While there he established in 1833 a Domestic Missions Program in Liverpool, modeled after the ministry-at-large in Boston. When he returned home in 1834, he found that the Unitarian Churches of Boston had formed a consortium in support of his ministry, naming it the Benevolent Fraternity of Unitarian Churches. Two additional ministers-at-large, the Revs. Frederick T. Gray and Charles Barnard, had been hired to assist him with the work and were ordained jointly in 1834. William Ellery Channing spoke at the service, calling attention to the remarkable shift in thinking that was evident in the ministry-at-large and proclaiming its emergence a "grand and holy revolution."[92] Similar formulations of the minister-at-large concept soon appeared in other East Coast cities, prompted by the deleterious effects of the financial panic of 1837 and the arrival of impoverished immigrants in the 1840s. In 1841, a new journal appeared—*The Journal of the Ministry-at-Large*—which published articles by and about persons serving in that capacity. In 1850, the Association of Ministers-at-Large in New England was founded, bringing ministers together quarterly to discuss their work on behalf of the poor. The Benevolent Fraternity expanded its services to address the needs of arriving immigrants and to provide Sunday Schools and chapels, a gymnasium, classes and clubs, and a fruit and flower mission.

As for Tuckerman, his health was failing by 1838. In that year, too, his second wife died. With an eye toward recuperation, he went to Cuba, but he worsened in Havana and died soon after arriving in 1840. His lifelong friend Dr. Channing eulogized him, saying, "his love was founded on a deliberate perception of the spiritual nature of a human being."[93] On Tuckerman's time-worn headstone in Mt. Auburn Cemetery are inscribed the following barely legible words: "For twenty-five years, a faithful minister of Jesus Christ in the village of Chelsea, and for fourteen years, a devoted Missionary to the suffering, and neglected of the City of Boston, his best monument is the Ministry-at-Large, his appropriate title, Friend of the Poor."

This chapter has examined three Unitarian ministers — Buckminster, Channing, and Tuckerman—who exemplify the early liberal Unitarian moralists. The fourth contemporary to be included in this category is Henry Ware, Jr., whose ethical vision of Christian Unitarian belief guided his ministry of teaching. Among the subjects recommended for inclusion in the curriculum at the new Harvard Divinity School was "pastoral theology." The obvious person to assume this position was Henry Ware, Jr. The younger Ware had completed his studies at Harvard in 1812, the year Buckminster died, and was installed as minister of the moribund Second Church of Boston in 1817. He proved to be a remarkably effective minister, demonstrating high gifts of preaching and great personal warmth in pastoral work. With the eloquence of his preaching, Ware held a reputation in Boston second only to Channing. With regard to pastoral care, he had no equal.[94]

Ware accepted the appointment of Professor of Pulpit Eloquence and Pastoral Care at Harvard in 1830, leaving the Second Church to the ministerial leadership and pastoral presence of his younger colleague, the Rev. Ralph Waldo Emerson. At Harvard, Ware became a popular professor, giving practical advice to students out of his own experience. In his *Hints on Extemporaneous Preaching* (1831), he wrote with respect to baptism, "The dropping of the water upon the child's face may cause a disturbance and this is the reason the closing prayer should be brief." Ware became as well a beloved mentor, giving pastoral care to his students in the way he had done with his parishioners. In 1831, he helped the students form the Philanthropic Society for benevolent action; he led "conversation meetings" on religious and moral topics; he offered spiritual counsel to his students, as the Corporation intended; his wife helped nurse them when they were ill. Unfortunately, Ware suffered from poor health, which forced him to retire in 1842. His students wrote to him, "Your example, beloved Sir, even more than your instruction, has taught us the greatness and beauty of a Christian life."[95]

The younger Ware practiced an emotional pietism that his father did not. He held that religion should begin with the truths revealed by the Gospel, but he spoke against reliance on the "cold judgment of the intellect." There must be a "warm, glowing feeling of preference and desire; a feeling which attaches itself in love to the Father of all, and to all good beings . . . which prefers and delights in that which is well pleasing to God, and takes an affectionate interest in the things to which the Savior devoted himself."[96] Wright offers, "To Ware, religion meant piety, not social convention; and a spiritual quality pervaded his personality which communicated itself to his students." He adds, "It is useful to keep Henry Ware, Jr. in mind when one is tempted to accept without qualification Emerson's references to "the pale negations of Boston Unitarianism" and "the corpse-cold Unitarianism of Brattle Street."[97]

Ware became involved in numerous humanitarian causes, including Sunday Schools, temperance, anti-slavery, and ministry to the poor.[98] He also wrote a great deal—many sermons, of course, but also poetry and fiction, and in 1831, the devotional manual *On the Formation of the Christian Character*. In the latter work, he advised that the aim of religion is "the cultivation of the ability to give your heart a permanent bias toward God."[99] One year after he retired, Ware died at the age of 49. His emphasis on expressive moral piety is indicative of the ideal espoused by his generation of liberal Christian Unitarians.

Among the Universalists, Hosea Ballou and Thomas Whittemore exemplify a moral pietism comparable to their Unitarian contemporaries. Whittemore, a writer and editor, became a Universalist minister under the encouragement and tutelage of Hosea Ballou, a circuit-riding Universalist preacher. Ballou is significant in having promoted a shift at the turn of the nineteenth century toward a less Calvinist and less Trinitarian view of Universalism than was articulated by John Murray and his peers. In 1803, a meeting of the New England Convention of Universalists created a summary of Universalist beliefs known as the Winchester Profession, so named for the town in New Hampshire where they met. The essential premise was that, while all humans were sinners, God would inevitably "restore the whole family of mankind to holiness and happiness." Encapsulating the eighteenth-century Universalist message, this was simply "Calvinism with a new conclusion," as David Robinson phrases it.[100] Ballou agreed that all humans would be saved, but he objected to the assertion that "infinite sin against an infinite God required an infinite sacrifice, the death of Christ. . . ."[101] In the winter of 1804–1805, Ballou wrote his *Treatise of Atonement*, which offered a concept of sin that drew on the Arminian concept of salvation as character formation. Ballou's version of the atonement process was essentially moral. He wanted to correct the view that God was intent on punishing the sinner; rather, "the consequence of the atonement is the universal holiness and happiness of mankind."[102]

Thomas Whittemore was a protégé of Hosea Ballou. Ministry would be the primary platform from which Whittemore would engage in many pursuits, including writing and finance. Whittemore's father died when he was fourteen; during an apprenticeship to a boot maker, he had the opportunity for three months of formal schooling.[103] The young Thomas's facility with numbers and finance came to the attention of Mr. Baker, his master, who turned all of his books over to him. During these years, Whittemore also began singing in several church choirs and was soon invited to sing in the Boston Handel and Haydn Society. After taking lessons in harmony, he produced a 350-page book of hymns entitled *Songs of Zion or the Cambridge Collection of Sacred Music.* It had "a large circulation and was used quite extensively in churches of the different Christian sects."[104] It was at this time that Whittemore came to know the Rev. Ballou, who rented a room from Mr. Baker in 1820. Upon hearing Ballou preach, Whittemore began collecting his writings, and soon they became friends.

The relationship between Whittemore and Ballou deepened. As Whittemore's thoughts turned more toward religion, Ballou began teaching him how to preach a sermon. After only three months of training, Whittemore was called to be the minister to a newly formed congregation at Milford, Massachusetts. He was formally ordained to the Universalist ministry in June 1821, and a year later accepted a call to the First Universalist Society in Cambridge. Whittemore found great joy in parish ministry as he enthusiastically preached twice each Sunday to his own congregation and once to an outlying church. He was also able to use his skill with finances to better manage the church's assets. But parish ministry was soon shared with ministry of another kind: writing and editing.

While living in Cambridge, Whittemore became co-editor with Hosea Ballou and Hosea Ballou 2nd of the *Universalist Magazine.* In time, Whittemore purchased the magazine and renamed it the *Trumpet and Universalist Magazine.* Under Whittemore, the magazine became more assertive in its defense of Universalism. It also became more profitable as, over the next twenty years, subscriptions grew from 700 when he purchased it to nearly 6,000. Whittemore was unquestionably the leading Universalist newspaper editor of his day, well known for his "watchful warnings against the religious errors of the times"—namely, "Restorationist" Universalism.[105] Whittemore shared Ballou's "Ultra-Universalist" idea that sin was not punished after death, but during life on earth. "Ballou's denial of suffering after death was based on his insistence of the natural and more immediate suffering that sin causes in life itself."[106] Whittemore also wrote several books on Universalist theology and history, including the four-volume *Life of Rev. Hosea Ballou*, published in 1854–1855, and later his own autobiography, *The Early Days of Thomas Whittemore*, published in 1858.

Besides his work as a writer, Whittemore served in the Massachusetts legislature, having been elected to office in 1831. He served for five years and was especially influential in pushing the passage of a bill to disestablish the Congregational and Unitarian churches. Passed in 1833, this measure finally made Massachusetts the last state in the union to come into compliance with the First Amendment, ending tax support for the churches. While in the legislature, Whittemore played a central role in crushing a move to divide Cambridge in two. He attributed this plan to a desire by some "to incorporate the wealth into one town and the expenses into the other."[107] Instead he advocated that Cambridge be incorporated as a city, and he guided that effort to passage. Whittemore became a highly successful businessman, eventually assuming the presidency of the Cambridge Bank and later the presidency of the Vermont and Massachusetts Railroad.

Whittemore was a strong-minded but genial man. According to Hosea Ballou, he drew "hosts of friends" into his life and demonstrated "humanitarian sentiments that extended to the rudest elements of society." He believed there should be universal education for all, advocated temperance, and opposed capital punishment.[108] Ultimately, he denounced the slave trade and condemned the Fugitive Slave Act of 1850, which empowered special federal courts and agents to retrieve fugitive slaves in the north and return them to slavery in the south.[109] Whittemore died in 1861, having suffered a series of paralytic strokes in the last years of his life. The Rev. A. A. Miner eulogized him, saying, "With many hours and toils that would have absorbed the entire energies of most men, you have met with him in the editorial chair, and as an author, appealing to the religious mind, and as a preacher welcome everywhere, in all our churches." He was a "man for all seasons," fully living an Ultra-Universalist ministry of high energy, multi-dimensional intelligence, conscious intent, and moral action.

CHAPTER THREE

The "New Religion"
Authorship and Oratory
as Public Ministry

Ralph Waldo Emerson ushered in the "New Religion" —what he liked to call "Idealism" and others called "Transcendentalism." Perhaps he was only one of the most articulate spokespersons, most prolific writers, and most passionate visionaries of an idea that was "in the air." There is no mistaking that he was quintessentially the individual who gave voice and shape and religious meaning to a mid-nineteenth century shift away from biblical revelation in American Unitarianism. What he offered instead was a radical re-thinking of the divine presence in human experience and inner consciousness.

Emerson was born the son of a minister who had led his congregation at Boston's First Church to accept Unitarian belief, probably in Channing's mode of Bible-based Arian (non-Trinitarian) Christianity. Emerson's father died when he was only eight, but his connection to the religious milieu of his father's peers continued due to family and friends. Of special influence was an aunt, Mary Moody Emerson, who encouraged him, at the age of fourteen, to keep a journal. In the volumes of intimate reflections collected over a lifetime, it is possible to see the private pain and struggle through which he honed his public views. Mary was a Bible theist, but she was also open to direct experiences of God in solitude and nature.[110]

Emerson graduated from Harvard College at age eighteen and taught school for a few years before entering Harvard Divinity School. A winter in Florida enabled him to recover from certain early signs of tuberculosis, before he undertook a brief stint of itinerant preaching in the Boston area. When he married his beloved Ellen Louisa Tucker, he accepted a permanent post at the Second Church of Boston, where he had been assisting his friend and mentor Henry Ware, Jr. Ware, it will be recalled, accepted a professorship at Harvard. It seems not to have been a surprise to Emerson when he discovered that the work of parish ministry did not suit him well. He loved preaching, but detested pastoral calling. When Ellen died from tuberculosis after only eighteen months of marriage, Emerson's overwhelming grief forced him to come to terms with his true calling. After a brief period of travel in Europe, he returned to New England in 1833 and embarked on a career as a public lecturer. In the words of Frank Schulman, he "exchanged his pulpit for the rostrum . . . and accepted a call to a much larger audience, the country."[111] He had become, in effect, a community minister.

Emerson devoted the next half-century to writing and public speaking on behalf of his philosophy of Idealism or Transcendentalism—a philosophy that had originated in Germany, denying the authority of the Bible as God's revelation, the miracles it records, and salvation by the death and resurrection of Jesus Christ,[112] and arguing rather that God is directly experienced in the present, in nature, and within the individual soul. In his first book, *Nature* (1836), Emerson wrote of the directness with which the individual might experience God in the natural world. "Standing on the bare ground—my head bathed by the blithe air, and uplifted into infinite space—all mean egotism vanishes. I become a transparent eyeball; I am nothing; I see all; the currents of the Universal Being circulate through me; I am part or particle of God."[113] Though *Nature* sold only 500 copies, Emerson acquired considerable notice, and in March 1838 he was invited by the graduating class of Harvard Divinity School to speak at their commencement. He accepted the invitation, saying, "In the good hope of our calling, I am your friend and servant."[114]

The speech Emerson delivered that day in July 1838 has been known forever after as the Divinity School Address. In it he argued his objections to the continued liberal Bible-based Christian influence in Unitarianism. "I shall do my duty to you, on this occasion, by pointing out two errors," he began. First, allowing that Jesus was a true prophet who saw with open eye the mystery of the soul, Emerson denounced the word "miracle," as understood by Christian churches, as "a Monster" that was in no way equal to the real miracles of blowing clover and falling rain. "So the first defect of historical Christianity is . . . that it has dwelt with noxious exaggeration about the person of Jesus. The soul knows no persons."[115] The second defect, deriving from the first, was that "the Moral Nature, whose revelations introduce greatness into the open soul, is not explored as the fountain of teaching in society."[116] "The man on whom the soul descends, through whom the soul speaks, alone can teach," asserted Emerson.[117] He admonished his listeners finally to "go alone, to refuse the good models," and as a "newborn bard of the Holy Ghost" to "acquaint men at first hand with Deity." In the end, Emerson did not advise his audience of ministerial candidates to leave the church, even though that is what he had done. Rather he challenged them to breathe new life into it. The remedy to the deformities in the church, he said, was "first, soul, and second, soul, and evermore, soul."[118] The Harvard faculty and dean were hurt and appalled; some students felt uncomfortable; others came away enthralled. The Divinity School Address was a defining moment. It marked the beginning of the second controversy in Unitarianism, whether Unitarians would continue to follow the Bible-based Channing view or take the Transcendentalist path.

Scott Russell Sanders argues that Emerson wrote *Self-Reliance* (1841) as a defense against the storm of criticism occasioned by his Harvard speech.[119] Here he "marshaled his arguments for trusting one's inner light," not because it came easy for him, says Sanders, but "because it came hard." *Self-Reliance* reads, "Trust thyself: every heart beats to that iron string. . . . Nothing is at last sacred but the integrity of your own mind." Emerson's struggle is evident: "What I must do is all that concerns me, not what people think. . . . It is harder because you will always find those who think they know what is your duty better than you know it."[120]

Emerson was not arguing for a self-centered approach to life. To understand God in the self was to diminish the self and enlarge one's responsibility for moral action. One could only "arrive at the voice of God" by "patient listening to your own conscience."[121] As early as 1831, Emerson spoke out against the unjust treatment of Native Americans, calling such treatment a "bare-faced trespass of power upon weakness" and "an alarming symptom of how obtuse is the moral sense of the people."[122] In an 1838 letter of protest to President Martin Van Buren, very probably encouraged by his second wife Lydian, he expressed indignation over the plan to remove the Cherokee from Georgia. "In the name of God, sir, we ask you if this is so? . . . You sir, will bring down that renowned chair in which you sit into infamy . . . and the name of this nation will stink to the world."[123]

Lawrence Buell observes that Emerson recognized in his world "a sense of unprecedentedly vertiginous social upheaval . . . of living in an age of revolution."[124] In the introductory lecture in a series entitled *The Times* (1842), Emerson wrote, "We are not permitted to stand as spectators in the pageant which the times exhibit; we are parties also, and have a responsibility which is not to be declined."[125] Here appears in greater measure by the 1840s what Robinson calls "the political Emerson." The crisis that was "not to be declined" in Emerson's day was the cause of anti-slavery. In 1844, he accepted an invitation to speak at the occasion of the tenth anniversary of the British emancipation of slaves in the West Indies. What Emerson learned in preparation for his talk aroused his consciousness to the realities of slavery and secured his permanent commitment to the anti-slavery cause. He spoke, "From the earliest time, the negro has been an article of luxury to the commercial nations . . . I am heartsick when I read how they came there and how they are kept there." He itemized the cruelties of slave treatment—"the whip applied to old men and tender women," and "the pregnant women set to the treadmill"—and spoke of slavery as fundamentally contrary to all sense of human morality. "The stomach rises in disgust."

In *American Slavery* (1855), Emerson joined the voices of growing frustration amplified in reaction to the Fugitive Slave Act. "This filthy act," as Emerson termed it, was enacted as part of the Compromise of 1850 that brought California into the Union. It provided federal funds to pay federal agents to retrieve runaway slaves in the northern states, with the assistance of local northern law enforcement officials. Magistrates were paid $10 for each captive determined to be a runaway, $5 for each captive determined not to be a runaway. Captives were not permitted to speak on their own behalf. Thus the 1850s became a time of terror for all black persons in the north, whether they were runaway slaves or not. For northerners, their compliance in the capture and return of runaway slaves felt like complicity, and the law inadvertently increased the number of northern abolitionist converts. "The subject seems exhausted," sighed Emerson. "An honest man is soon weary of crying 'Thief!' One must write with a red hot iron to make any impression."

Emerson connected the problem of slavery to the larger problem of the political parties' unwillingness to address the crisis. "Does Democracy really stand for the good of the many? For the poor? For the elevation of entire humanity? The Party of Property, of education, has resisted every progressive step . . . [These conservatives] would nail the stars to the sky. . . . They wish their age should be absolutely like the last." He singled out the motivations of commerce. "Our merchants do not believe in anything but their trade. . . . And the power of money is so obtrusive as to exclude the view of the larger powers that control it."[126]

"Liberty," he concluded, "is a very serious thing. It is the severest test by which a government can be tried. History shows that it is the measure of all national success." Here, then, Emerson brought the issue into a larger light: the prospect of success for the country as a free nation was being jeopardized by the presence of slavery, and by the apparatus of laws erected among free citizens to protect it. In 1860, Emerson wrote to honor the sacrifice of John Brown, whom he regarded as a heroic martyr for abolition. Deriding the "blind statesmen" who hunt down the heresy of support for Brown's "treason," Emerson wrote, "They will need a very vigilant committee indeed to find its birth place." And now he raised the issue to an even higher dimension of ageless human moral capacity. "For the Arch-Abolitionist, older than Brown, older than the Shenandoah Mountains, is Love, whose other name is Justice, which was before Alfred, before Lycurgus, before Slavery, and will be after it."[127]

The place of Ralph Waldo Emerson in this study of community ministry is pivotal to our appreciation of much of what follows. After this, expressions of Unitarian belief fell somewhere on a continuum marked by degrees of appropriation or not of Emerson's views of innate divinity and the soul in direct communion with God in nature. The spread of Transcendentalist ideas was facilitated by the fact that members of the literary and religious elite found them so compelling. They wrote about the "new views," discussed them in the Transcendentalist Club, and preached them from their pulpits. Transcendentalist ministers had the effect of expanding the non-creedal scope of Unitarian thinking because, for the most part, they did not leave the denomination.[128] Moreover it will be seen that what they believed intensified the liberal call to moral concern, moral action, and, as in Emerson's case, moral prophesy. Their call for the integrity of all souls carried over into practical religious aims, which is why their story is vital to this history of community ministry in Unitarian Universalism. Of immediate importance are Margaret Fuller and James Freeman Clarke; others among them—George Ripley, Theodore Parker, and Thomas Wentworth Higginson—are more fully known for their ministries of communalism (Ripley) or reform (Parker and Higginson), and will be discussed in succeeding chapters.

Probably the most influential American woman of the early nineteenth century was the writer and teacher Margaret Fuller.

According to Elizabeth Cady Stanton and Susan B. Anthony, Fuller "possessed more influence on the thought of American women than any woman previous to her time."[129] The roots of her later accomplishments are found in her early training as a child. Margaret was educated by her father, who imposed "discipline of considerable severity" on her studies, drilling her in the night long past her bedtime. It was a regimen that gave her nightmares, yet she had great aptitude for learning. The effect was to create in young Margaret strength of purpose and precision about her life—she identified with the "gladiators of Rome"—but at the same time to deny those feminine patterns of speech and manner cultivated by her female peers. Her erudition made her bright and engaging to a small number of adult intellectual peers, but out of place with youthful companions. At the age of twelve, she believed her choices were, in her words, "to be feminine and less bookish" or "to be bright and ugly." She resolved to follow the latter course.[130]

From her lonely teenage years, Fuller emerged into adulthood as the most intellectually brilliant woman (some would say person) of her day. Now she became acquainted with the likes of Lydia Maria Child, James Freeman Clarke, Henry Hedge, and Harriet Martineau, who introduced her to Ralph Waldo Emerson. In 1838, Emerson invited Fuller to join the circle of Transcendentalist thinkers and writers. Within a year, she agreed to edit the *Dial*, the Transcendentalist journal, and became a contributor to it herself. It was during these years that she wrote of her own faith needs, stating that she believed in Christ. Even though she could do without him, she said, "I do not wish to do without him. He is constantly aiding and answering me." Beyond Christ, however, she looked for meaning in the "symbolical forms of human life" seen in the "fullness of a Greek god" and the "deep consciousness of a Moses." While she did not reject the church, she also wrote, "the blue sky . . . preaches better than any brother."[131]

Fuller could be intimidating. Unitarian minister William Henry Channing confessed that he initially avoided one "so armed from head to foot in saucy sprightliness."[132] James Freeman Clarke stated that a conversation with Margaret "could not merely entertain

*Kate's comments
home so middle
so each other deeply*

and inform, but make an epoch in one's life." She was nonetheless earnestly convinced that her knowledge and understanding would be of use especially to women in helping them to "nurture their serious responses to each other."[133] To that end, she initiated her famous "Conversations" with "well-educated and thinking women" of Boston to help them "systematize thought and give a precision and clearness in which our sex are so deficient, chiefly, I think because they have so few inducements."[134] Held in 1839 and 1840, these conversations drew between twenty-five and forty women. Participants paid a small fee and met with Fuller at Elizabeth Peabody's foreign language bookstore. They were encouraged to discuss such topics as mythology, art, ethics, education, faith, health, women's rights, and the lives of great women and men.[135] "My ambition," Fuller wrote, "is to pass in review the departments of thought and knowledge and endeavor to place them in due relation to one another in our minds." To Emerson she confessed, "My class is prosperous. I was so fortunate as to rouse, at once, the tone of simple earnestness, which can scarcely, when once awakened, cease to vibrate. All seem in a glow and quite receptive as I wish."[136]

Fuller's Conversations influenced her subsequent writing. In July 1843, the *Dial* published her groundbreaking essay "The Great Lawsuit: Man vs. Men and Woman vs. Women." In this essay, Fuller applied Transcendentalist tenets to women, particularly the universal sacred right and duty to develop fully one's nature. This was a break from Emerson's Transcendentalism, produced at the very moment in time when Fuller's friendship with Emerson was strained by their very different temperaments—hers more social and dynamic, his more inward and ascetic.[137] Fuller's arguments in "The Great Lawsuit" were but a prelude for what was yet to come: her profound life-changing work, *Woman in the Nineteenth Century*, published in 1845. In this work, Fuller revealed an evolving consciousness of her own feminism, before there was even such a word. Having earlier criticized her father's "mistakes" with her strict upbringing, she now said his approach stemmed from his belief in the "equality of the sexes." For women, Fuller stressed the independence of self-reliance, heeding one's inner voice and conscience, and taking action as needed to address social reforms. Here she praised female abolitionists Angelina Grimke and Abby Kelley Foster, and called upon women to resist the annexation of Texas.[138] At the same time, she scorned the idea that women should remain cloistered in a domestic sphere. Here was a radicalism that reached beyond Transcendentalism and led to a career in journalism, in which she wrote weekly columns on issues of social reform.[139] Upon completing her book, Fuller described feeling "a delightful glow as if I had put a good deal of my true life in it, as if, suppose I went away now, the measure of my footprint would be left on the earth."[140] These words would prove prophetic.

Writing for the *New York Tribune*, Fuller was sent to Europe as a foreign correspondent. There she witnessed a kind of poverty she claimed exceeded anything she had ever witnessed in the United States. Having met Giuseppe Mazzini in England, she traveled to Italy in support of his movement for Italian unification and independence. There she met and fell in love with Giovanni Angelo, the Marchese d'Ossoli. Ossoli served as a Guard in the revolutionary army, and Fuller volunteered in a hospital in Rome. She marveled at the heroic struggle of the Italian people and hoped to write their history. On September 4, 1848, Angelo Eugenio Fillippo Ossoli was born in the village of Reiti. Overwhelmed with joy on becoming a mother, Fuller nonetheless continued to send reports to the *New York Tribune* on events in Rome. On the eve of the declaration of the Roman republic in February 1849, Fuller published an appeal in the *Tribune* to the United States government to send a statesmanlike ambassador to the new nation. She added presciently, "Another century and I might ask to be made Ambassador myself."[141]

When the revolution ultimately collapsed, Fuller and Ossoli fled to Florence with their small son, and in May 1850, they sailed for New York. Unfortunately, the captain of the ship died of smallpox. The inexperienced mate left in charge of the ship inadvertently grounded the ship on a sandbar within sight of Fire Island just as a hurricane descended upon the area. Tragically, Margaret Fuller, Ossoli, and their son were lost in the shipwreck that followed. Their remains were never found, nor was Fuller's manuscript, an account of the revolution in Italy. Her early death was a shocking personal loss for those who knew her. It also brought to an abrupt end her transformation into a woman of high political conviction and radical social purpose. The writing she left behind was indeed the final "measure of her footprint"—a formative ministry of empowerment for women in her time and our own.

An endnote to Fuller's story offers some sense of the gender limitations she faced, even in the end. After her death, Emerson accepted the task, with James Freeman Clarke and William Henry Channing, of gathering her papers into a published volume. This work appeared as *Memoirs of Margaret Fuller Ossoli* in 1854. Strangely her editors minimized her work as an editor and visionary writer, perhaps due to popular suspicion that she had borne her child out of wedlock.[142] Indeed, while she was still in Italy, Emerson had cautioned her not to return. Emerson would speak on behalf of women's rights in 1855, at his wife's urging, but for Fuller he was yet a man of the times. Praise for Fuller's influence, voiced thirty years later by Stanton and Anthony, is better understood for what it meant in that context.

James Freeman Clarke's contributions to Unitarianism in the nineteenth century are nearly unmatched.[143] Like Emerson, Clarke read and embraced the German literature that first articulated Transcendental thought. Unlike Emerson, Clarke did not reject historical precedents such as Jesus. Further, he was committed to working within the institutional framework of the Unitarian denomination, despite the condemnation expressed by prominent Unitarian ministers of the "latest infidelity" called Transcendentalism. Clarke would expand the parochial boundaries of Unitarianism in its theology, geography, constituency, and mission to the community.

Clarke chose a career in Unitarian ministry through the influence and financial support of his grandfather, the Rev. James Freeman of Boston's Kings Chapel. Upon completion of his studies at Harvard in 1833, he applied to be fellowshipped as an "evangelist" to the "West" and accepted an appointment in Louisville, Kentucky. This western part of the country was as yet rude and rugged frontier; Clarke told of its hazards in his autobiography, recounting such episodes as overturned stagecoaches in unpaved rutted roads and, worse than anything, the isolation.[144] For Clarke it was an opportunity to bring Unitarian belief to the unlettered families of the frontier. In the absence of any intellectual stimulation in this environment, Clarke founded with Ephraim Peabody in Cincinnati, Ohio the *Western Messenger*, a Unitarian periodical that published writings by and for Unitarians in the west. It was the first periodical to publish Emerson's poetry; Clarke also used it to defend Emerson's *Divinity School Address*. When Clarke resigned his Louisville position in 1840, he carried with him a sense of regret that he had not fulfilled his mission. But his calling led elsewhere.

While out west, Clarke met the family of Harm Jan Huidekoper in Meadville, Pennsylvania. Huidekoper was a Dutch land agent who had done well and had financed the 1836 founding of the Independent Congregational (Unitarian) Church of Meadville. Clarke fell in love with Anna, Harm's daughter, and the two were married in 1839. Meanwhile Clarke longed to return to the more cosmopolitan setting of eastern Massachusetts, and in 1840, he and Anna moved to Boston with their infant son, Herman. With initial financial backing from Huidekoper, Clarke was able to start the Church of the Disciples, a community-based church of which he had always dreamed. It was to be a church open in theology, drawing its members from the city at large, and engaged in practical service to the community. Attendance grew to 700 by 1845, at which point the congregation built a meeting house.[145]

From the beginning, the church was actively committed to social justice. The congregation became involved in the charity work of the Boston Port Society and established its own charity for poor women. Clarke became an outspoken advocate for social reforms, including woman suffrage, temperance, educational reform, prison reform, peace and unions. He lobbied hard to end the death penalty, and by the mid-1840s, he had joined the call to end slavery. Indeed, in 1836, he had reviewed Channing's work, *Slavery*, for the *Western Messenger*, which had a formative effect on his views. With Channing, he felt that the slave system should be

condemned, but not slave owners. His views had been shaped, as
well, by having seen slavery first hand, and having met kind slave
owners, in Louisville. Later, when he realized that slavery would
not end gradually on its own, he became more outspoken. In 1845,
he drafted a letter to protest slavery as a violation of the principles
of the Unitarian faith. It was signed by 173 Unitarian ministers.[146]
During the Civil War, Clarke worked hard on behalf of the Union
cause and joined Henry Whitney Bellows in raising funds for the
Sanitary Commission. In 1883, late in his life, Clarke wrote a history of the struggle to end slavery: *Anti-Slavery Days, A Sketch of the
Struggle Which Ended in the Abolition of Slavery in the United States.*

It is important, finally, to appreciate the range of Clarke's theology and scholarship, which is evident in his published sermons
and numerous other writings. From his more moderate Transcendentalist view, Clarke studied all religious traditions and determined that Jesus Christ "embodied what was best in other world
religions." He accepted the need for historical precedents in religion, which separated him from his friend Emerson. Clarke consciously assumed the role of a bridge between factions. When most
of the Unitarian ministers of Boston voted to deny Theodore
Parker access to their pulpits after his 1841 address "The Transient
and Permanent in Christianity," Clarke refused to go along.[147] Out
of friendship and principle, he opened his pulpit to Parker, though
twelve families left his congregation as a result. At the same time,
Clarke became known in later years as "one of the great protectors
of the Christian Center of Unitarianism." He was recognized as a
member of the Broad Church Group, which was neither liberal nor
conservative. He was a peacemaker, looking for pragmatic compromise and committed to the larger work of moral reform through
the workings of the church.[148]

In 1867 Clarke was invited to serve as Professor of Natural
Theology and Christian Doctrine and later as Professor of Ethnic
Religions and Creeds of Christendom at Harvard Divinity School.
As a member of the Board of Overseers, he envisioned the school
as a "university of theology" with every Christian sect represented
and attention given to non-Christian religions as well. The idea

that other religions would offer some kind of partial truth was, in Clarke's time and in this setting, a radical view.[149] He was a popular innovative lecturer at a time when Harvard Divinity School was in a period of malaise, with professors of the "old regime" resisting the move toward a more open theological model. It would not be until 1880 that the Divinity School would become an "unsectarian school," no longer taught exclusively by and for Unitarians."[150] In that time, Clarke published his influential, though admittedly optimistic, "Five Points of the New Theology," which included "the fatherhood of God, the brotherhood of man, the leadership of Jesus, salvation by Character, and the continuity of human development in all worlds." Two years later he died, his life a voice for both innovation and institution-building, someone whose larger sense of ministry had no real parallel in the Unitarianism of the nineteenth century.[151]

Community Ministers-at-Large in the West

By the late 1820s, prominent eastern Unitarian clergy recognized the need to establish churches in the western territories of Ohio, Kentucky, Indiana, Illinois, and Missouri. This region has been identified as the "First West" or Trans-Allegheny West. Large centers of manufacturing and commerce developed in this area by virtue of their accessibility to river, canal, national road, and eventually rail. They ranged along an axis running south from Buffalo to Erie and Pittsburgh and west along the Ohio River toward Cincinnati, Louisville, and St. Louis. Few Unitarian ministers stayed long in these remote locations, where one was likely to encounter hazardous travel, low and uncertain pay, cultural alienation, and social isolation.[152] In this context, western ministers-at-large played a valuable role in starting new churches and organizing networks of support among themselves. They also assumed other functions, as in the founding of the Meadville Theological School in Meadville, Pennsylvania and the Washington University in St. Louis, Missouri. Worthy examples are seen in the work of William Greenleaf Eliot, Mordecai De Lange,

Frederic Huidekoper, Ephraim Peabody, Robert Collyer, Thomas
Starr King, and Quillen Hamilton Shinn.

William Greenleaf Eliot was unique among eastern establishment clergy. He had seen editions of the St. Louis newspapers as
a teenager and become captivated. St. Louis had sprouted up at
the impressive confluence of the Mississippi and Missouri Rivers
where once had flourished the late medieval Indian empire known
as Cahokia.[153] Eliot graduated from Harvard Divinity School in
1834 and was ordained at the Federal Street Church in Boston,
being commissioned as a minister-at-large to plant a church in the
place so long an object of his fascination. He announced, "Let them
know that a youngster is ready to come there and live and to spend
his life among them. I come to remain and to lay my ashes in the
valley of the Mississippi."[154] This path was for him what Earl Holt
believes was "a consecrated course" from which he would never be
swayed, despite attractive offers to return east.[155]

Eliot's experience in the west began like so many others.
There were times, he reported, when he preached to only eight persons. The First Unitarian Church that was founded in 1835 under
his leadership would eventually become one of the most influential
churches in the early west. Beyond the work of his parish, Eliot
embraced the role of western outreach, bringing encouragement to
lonely and embattled Unitarian ministers in New Orleans, Chicago,
Milwaukee, and other cities. His work in the larger community
included serving on the school board for the city of St. Louis. By
1854, he was instrumental in the founding of Eliot Seminary,
which eventually became known as Washington University. Holt
states, "[Eliot] envisioned a truly national university in a St. Louis
that would be the central city of the great new American republic growing in the west. Washington University would become a
primary spiritual resource shedding its influence throughout the
land, even as St. Louis was the center through which the natural
resources of the prairie would feed the nation."[156]

Eliot's mind and spirit would somehow capture the heart of
a Jewish man living in St. Louis in the early 1840s. Mordecai De
Lange converted to Unitarianism under Eliot's mentorship and

soon thereafter journeyed to Meadville, Pennsylvania, where the new Meadville Theological School had opened in 1844. Upon completing his studies at Meadville, De Lange was ordained as a minister-at-large with the understanding that he would travel across the west establishing new churches. In 1849, he went to Pittsburgh, as recommended by Eliot, to revive a church that had died out due to transient ministerial support and loss of membership. Eliot had once described Pittsburgh as "the nastiest place in creation."[157] As it turned out, De Lange stayed in Pittsburgh for eleven years, reviving the small society there and running for ten years a merged Unitarian and Universalist Sunday school. From Pittsburgh, he continued his engagement in the larger arena of western churches, building connections between ministers situated in remote western locations. In 1849, De Lange and others resolved to found a Western Conference of Unitarian Churches. William Eliot resisted this move, and it is thought that De Lange's 1850 meeting with Eliot in St. Louis may have helped to sway him on the idea. The Western Conference met for the first time in 1852 in Eliot's First Unitarian Church in St. Louis. It would become the organizational source of support and connection for the fledgling western societies for many years to come.[158]

The work of the Western Conference, as well as the work of ministry in the regions of early western development, was greatly facilitated by the founding of the Meadville Theological School in Meadville, Pennsylvania. Meadville had become the "western center" of Unitarian activity under the inspiration and financial support of Harm Jan Huidekoper, the Dutch immigrant land agent who had supported the work of James Freeman Clarke. After converting to Unitarianism in the 1820s, Huidekoper recruited ministerial students from Harvard to serve two functions: to pastor the Independent Congregational (Unitarian) Church he had founded in 1835, and to tutor his children. The Huidekoper household offered an environment of high theological discussion, from which Huidekoper's son Frederic grew up to pursue theological studies at Harvard and in Germany.[159] Frederic Huidekoper returned to Meadville to be ordained in 1844 as a minister-at-large. At Frederic's ordination, the Rev. George Hosmer of the Unitarian Church in Buffalo gave the charge and suggested that Frederic should consider a career in teaching (since his visual handicap precluded a career in ministry) at a Unitarian seminary to be established in Meadville. It was to be a school that would train ministers to serve in the west, where there was indeed a dire shortage. Henry Bellows, long-time minister to the First Congregational Church in New York City, described the Meadville school in 1850 as a "missionary institution." It was a school that in his mind "educated no one to expect a high salary, aspire after literary fame, or claim the honors of theological science."[160] Writing in the *Christian Register* in 1867, Rufus Stebbins, former president of Meadville Theological School, reflected a similar view: "The one great error of the hour is the attempt to make all ministers scholars."[161]

Due to his weak eyes, Frederic restricted his period of study for years to ten minutes each day. Remarkably, in spite of his handicap, he was highly knowledgeable. About him it was written that he "knew the literature and events of the first three centuries [of the Christian era] with an accuracy and fullness that was astounding."[162] Frederic would teach at the Meadville School for thirty years, until he went completely blind. His work as a minister-at-large in the Midwest served a remarkable and vital purpose: to educate ministers who would commit their talents, training, and love to western communities. The Meadville School brought to the west what Harvard was not well suited to provide in any kind of sustained way—not that eastern Unitarian leaders and educators were unsympathetic. In August 1844, the American Unitarian Association did commit $500 a year for five years toward the salary of a well-trained director of the Meadville School.

Among the few eastern ministers who gave of their early years to the west was Ephraim Peabody. Of special importance to this story is the fact that Peabody's first call was in 1830 as pastor to the church at Meadville and tutor to the Huidekoper children.[163] Two years later, he accepted a call to the First Congregational (Unitarian) Church in Cincinnati. While there he linked up with Clarke, minister to the church at Louisville, Kentucky, to edit the

Western Messenger, their publication for Unitarian writings in the west. After two years in Cincinnati, his failing health compelled him to return east where he would serve established churches in New England under more favorable circumstances.

Though primarily a parish minister, Peabody implemented important strategies by which parish ministers served the larger community. In discussions with the Rev. Frederick Gray, Peabody learned about the Benevolent Fraternity of Churches in Boston, which deepened his concern for people living in poverty. He perceived that cities presented individuals with new and complicating forces that challenged their ability to make sound moral choices. Known for his sensitivity and compassion, he "became a pioneer in social work, which for him encompassed everything from pastoral care to social justice."[164] As minister to King's Chapel in Boston (from 1846), he encouraged his congregation to give more support to the Benevolent Fraternity; he also started other programs to address issues of poverty. One program set up a system of districts wherein local administrators were given responsibility to distribute relief. Another program founded a school for adult education and helped in the establishment of public schooling for children and youth. In these ways, people would be enabled to help themselves. Public education was a nineteenth-century reform that religious liberals like Unitarian Horace Mann and Universalist minister Thomas Whittemore viewed as "the great equalizer of the condition of men."[165] Besides promoting education Peabody also preached character development, to help persons acquire, in his words, "a moral sense of self-respect." Peabody died in 1856 of tuberculosis. His legacy to community ministry is important for the work he did in the west; it is also important for the insight and energy he brought to his work on behalf of the urban poor in Boston.

The occasions in which persons served as ministers-at-large seem to have developed when an exposed need made itself felt at the very point in time when an able and inspired candidate appeared ready to take it on. So it seems was the case with Tuckerman, Whittemore, Clarke, Eliot, De Lange, Huidekoper, and

Peabody. When Robert Collyer came to Chicago in 1859, the scenario reversed this pattern. Here the Rev. George Noyes of the First Unitarian Church of Chicago had persuaded his congregation to sponsor a volunteer-based ministry-at-large to engage in social service work in the city. This was the earliest instance of a congregation-based community ministry in the west. After the ministry was in operation—reportedly the only private agency for general relief in the city at the time—the congregation decided to hire a director.[166]

English-born Robert Collyer had turned to Methodist lay ministry soon after his wife died in childbirth. Having immigrated to the United States in 1850 with his second wife, Collyer found himself at odds with authorities in the American Methodist denomination over his growing Unitarian views and his opposition to slavery.[167] In the course of a trial for heresy, Collyer resigned his Methodist affiliation and began to preach and speak independently. Lyttle writes that though Collyer was lacking in formal education, he had "a genius for speaking and writing lucid, graphic English." Great-hearted and massively built, he exuded warmth and generosity with his audiences.[168] In Philadelphia William Henry Furness, who had once opened his Unitarian pulpit to Collyer, recommended that he take over the Unitarian Ministry-at-Large in Chicago, to which Noyes' congregation agreed.[169]

As director of the Ministry-at-Large in Chicago, Collyer ran a Sunday school specifically intended for children living in poverty and soon had 200 pupils. He also ran a day and evening school, offered sewing classes, found 150 jobs for the unemployed, administered a bureau to place children and elderly persons in foster homes, visited prisoners, and engaged in other forms of relief work. In one account he reported, "The ministry-at-large is devoted to the poor—to their help in every possible way. All the publicans and harlots are members of my 'parish'—when the churches turn them out and they are lost to society, I am here to help them to themselves and to God." His notes give an idea of how this ministry looked in practical terms: "Just as I sit down to write this I have been out (nine at night) to get a poor woman an extension on two pawn tickets—to read and pray with a young man in consumption [tuberculosis]—and to buy meat, bread, and sugar for a woman quite sick and destitute, with a drunken husband."[170] Collyer's ministry should be remembered as the first urban social-action ministry-at-large in the West and the first of several to operate out of the First Unitarian Church of Chicago.

To the far west would go Thomas Starr King. Physically frail and small in stature, hobbled economically by his father's early death, Starr King utilized his energy, determination, magnetism, and intelligence to become one of the most revered and loved Universalist, and Unitarian, ministers in the nineteenth century. King aspired to be a Universalist minister like his father. Indeed, at the age of thirteen, he had already published a sermon. When his father died unexpectedly two years later and there was no money for college or divinity school, he was forced to take a job in the Charlestown Navy Yard to support his family. He found time, however, to attend lectures at Harvard College and to pursue considerable study on his own. Without a formal degree, he was called to the Charlestown Universalist Church in 1846. Through his eventual acquaintance with Henry Whitney Bellows, King obtained recognition and contacts with notable Unitarian ministers in the Boston area and began preaching at the financially destitute Hollis Street Church. In 1847, he began public lecturing to augment his salary and was soon a much sought after lecturer, traveling a circuit from Bangor, Maine to St. Louis, Missouri, speaking on such topics as "Existence and Life." Meanwhile, the Hollis Street Church overcame its financial difficulties under Starr King's leadership. In 1850, Harvard College awarded Starr King an honorary Master of Arts for his achievements as a scholar and minister.[171]

In 1860 Starr King accepted a call to serve a Unitarian church in San Francisco. Given other choices that surfaced at that same time, California presented, he said, "the more crying call." He was soon a minister-at-large to the far west, serving, as he viewed it, a Unitarian congregation, a community, and a state. King was an exceptional orator; people traveled from near and far to hear him preach. He believed that God's spirit was to be found both inside and outside the church, even in the secular arenas of art, music, and public expression. With that in mind, he turned his eye toward the state, building up Unitarian institutions on the West Coast, hoping to foster "a larger reality of spiritual development."[172] During the Civil War, King traveled the length of the state, speaking in favor of the Union, and was credited by Abraham Lincoln with saving California from becoming a seceded republic. King also headed up the Pacific Branch of the Sanitary Commission during the war, a story that appears in the chapter on the Civil War Era in this book. Behind Starr King's community ministry lay his idea that Christianity existed "not as a creed, but as a spirit, a 'secret agency'" to be found in all of public life.[173] The spiritual Christianity about which he preached was surely evident in his ministry before and during the war.

Finally, there was Quillen Hamilton Shinn. Here was a Universalist minister with the inspiration and inclination to spread the message of Universalism to remote communities across the country, most especially in the "untouched territory" of the South. Shinn had been born in 1845 in a town called Bingaman, in a part of Virginia that would in 1863 become West Virginia. At that time, this was frontier country.[174] West Virginia comprises the counties that refused to secede from the Union in the Civil War, and Shinn served with the West Virginia Volunteer Infantry through twelve engagements. Wounded once and held as a prisoner by the Confederates until ransomed, he fought at Appomattox and witnessed Lee's surrender. The war had a lasting impact on his life. In later years, he was chaplain to several units of the Grand Army of the Republic, always counseling understanding and good will toward those who had served in the Confederacy. His work with these veterans of the Civil War became an extension of his community ministry.

When the war was over, Shinn enrolled at St. Lawrence University, in Canton, New York, one of two Universalist theological schools founded in the nineteenth century.[175] From the very beginning, Shinn established himself as a uniquely promising candidate for ministry. On his way to the school, he stopped in

Baltimore to attend the Universalist General Convention then in session and engaged in debates over the Winchester Profession. Shinn was so appalled at what he heard that he stood up and addressed the convention without delegate status. What he was hearing nearly convinced him to give up on his plan to be a minister. Openly he called for harmony among the assembled ministers, which reportedly turned the "Baltimore bedlam" into a "love feast."[176] As a student at St. Lawrence, Shinn set up a ministry to the poor, and after graduating in 1870, he developed a ministry-at-large that inspired his work in prison reform, public works for the poor, and treatment of mental illness. Having been fellow-shipped by the Vermont Convention, he served briefly in a number of churches in New England, but never really settled down. Indeed, he was not content to serve one church at a time and organized circuits wherever he went. His missionary talents came to the attention of others, and in 1895 he was made the General Missionary by the Universalist General Convention, at an annual salary of $3000.

Russell Miller writes that Shinn's enthusiasm for missionary work was apparent from the first. He was unequivocal in his devotion to Universalism; he had an outgoing personality, and at the same time a knack for organizing and fund raising. As a missionary evangelist, he preached and organized, eventually setting up churches in states across the Midwest, Far West, and South. He followed a pattern that becomes identifiable upon studying his notes and the reports he filed with the Universalist General Convention. Estimates are that he traveled over 500 miles a week or 25,000 miles a year, his hand luggage full of denominational literature. He wrote his sermons on scraps of paper on trains, in hotel rooms, and in backwoods cabins. Upon arrival at his destination, he sought out families who might listen to him preach, believing that even if only one or a few families were convinced of his call to "the glorious faith," a church should be organized. Accordingly he helped establish Ladies' Aid societies and church building fund committees. One 1893 critic scornfully referred to Shinn as the "grasshopper missionary" whose brief stays in any one place made it impossible to establish permanent results. In fact, between return visits, Shinn relied on lay leadership to run these small societies until a permanent minister could be found. Shinn's biennial report to the General Convention in 1897 reveals an impressive record of activity. In less than three years, he had worked in thirty-four states, the District of Columbia, and two Canadian provinces, traveling a total of 15,000 miles. Altogether, he had organized eight churches, four state conferences, six Ladies' Aid societies and three mission circles. Indeed, at his death in 1907, it is estimated that he established at least forty churches.[177]

Shinn's sincerity sprang from his Bible Universalism, which was the basis of all his preaching. During the Civil War, he carried a Bible in his pocket and committed many passages to memory. In later years, his detailed knowledge of the Bible helped him deflect the criticism aimed at him by orthodox Christians. Significantly, though he was not orthodox, he had no use for Higher Criticism of the Bible or for the religious liberalism professed by many Unitarians. Indeed, Shinn had referred to Unitarianism as the "go-as-you-please church," and for that reason refused to identify Universalism with the label of "liberal" religion.[178] Further, even as some Universalists rejected Trinitarian language in the early twentieth century, Shinn still recognized God as savior and Christ as divine. He also preached the evils of alcohol and tobacco, discouraged the use of profanity, and advocated an end to the death penalty.

As an itinerant missionary Shinn was probably the single most recognizable figure among Universalists in his time. Robinson states, "He took the whole nation as his parish."[179] In his later years, some in the financially worried Universalist General Convention considered that his work was not worth funding. Baltimore's parish minister, Anthony Bilkovsky, charged, "A hundred churches of great strength would be superior to a 'myriad of feeble parishes scattered up and down forty-five states'. . . . The day of little things is gone." The exchanges between Bilkovsky and Shinn were printed in the newspapers, which elicited popular support favoring Shinn. The result was that he continued in his position until his death in

1907. "My way," Shinn had said, "is to go wherever a hungry soul calls for our message."[180]

PART II

Liberal Religion and Antebellum Reform

In the decades preceding the Civil War, a time known as the antebellum period, Unitarian and Universalist reformers dramatically drew attention to the need for temperance, public schools, rehabilitative prisons, an end to the death penalty, and humane asylums for the insane. A courageous few devoted their lives at great cost to the moral cause of the hour—the abolition of slavery. It is conceded that Unitarians and Universalists went further in the range of their reforms than did their evangelical counterparts. During the war, they were inseparable from the inception and operation of the U.S. Sanitary Commission. These chapters identify the reform work of Unitarians and Universalists in these antebellum years as forms of community ministry.

CHAPTER FIVE

Utopian Societies as Community Ministry

I t is estimated that there were approximately 100 communitarian societies in America between the time of the Revolution and the Civil War. The greatest wave of them occurred in the 1840s in response to the hard times that resulted from the Panic of 1837.[181] These societies could be run on either religious or secular grounds, though most were conceived at varying levels as both. Some were community ministries in that their repudiation of competitive economic individualism and its attendant disparities in wealth modeled an inspired vision of fairness and egalitarianism. Communitarian reformers were few in number, because they were trying to restructure the social and economic order. The utopians perceived a profound unfairness in the new factory system of labor. They were also generally uncomfortable with commercialism and its attendant emphasis on material wealth. Finally, some questioned traditional marital laws that typically put women at a disadvantage with regard to legal rights and property.

There are two well-known utopian leaders from this period who came out of Unitarian and Universalist faith traditions: Adin Ballou,

Universalist founder of Hopedale, and George Ripley, Unitarian and Transcendentalist founder of Brook Farm. These two societies were contemporaries of each other, though Hopedale was larger and lasted a good bit longer than did Brook Farm.

Adin Ballou's Universalist ministry was characterized by his intensely conscientious evolution in thinking. In each phase of his development, Ballou acted on the deepest insights of his faith in ways that were distinct and purposeful. Early in his career he was engaged in ecclesiastical debates over punishment after death. Ballou broke with Whittemore Universalists in 1830 in asserting that after death there would be a time of punishment before one could enter heaven. Restorationist Universalists, like Adin Ballou, contended that the second article in the Winchester Profession ought to read, "God will finally restore all men to holiness and happiness."[182] Mocked and condemned by traditional (Whittemore) Universalists, Ballou joined with others like himself in forming the Massachusetts Association of Universal Restorationists (MAUR). Like other Restorationist Universalists, Ballou saw an affinity between his views and those of the Unitarians who believed in a benevolent God.

When his closest friend, Unitarian minister Bernard Whitman, died suddenly, Ballou turned away from these ecclesiastical issues and focused instead on the idea of Practical Christianity. Here his religious focus was less about theological debate and more about what good could be done in the world. He turned his attention to the social reforms of temperance and abolition. Temperance was a popular reform that galvanized the support of people at nearly all levels of society. Curbing alcohol consumption would prevent drunken husbands from beating their wives or wasting the household money on drink. It would also bring order to people's lives. Abolition, on the other hand, was very unpopular, especially in the 1830s. People who advocated the abolition of slavery provoked scorn and animosity, even violent reprisals, from most anyone of respectability and standing.[183] Southern slave owners did not want to lose the money invested in their slaves; northern mill owners knew their profits depended on a steady supply of cheap cotton. In the face of certain condemnation Ballou argued that slavery was the "sum of all human wickedness."[184]

In 1838, Ballou came out in favor of Christian nonresistance, his name for civil disobedience when laws were perceived to be wrong. Nonresistance was in keeping with a kind of "perfectionism" that motivated the most ardent of reformers, whether they were evangelicals or secularists, or something in between. Ballou sought a way by which his Practical Christianity could be applied to nonresistance and lived out in real terms. Soon he and his fellow Practical Christians conceived of a plan to build a communitarian society. In 1841, they purchased a farm in Milford, Massachusetts, and named it Hopedale. The Hopedale members comprised the most radical reformers among the Universalist Restorationists. The life of the community was guided by Ballou's *Standard of Practical Christianity*, at least in theory. Its opening lines reversed standard notions of power: in the "kingdom of righteousness," greatness was to be found in humility, preeminence in service, patriotism in love of enemies, glory in self-sacrifice, and wealth in charity.[185] Ballou's ideas of Christian nonresistance are known to have had a profound influence on Leo Tolstoy, who reportedly named Adin Ballou the foremost writer in American literature. Tolstoy wrote that he was especially impressed with Ballou's proof of the necessity of nonresistance even, or especially, in the most impossible of situations.[186] Tolstoy in turn influenced Mohandas Gandhi, who in his turn influenced Martin Luther King, Jr.

Communitarian societies faced a dilemma. If they imposed strict rules of communal property, they risked destroying the features of individuality and private gain that some members sought to retain. If they allowed for more individuality and private gain, they risked breaking the cohesive bond that fulfilled the communitarian purposes of the society as a whole. As head of Hopedale, Adin Ballou took a moderate position on the issue of private property and, unlike some other utopian leaders, he held a conventional view of marriage. Thus members of the community invested in the properties and businesses at Hopedale and practiced traditional family commitments. Over the course of its fifteen years of operation, the community grew to 300 residents living on 600 acres of land and running a collection of shops, mills, and farms. Unfortunately, the investment scheme led to the community's collapse, when two majority investors, George and Ebenezer Draper, withdrew their shares due to what they claimed were faulty business practices on the part of the community. For Ballou, this was the overthrow of his "most cherished hopes for the regeneration and progress of individual and social humanity." At some point after that, he accepted Unitarian fellowship and served until 1880 as minister to the remnant of his community in the Hopedale Unitarian Church.[187]

Unitarian and Transcendentalist minister George Ripley was founder in 1841 of the Brook Farm commune. Ripley's ministry and the terms under which Brook Farm was founded differed in theory, if not in form, from the practical purposes embodied in Adin Ballou's work and the Hopedale Community. Ripley was a leading voice in the radical wing of Unitarianism, which also included Transcendentalists like his friend, Ralph Waldo Emerson. As we have seen, Transcendentalism emerged in the 1830s as an idea that profoundly changed New England theological discourse. In 1836, an informal discussion group met and soon took the name of the Transcendentalist Club. Those in attendance over time included George Ripley, Theodore Parker, Ralph Waldo Emerson, Margaret Fuller, Elizabeth Peabody, Bronson Alcott, Nathaniel Hawthorne, and others.[188] While Transcendentalism is understood to have promoted individualism, Emerson's call for "self-reliance," as we have seen, encouraged a willingness to challenge authority and the power of traditional institutions. This is the reason, contends David Robinson, why Transcendentalists became linked to causes of reform.[189]

George Ripley had become minister to the newly formed Purchase Street Church after graduating from Harvard Divinity School in 1826. This church offered a welcome environment of theological scholarship for this student of the liberal religious thought coming out of Europe. At the Purchase Street Church, however, Ripley became dissatisfied with parish ministry as a vehicle for social reform.[190] Meanwhile, he had become engaged in a movement called Associationism, an early form of socialist theory stressing cooperative, non-competitive living in order to bring about harmony in society. Amid talk of reform and other experimental communities among Boston's intellectuals, Ripley announced to the Transcendentalist Club in 1840 his desire to create an intentional community that would emulate in real life the values of Associationism and Transcendentalism. He would call it Brook Farm Institute for Education and Agriculture. It would be a society in which agricultural labor and intellectual pursuits would be evenly shared and equally valued. Beside the farm, there would be a school offering the full range of instruction, "from the first rudiments to the highest culture."[191] This arrangement would "guarantee the highest mental freedom, by providing all with labor . . . and securing them the fruits of their industry." Established under these high ideals, and in keeping with the Articles of Agreement and Association, its members expected their endeavor to "impart a greater freedom, simplicity, truthfulness, refinement, and moral dignity to our mode of life."[192]

Brook Farm remained small in size, its membership never exceeding 150, and only lasted five years. It became one of the most noteworthy of the communitarian experiments because of the Transcendentalist writers who stayed there and wrote about their experiences.[193] What may have contributed to its premature demise in 1846 was Ripley's decision in 1844 to restructure the community along lines laid out by the French utopian social theorist Charles Fourier. Ripley had read of Fourier's ideas, as presented in Albert Brisbane's compendium *The Social Destiny of Man.* Fourier believed that the cause of conflict and suffering was due to the perversion of human goodness by faulty social organization. He advocated small planned communities, each one its own "phalanx" with membership limited to 1620 and coming from all strata of society. Brisbane visited Brook Farm many times, and then stayed for several months to work on his translation of Fourier's works. It is thought that Brisbane was instrumental in persuading Ripley to adopt the Fourier plan to achieve greater prosperity. On January 18, 1844, Ripley consented to turn Brook

Farm from what Russell Miller termed a "Transcendentalist picnic into a regimented Phalanx."[194]

To implement the plan, the community built a large building called a phalanstery and set up a system of rotating tasks. The Transcendentalist *Dial* ceased publication in 1844, replaced in June 1845 by the *Harbinger*, a journal that spoke not for Brook Farm but for Fourier and international socialism. In its pages, Ripley set out the philosophy of the new arrangement and the new journal. "The interests of Social Reform will be considered paramount to all others in whatever is admitted into the pages of the *Harbinger*." He continued, "In this reform, we are conscious that we are devoting our best ability to the removal of oppression and injustice among men, to the complete emancipation of the enslaved, to the promotion of temperance, and to the elevation of the toiling and downtrodden masses to the inborn rights of humanity."[195]

Unfortunately, these high aims for humanity soon met with tragedy and loss. After a celebration of the near completion of the new phalanstery, a small fire intended to dry out the plaster spread into the building and burned it to the ground. This was an uninsured loss from which the community was unable to recover. The remaining buildings were sold for $20,000, a fraction of what they were worth.[196] To help defray these costs, the intellectual Ripley sold his library. As the last of his books were carted away, he mourned, "Now I understand how a man would feel to be present at his own funeral." The *Harbinger* was moved to New York and lasted only until 1849.

The communitarian experiments of the nineteenth century were inspired attempts to contemplate and construct humane egalitarian approaches to life. Hopedale and Brook Farm embodied forms of community living that offered—not only for their members but for the rest of the world—radical lessons about religion and its relationship to human experience and human connection. Hopedale's Practical Christianity defined any form of power as the self-serving antithesis of authentic love; Brook Farm's Transcendentalist and Fourieristic ideals were based on the complementary ideas that each individual embodies an inner essence of higher truth, and that, working in cooperation, small societies can over-come the causes of conflict and suffering. The idioms of expression were seemingly distinct for each community. Importantly, how-ever, they stood on common ground in their determination to overcome the alienation of a modern material worldview. More-over, each society offered a benevolent egalitarian formula for living out the moral imperatives of Universalist or (Unitarian) Transcendentalist religious practice.

CHAPTER SIX

Ordained Ministers
as Reformers

This is a good place to look more carefully at the reform ministries of the 1830s through the 1850s. In the thirty years preceding the Civil War, trends in urbanization, immigration, and early industrialization presented Americans with new problems and challenges. At the same time, a Second Great Awakening of religious fervor, as well as rational thought, further opened the doors of orthodoxy and sent believers in evangelical, liberal, and secular directions. In all cases, followers embraced a perfectionist impulse that more broadly undermined the Calvinist premise of total depravity. To address issues of social dislocation, economic collapse, alcoholism, and sexual vice, reformers assumed that people were not trapped in their failings. They could substantially improve themselves and their society. This idea galvanized a generation of reformers, both lay and clergy, in the early decades of the nineteenth century. Included among them were many Unitarians and Universalists, whose ideas of "self-culture" emphasized, in the words of William Ellery Channing, "the spiritual capacity of the soul." "The purpose of a religious life," lectured Channing in 1838, "is to do whatever we can to unfold all our powers and capacities."[197] Such ideas became the basis for "self-culture" and helped inspire the reform activities that proliferated in the decades leading up to the Civil War.

Dennis Landis refers to Samuel Joseph May as "one of the greatest social and educational reformers of the nineteenth century."[198] From the time of his younger brother's accidental death, May adopted a seriousness of purpose that guided him throughout his later life and ministry. While at Divinity School, May set aside his Trinitarian views to become a Unitarian, and in 1822 he accepted a call to a liberal Congregational church in Brooklyn, Connecticut. From this parish, May wrote, "I determined to make [the] words and character [of Jesus of Nazareth] the standard of my faith and practice."[199] In 1826, he helped found the Windham County Peace Society and, soon after, organized a local temperance society.

The work for which May would be most widely known came after he heard William Lloyd Garrison speak in Boston in 1830. At that point, he was converted from his lukewarm support for anti-slavery and called for the immediate emancipation of slaves everywhere in the United States. This put him in line with the radical views of Garrison, who opposed the gradualist and partialist views of the moderates. He would continue to work with Garrison and other abolitionists to support the cause of anti-slavery, traveling widely as a speaker for the cause and aiding fugitive slaves in their escape to Canada. In 1833, he became intensely involved in the cause of a schoolteacher in Canterbury, Connecticut, when local townspeople forced her to close her school for "Ladies of Color."[200] When even churches were closed to Prudence Crandall and her students, May invited her to bring her students to his church. Years later, when the 1850 Fugitive Slave Law was in force (see an explanation of the law in the discussion of Emerson), May was known to have escorted escaping slaves along the Underground Railroad and to have personally inspected living conditions at Canadian destinations.[201] In 1851, he participated in a "Jerry Rescue," helping to free runaway slave William "Jerry" McHenry. May was a principal in the plan, but the district attorney chose not to bring a case against him.

It was an episode that would be repeated elsewhere by others, so great was resistance in the North to the Fugitive Slave Law.

In 1845, May began a ministry at the Church of the Messiah in Syracuse, New York. Here he became more acquainted with the cause of women's rights and delivered in 1846 his memorable address on the *Rights and Condition of Women,* asking why "half the people have the right to govern the whole."[202] Soon he was well known among the likes of Susan B. Anthony and Elizabeth Cady Stanton. In 1850, he spoke at the National Woman's Rights Convention, held in Worcester, Massachusetts, saying "Humanity is dual, and yet when perfected it is one." Having witnessed the conditions of labor for needle-women in Syracuse, he assisted in 1854 in the formation of an early union, the Sewing Female Protection Society. Thus, his reform impulses broadened to include the causes of woman suffrage, as well as workers' rights, and the redistribution of wealth through a graduated income tax. On this last measure, he pre-dated American policymakers by at least thirty years. In 1855, he delivered a controversial Berry Street Lecture to Boston Unitarian ministers in which he addressed fundamental economic unfairness and called for a redistribution of wealth in a socialist government.[203] In this campaign, as in others, he was ahead of his contemporaries, and more in league with a later generation of nineteenth-century socialist visionaries.[204] May's life and work would touch the lives of untold numbers of people well beyond his parish. When he died in 1871, Andrew Dickson White, president of Cornell University, called him "the noblest man and the best Christian that I have ever known."

There were other ministers besides May who traveled the knotty roads of reform, well outside the confines of traditional parish claims—in particular, Charles (b. 1803) and John Murray (b. 1804) Spear. The Spear brothers were born into a Universalist family in Boston and raised in the earliest of the Universalist churches led by John Murray and Hosea Ballou. Both brothers grew up to become Universalist ministers, serving parishes in various locations within Massachusetts, and devoting much of their time to important reform causes. Charles had been inspired by the

Marquis de Lafayette, who had lectured: "I shall ask for the abolition of the Penalty of Death until I have the infallibility of human
judgment demonstrated to me."[205] From this moment, Charles
began writing against capital punishment, while his brother John
urged the Massachusetts legislature to pass resolutions against it.
Giving added weight to their convictions, Charles and John became
founding members in 1839 of the New England Non-Resistance
Society. This organization, led by William Lloyd Garrison and Adin
Ballou, renounced violence of any kind and repudiated all world
governments because they used force to preserve a social order that
was cruel and unjust. Many non-resisters, for instance, refused to
vote, because doing so would give credibility to the government.[206]

Charles Spear was appointed General Agent of the Massachusetts Society for the Abolition of Capital Punishment. In his
Essays on the Punishment of Death, he outlined his belief that because
human life is sacred and capital punishment is irreversible, execution
is a blasphemous appropriation of divine power. He began to edit
the *Hangman*, later named *The Prisoner's Friend*, a journal that urged
a changed ethos in prisons, from punishment to rehabilitation. In
this he became part of a movement, joined by others, including
Dorothea Dix, whose reform ministry is included in the next chapter of this history. Besides writing, Charles engaged in lobbying for
improved conditions in prisons, visiting prisoners, helping parolees,
and running halfway houses for ex-convicts. During the war, he
developed his ministry as an Army chaplain, serving in the hospitals, churches, and military encampments of Washington, DC.[207]

Near the end of his life, Charles' reputation began to suffer
from his being confused with his brother John Murray Spear. John
had long shared in Charles' labors to end capital punishment—
what he called his "mission of love." John had also played a hero-
ically active role in the abolitionist movement. He organized the
first Universalist anti-slavery conventions, despite opposition from
many Universalists. While on an anti-slavery tour in Portland,
Maine, John was attacked by a mob and sustained serious head
injuries from which he took months to recover. After helping a
slave girl gain her freedom, he was vilified in public with racist

epithets, which forced him to resign his pulpit in New Bedford.[208] With the passage of the Fugitive Slave Law in 1850, John was among the organizers of the Boston Vigilance Committee, dedicated to helping slaves escape to Canada. By the 1850s, these activities placed John Murray Spear well within reform traditions that did not in themselves alienate him from his reform-minded peers. It was John's turn to Spiritualism, however, that brought his personal reputation into question, even among reformers. Spiritualism rested on a belief that the line separating this world from the next was more permeable than ordinarily assumed. Clients sought to contact the spirits of their departed loved ones through a medium who "facilitated" the connection.

Perhaps it was the way in which John Spear propounded his Spiritualist beliefs that so dismayed his family and friends. He believed he was the general agent on Earth of the spirits of John Murray, Thomas Jefferson, Benjamin Franklin, Benjamin Rush, and other distinguished elites who had formed a "Congress of Spirits." This Congress, announced Spear, would make known their plans through him for the remaking of society. Spiritualism reached a peak of popularity from the 1840s through the 1860s, in part due to grieving mothers desperate to contact their lost sons during the Mexican War and the Civil War. Unfortunately, its dubious premise, compounded with the fakeries and delusions of its practitioners, undermined any legitimacy it might have enjoyed. In this instance, John Murray Spear lost the support he earlier had acquired for his reform ministry, especially after he also turned to "free love," which, not surprisingly, led to the breakup of his marriage. His peculiar story is worth telling because it is indicative of the experimental quality of some reform movements in this period. He should also be remembered for his work on behalf of ending capital punishment and slavery.

The ministry of Thomas Wentworth Higginson took him into most of the powerful reform movements of his day, especially temperance and abolition. In the world of nineteenth-century social reform, temperance was the most popular cause, consisting of a range of movements aimed at curbing drink to a greater or lesser degree. As a reform cause, its advocates crossed all sectional, class, and religious lines. Reducing alcohol consumption would help eliminate poverty and reduce instances of drunken husbands beating their wives. Further, it would prevent vice and moral decay in the nation's cities. Finally, signing pledges of abstinence would raise the social status of those who aspired to be upwardly mobile.[209] It will be remembered that it was eighteenth-century Universalist physician Benjamin Rush who influenced a change in thinking— to see alcohol addiction as a condition to be treated, a disease rather than a sin.

For Unitarians and Universalists, the most visible temperance organization was the Massachusetts Society for the Suppression of Intemperance. Formed in 1813, more than 40 percent of its founders were Unitarians.[210] Higginson, minister of the Free Church in Worcester, Massachusetts, was Secretary of the Massachusetts Temperance Society, which organized a successful campaign for the prohibition of the sale of alcohol in the state. He also organized a Carson League, a "private police force" that could be employed to enforce the law in Worcester. Indeed, Higginson used undercover agents to buy drinks in the Irish shantytowns; such agents would then testify against the sellers. It may seem an unworthy business when one considers that sellers could easily include a poor widow trying to support herself. Higginson and others like him found justification for their actions in the writings of Benjamin Rush. Indeed, imbued with a sense of the rightness of the campaign, Higginson reflected that even partial suppression was a blessing. "How many does it save from the beginnings of vice?"[211]

In his day, Higginson would have been known as an "Ultra"—someone unwilling to compromise on his principles.[212] Any Ultra would have actively resisted the Fugitive Slave Law, and Higginson was no exception. When Boston resident and Baptist minister Anthony Burns was taken captive, Higginson and other abolitionists staged an unsuccessful attempt to rescue him from prison in May 1854. Hundreds of Boston's citizens watched in horror, shouting "Kidnappers!" as soldiers and marines paraded Burns down the street toward the ship that President Franklin Pierce had ordered to return him to slavery. Boston buildings were draped in black for the occasion and church bells tolled across the city.[213] Higginson was apparently well loved for his part in the Burns rescue attempt, even though the break-in resulted in the wounding and subsequent death of a prison guard. When a U.S. Marshal arrived to investigate Higginson's involvement, Worcester citizens both black and white mobbed the Marshal. From his pulpit, Higginson preached on "Massachusetts in Mourning," challenging the citizens of Worcester to make their city the Canada of the Fugitive Slave movement. There is no doubt that Higginson was one of the most radical men of his time, financing John Brown's raid on Harper's Ferry as a member of a secret committee to support Brown, later known as the Secret Six. When the raid failed, Higginson berated those on the committee who sought to deny their culpability.[214] He, on the other hand, publicly announced his support for Brown, the so-called "fanatic," whose execution made him a martyr for the anti-slavery cause.

Theodore Parker was addressing a rally at Faneuil Hall, called to protest Anthony Burns' arrest, at the moment that Higginson and others were trying to free him. Parker's 1850 *Sermon of Conscience* had called for open defiance of the Fugitive Slave Law. Indeed, he had served as minister-at-large to the fugitive slaves in Boston and chaired the Boston Vigilance Committee, which provided material aid, legal assistance, and help with avoiding capture. The capture of escaped slave Anthony Burns occurred shortly after Congress passed the Kansas-Nebraska Act, which potentially opened up the northern territories of Kansas and Nebraska to slavery through the dubious mechanism of popular sovereignty, in defiance of previous compromise bills.[215] This bill threw the North into an uproar, split the Whig party, and spawned the new Republican Party, which was dedicated to preventing the spread of slavery into the western territories. Subsequent to Burns' extradition, Parker publicly condemned the Slave Commissioner Edward G. Loring, a conservative Whig, who had ordered that Burns be returned to his master. Parker was indicted before a federal grand jury for obstructing the execution of federal law.[216] As with Higginson, popular opinion in Boston made prosecution a practical impossibility. In 1855, the charges against Parker were dismissed on a technicality.

Parker's opposition to slavery had grown in part out of his belief that slavery was the greatest obstacle to achieving the promise of industrial democracy. He denounced America's war with Mexico (1846–1848), as had many Northern Whigs at the time, as an aggressive action undertaken to gain territory for the spread of slavery.[217] When violence erupted between pro-slavery and anti-slavery advocates in Kansas Territory in 1854, Parker raised money to buy weapons and supplies for the free-state militias.[218] Finally, along with Higginson, Parker participated as a member of the Secret Six who helped finance John Brown's raid at Harper's Ferry. He saw a mighty struggle at work in the country between the forces of freedom and the forces of despotism. On the latter side stood both the slaveholders of the South and the wealthy powerful classes of the North. Parker denounced slavery as a violation of Christian ideals. It was a characteristic of the Transcendentalists that they spoke so openly against slavery. Like Emerson and Higginson, Parker could not proclaim the latent divinity of the individual and at the same time condone the personal degradation of enslavement.[219]

Theodore Parker must be understood as one of the most vital figures in nineteenth-century Unitarian history. Being too poor to enroll in classes at Harvard, he nonetheless passed the entrance exams and read the complete curriculum on his own. Over the course of his life, Parker collected a library of some 14,000 volumes and is thought to have read them all. Moreover he wrote voluminously, producing thousands of pages of text in sermons, pamphlets, articles, and books. In keeping with Transcendentalist ideas, Parker held that revelation did not depend on some historical record, but grew out of a "deep internal sense of the sacred and holy dimension of existence."[220]

In 1841, he preached a controversial sermon—*A Discourse on the Transient and Permanent in Christianity*—in which he argued that the religion of Jesus was the Absolute Religion, which would never go away. Jesus was "the perfect moral and religious incarnation of God," but the biblical miracles and the miraculous authority of both Jesus and the Bible were not to be taken as factual or permanent. From this point on, Parker was nearly completely ostracized by the Boston ministers, who denied him access to their pulpits. Pulpit exchange, it should be noted, offered an important social and theological entry-point into the privileged status and society of ministers.[221] Forced to stand outside that circle, Parker developed a following of his own, organized as the 28th Congregational Society. He preached to standing-room-only audiences at the Melodeon Hall, until attendance surpassed 2000, prompting a move to the more spacious Boston Music Hall.

Parker preached on behalf of many reforms. He supported temperance because drunkenness produced widespread spiritual destruction; he supported public schools for girls as well as boys; he spoke for women's rights in many sermons, even addressing God as "Mother" as well as "Father." By the time of John Brown's raid at Harper's Ferry, Parker was in Italy dying of tuberculosis. His clergy peers withheld any official expression of sympathy until after his death in May 1860. No eulogy was spoken at his graveside; rather, the first eleven verses of the Sermon on the Mount were read, as he had requested. Younger Unitarian ministers would honor him as a prophetic figure and value his insistent commitments to a just society. Emerson accurately predicted that "coming generations" would learn from "the plain lessons of Theodore Parker . . . the true temper and authentic record of these days."[222]

In keeping with Neil Shadle's analogy, it may be said that these nineteenth-century minister reformers—Samuel May, Charles Spear, John Murray Spear, Thomas Wentworth Higginson, and Theodore Parker—illustrate the old Puritan covenantal model of parish ministry, with the parish expanded to include the larger community. Whereas their Puritan forebears were concerned with sustaining theological conformity, these latter-day ministers challenged it, realizing expansive liberal theological innovations in meeting their call to serve the world. For them, the line between the church and the world became blurred, nearly indistinct, as they responded to the social justice imperatives of their day.

CHAPTER SEVEN

Reform Work as
Lay Community Minstry

There were Unitarian and Universalist laypersons who also dedicated their lives to the reform movements of this time. As with parish ministers who took on reform work, lay ministers worked for temperance, eradication of the death penalty, prison reform, asylums for the insane, educational reform, and abolition. Like parish minister reformers, lay reformers were alert and vigorous people responding to the social ills they witnessed, pursuing community ministry as a life's work—sometimes without remuneration. Ronald Walters argues that the reform impulse was encouraged by a Protestant perfectionist impulse that owed much to the revivalism of the 1820s and early 1830s. Reform energies, claims Walters, soon surpassed in direction and scope the narrow vision of most evangelicals. The Unitarians and Universalists were among the more progressive reformers, committed to advancing their aims for the sake of "improving the human situation."[223]

In 1833, popular writer Lydia Maria Frances Child implored her readers "not to throw down this volume as soon as you have glanced at the title." She was referring to her book *An Appeal in*

Favor of that Class of Americans called Africans, which described the abuses of slavery and put forward an argument for why it should be abolished. This was indeed a departure from her former fare, which included the highly popular *The Frugal Housewife* (1829), other household manuals, historical novels, and children's magazines. Since Child had been accustomed to supporting herself and her somewhat improvident husband, David Child, on the income from her writing, she dearly understood what she risked in exposing her radical politics. Predictably, publication of *An Appeal* cost Child most of her wide readership. Yet she could not do other than write what was in her heart. William Lloyd Garrison, Child later wrote, had "got hold of the strings of my conscience and pulled me into Reforms."[224] Joan Goodwin writes that *An Appeal* converted more people to abolition than any other publication. It is known, for instance, to have had a deep effect on William Ellery Channing, whose anti-slavery views prior to reading *An Appeal* had been more moderate. From 1841 to 1843, Child turned her attention to editing the *National Anti-Slavery Standard*, a weekly publication of the American Anti-Slavery Society. When the anti-slavery movement split over Garrison's position of "non-resistance," Child left the paper and the movement. Non-resisters, as we have seen with Adin Ballou, refused to acknowledge the government, on the premise that governments used force to uphold unjust laws. In Garrison's case, he refused to vote, which alienated much of his support.

With the enactment of the Fugitive Slave Law of 1850, Child was compelled to return to the cause. It was during the years of the Fugitive Slave Law that Child became acquainted with a runaway mulatto slave woman, Harriet Brent Jacobs. Jacobs had publicly taken the name of Linda Brent to conceal her identity and elude capture by her former master living in South Carolina. Jacobs had written of her life in slavery, wherein she had spent seven years hiding in the crawl space above her free grandmother's kitchen, to escape the sexual demands of her master. Child served as editor of Jacobs' manuscript, only "for purposes of condensation and orderly arrangement," adding nothing to the telling of the story. It posed a "delicate subject," she acknowledged, but one that she

willingly exposed to view "for the sake of my sisters in bondage."
Also, she explained, "I do it with the hope of arousing conscientious and reflecting women at the North to a sense of their duty in
the exertion of moral influence on the question of Slavery" and
with the hope that "every man who reads this narrative" will swear
that "no fugitive from Slavery shall ever be sent back to suffer in
that loathsome den of corruption and cruelty."[225]

John Brown's massacre of pro-slavery settlers at Osawatomie
Creek in Kansas and his attempt to raid the federal arsenal at
Harper's Ferry to supply an army of escaped slaves were viewed in
the North with a kind of mixed admiration. We have seen that
ministers Thomas Wentworth Higginson and Theodore Parker
risked arrest in support of Brown. While Brown was being held in
prison, awaiting trial after his failed raid at Harper's Ferry, Lydia
Maria Child sent him a letter of sympathy, asking if she might
visit him and attend his wounds. She sent the letter via Virginia's
Governor Wise, requesting that he pass the letter on to the prisoner and grant permission for her visit. "I have heard that you were
a man of chivalrous sentiments.... Relying on these indications of
honor and justice in your character.... Will you have the kindness, after reading [the letter] yourself, to transmit it to the prisoner?" She allowed, "I deeply regret the step that the old veteran has
taken, while I honor his humanity towards those who became his
prisoners."[226]

The governor's response was "chivalrous" as well as critical of
Child's abolitionist views. Her lengthy response to him, outlining
a defense of abolition, was published, unbeknownst to her, by
reformer Horace Greeley in his *New York Tribune*. Readers in the
North offered admiration; readers in the South were indignant.
Calling Child a hypocrite, Mrs. Mason from Alto, Virginia, wrote in
defense of slave owners as people who cared for their servants. "We
endeavor to do our duty in that state of life it has pleased God to
place us." What had perhaps angered her was Child's accusation
that male slave owners engaged in sexual exploitation of their
female slaves. This was in fact a common practice about which
slave owners were most defensive. When war finally came, Child

continued with her anti-slavery activism and gathered supplies to send to the "contrabands," the runaway slaves who showed up in the ranks of the Union Army. She spent the last years of her life working on her own "eclectic Bible" of quotations from the World's Religions, explaining it was her task "to do all I can to enlarge and strengthen the hand of human brotherhood."[227]

Frances Ellen Watkins Harper was an African American woman born to free parents in Baltimore in 1825. A well-read woman, she became actively involved in the cause to end slavery, becoming one of the first female lecturers, black or white, to be invited by the abolitionist societies to speak publicly on her views. With the passage of the Fugitive Slave Law in 1850, the slave state of Maryland became unsafe for free blacks, and Frances Watkins moved to Ohio and taught sewing at Union Seminary. In 1851 she moved to Pennsylvania, where she worked with the Pennsylvania Abolition Society and helped escaping slaves along the Underground Railroad on their way to Canada.[228] It was here, in 1870, that she joined the First Unitarian Church of Philadelphia.[229] When her 1854 collection of poems, *Poems on Miscellaneous Subjects,* attracted critical notice and achieved commercial success, she donated most of the earnings to help free slaves. These poems and her other writings attacked racism and the oppression of women, and helped launch her on a career as a popular lecturer among anti-slavery audiences.

Watkins had known John Brown from the days when she had worked at Union Seminary and he was principal of the school. When Brown's unsuccessful raid at Harper's Ferry led to his arrest, she gave emotional support to Mary Brown during her husband's trial and execution. Grohsmeyer reports that a letter from Watkins was smuggled into Brown's prison cell. Writing from her experience as a free African American woman living in the North, Watkins' letter expressed in heartfelt words the depth of sentiment that empowered the anti-slavery cause and found its hero in John Brown. "In the name of a young girl sold from the warm clasp of a mother's arms to the clutches of a libertine or profligate—in the name of the slave mother, her heart rocked to and fro by the agony of her mournful separations—thank you, that you have been brave enough to reach out your hands to the crushed and blighted of my race."[230] Frances Watkins married Fenton Harper in 1860 and continued her writing and publishing, for which she was called the mother of African American journalism. Her career after the Civil War is described in more detail in the chapter on mid-century developments in community ministry.

Sallie Holley was a Unitarian woman from New York State who became active in abolitionism in the 1850s. When her father died in 1841, she moved to Buffalo to live with her sister and was baptized in the Unitarian church there. It was also in Buffalo that she attended anti-slavery meetings, which had a great effect on her. Indeed, she resigned her membership in the Buffalo church when President Millard Fillmore, a member, signed the Fugitive Slave Act of 1850 and the church issued no word of rebuke.[231] "I think I cannot consent that my name shall stand on the books of a church which will countenance voting for any pro-slavery presidential candidate."[232] Holley left Buffalo to enroll at Oberlin College, and while a student, she embarked on her career as an anti-slavery lecturer, a career she pursued from 1851 until the Civil War. Holley's ideas about slavery echoed the uncompromising views of William Lloyd Garrison, calling for an immediate and universal end to slavery.[233]

Among other significant Unitarian laypersons who worked to end slavery were a married couple, Samuel Gridley Howe and Julia Ward Howe. Samuel was a physician who had earned a medical degree from Harvard in 1824. He helped found the New England Institute for the Blind[234] and became a self-taught expert on educating blind persons and deaf-mutes. Julia was a poet, essayist, lecturer, and reformer who worked on behalf of abolition, women's rights, and international peace.[235] More is said on Julia Ward Howe in the chapter on Suffrage Pioneers in this book. Over the course of his career, Samuel Howe took an active interest in the several institutional reforms of his day: public education in Massachusetts, improved custodial care for people with mental illness, and rehabilitative penitentiaries for prisoners. Public schools would become the leveling agent of society; institutions for people with mental illness promised a cure if patients were given proper structure and kind treatment; penitentiaries offered wrongdoers the opportunity to contemplate their sins and reform their ways. An active member of the abolitionist movement, Samuel Howe edited the antislavery paper *The Commonwealth* and helped rescue fugitive slaves. When the passage of the Kansas-Nebraska Act in 1854 prompted a war between Free Soil and Pro-Slavery advocates in Kansas, both Samuel and Julia joined the hundreds who raised money to support the Free-Soil faction.

Of further importance to this period were Dorothea Dix and Mary Livermore. Dorothea Lynde Dix was part of the early generation of nineteenth-century reformers born at the turn of the century, like May and Child, who were deeply disturbed by the vast new difficulties that accompanied the emerging industrial economy. Though highly intelligent and well-read, Dix had an unhappy childhood. Her father was an itinerant hellfire-and-brimstone Methodist preacher, and her mother was "listless and self-absorbed." In 1814, at the age of twelve, Dix ran away from home, and within two years, she opened a private, academically demanding school. Later she balanced her daytime private school with a free evening school for poor children.[236] This pre-dated the arrival of free public schools, so long advocated by Unitarian Horace Mann.

Dix found her religious home among the Unitarians after hearing William Ellery Channing preach at the First Federal Street Church of Boston. She was profoundly influenced by Channing's vision of liberal Christianity; Channing was impressed by Dix's compassion and hired her as a tutor for his children. Still in her early twenties, Dix became part of the family, even traveling with them on vacations. Once the children were grown, however, Dix fell into what was likely a depression, at which point Channing arranged for her to recuperate with a friend in England. When she returned eighteen months later, she accepted an offer to teach a Sunday school class for women in the County House of Correction. This experience launched her into the work that would most distinctly mark her life.

Upon entering the East Cambridge jail, Dix was shocked at the conditions under which inmates were forced to live. There was no attempt to segregate hardened criminals from inmates who were considered "feeble-minded" or "insane," whether they were children or adults. Since it was assumed that the insane had lost their human capacities and could not feel cold, their quarters were unheated. Some had no blankets and most wore scant clothing. Dix soon managed to secure a court order mandating that heat and other improvements be provided to prisoners. She came to recognize that she had an ally in Horace Mann, a Unitarian layman who served in the Massachusetts legislature from 1827 to 1837. With Mann's encouragement, Dix embarked on a mission to investigate jails and almshouses across Massachusetts. Her report, entitled "Memorial," shocked legislators and citizens in Massachusetts. Additional money was soon appropriated to enlarge the State Mental Hospital that Mann had already founded in Worcester. From the success of this survey, Dix resolved to use the same strategy in other states. For the next twenty years she visited every state east of Colorado. Prison wardens were not always so anxious to have her see the worst cases, but eventually they relented in the face of her insistence. In the late 1840s, Dix formulated a plan in which a federal land grant of 12,500,000 acres would be parceled and rented or sold to fund schools for the blind, deaf, mute, and insane. The bill was passed by the Senate and House and would have been signed into law by President Millard Fillmore, had it reached his desk before he left office. Franklin Pierce, who won election in 1852, vetoed the bill.[237]

In the end, Dorothea Dix could legitimately claim credit for the creation of thirty hospitals for the treatment of people with mental illness. Of particular importance to Dix was the philosophy that institutions for the insane offer a "therapeutic setting for the curable insane and a humanely comfortable setting for those regarded as incurable."[238] Additionally, as a direct result of her work, fifteen states improved their supervision of penitentiaries, asylums, and poorhouses.[239] Having never married, Dix was financially free to pursue her community ministry of hospital reform due to a generous family inheritance. The asylums she helped establish offered structure and kindness, resulting in an estimated cure rate of fifty percent. Sadly, they became overcrowded by mid-century. Restraints and force replaced individual kindness as bureaucratic administrators treated their charges more like the unwanted outcasts of society. The rehabilitative idea that such human beings were curable or redeemable would be reborn, finally, with the new professionals at the end of the century.[240]

One of the most touching stories to grace the work of reform-minded ministry is that of Mary Ashton Rice Livermore. Raised in a Calvinist home, Mary had suffered much anguish over the doctrine of predestination. This reached a crisis stage when she worried that a sister who died was among the lost. It was not until she met Universalist minister Daniel Livermore, heard him preach, and read books from his library that she overcame her Calvinist anxiety and embraced a Universalist religious view.[241] Mary and Daniel fell in love and were married. But as a minister's wife, Mary was not particularly happy, and she turned to writing. Two of her early novels received awards: one a story on temperance, the other a story with autobiographical overtones on "changes wrought in one's life and character by a vital change of religious belief." Both Daniel and Mary held abolitionist views, and after a series of pastorates in New England, they moved to Chicago, where Daniel bought and edited a reform-centered Universalist newspaper, the *New Covenant*. Mary also wrote and edited significant portions of this paper and was able to begin reform work of her own, at first volunteering to help with the cholera epidemic and later heading up the Northwest Section of the Sanitary Commission during the Civil War. The story of the Commission, and the remainder of the Livermores' story, is told in the Civil War Era chapter of this history.

This discussion of lay reformers concludes with Horace Greeley, an important reform news writer and editor who, in 1841, founded the *New York Tribune*. Greeley was born into an itinerant farming family in New Hampshire. A voracious reader, he largely educated himself. He became interested in Universalist theology and adopted the Restorationist view of Adin Ballou, seeing the scriptures "happily blending inexorable punishment for every offense with unfailing pity and ultimate forgiveness for the chastened transgressor."[242] It was not until after he moved to New York City from Erie, Pennsylvania, that Greeley formally joined a Universalist church, that of the Rev. Thomas Jefferson Sawyer on Orchard Avenue.[243] In later years, Greeley's Universalism took on signs of Transcendentalism, as is evident in his statement that "an Omniscient Beneficence presides over the entire course of human affairs, leading ever onward and upward to universal purity and bliss."[244] He also moved toward anti-Trinitarianism, a view that generally distinguished Universalists of his day, he thought, from Universalists of the previous generation.

Greeley spent a great deal of time with the Rev. Sawyer and his wife, Carolyn, and was anxious to share with them his plan to start a new paper. The *New York Tribune* would absorb his two existing papers, the *New Yorker* and the *Log Cabin*. When the first issue came out in 1841, he handed a copy to Caroline and accurately predicted, "It shall be a power in the land." Under Greeley's editorship and management, the *New York Tribune* became an important voice for humanitarian reform, women's rights, and anti-slavery sentiment. Greeley hired top writers in the country as well as Transcendentalist literary figures like Margaret Fuller and George Ripley. It will be remembered that Margaret Fuller's fateful trip to Europe was taken on assignment for Horace Greeley and the *Tribune*.

Greeley's reform vision was consistent with the goals of his peers: he advocated an end to capital punishment, improved working conditions, and women's rights, the latter after being influenced by Margaret Fuller. After her death, he wrote a moderate endorsement of the 1850 National Women's Rights Convention, held in Worcester.[245] On the more radical side, Greeley also endorsed vegetarianism, communitarianism, socialism, and labor unions. About him it was written, "Greeley labored with the world to better it, to give men moderate wages and wholesome food, and to teach women to earn a living." He once described his own aims as creating societies that "shall ultimately result in universal holiness and consequent happiness."[246]

Actively engaged in politics as a Whig, Greeley helped organize the new Republican Party in 1856 and campaigned for Abraham Lincoln in 1860. He had long been opposed to slavery, and when the war began, he began pressing Lincoln to emancipate the slaves. His famous letter "A Prayer for Twenty Millions" was published in the *New York Tribune* on August 20, 1862. In it, Greeley charged Lincoln with being "disastrously remiss" in regard to his enforcement of the new Confiscation Act, which provided that runaway slaves would be granted immunity as contraband—that is, as appropriated enemy goods and property—if they showed up in Union camps. As Greeley tells it, army personnel had attacked arriving slaves and killed them, while Lincoln did nothing to reprimand them or enforce the law. Greeley berated Lincoln for being "unduly influenced by the counsels of certain fossil politicians hailing from the Border States" who still held slaves, while ignoring the presence of pro-Union sentiment in certain localities in the South. The Union cause would be futile without ending slavery, Greeley implored. "Every hour of deference to Slavery is an hour of added and deepened peril to the Union."[247] When Lincoln issued the initial phase of the Emancipation Proclamation in the next month, Greeley rejoiced. "It is the beginning of the new life of the nation."[248]

Reform in the antebellum years of the nineteenth century came as a natural consequence of the upheavals caused by industrialization, immigration, and rapid urbanization. New problems presented themselves and old problems acquired new urgency. Most critical of all was the call to stop the spread of slavery and ultimately to end it. Unitarian and Universalist clergy and lay leaders courageously assumed responsibility for bringing about change. Risking ostracism and arrest, they preached, they published books and articles, they joined protest organizations, they formed communal societies, they lobbied legislatures, and they employed civil disobedience to fight the fugitive slave law. The Civil War, when it finally came, ushered in new, more pressing claims for service. Community ministers turned their attention to the crisis at hand.

Community Ministry in the Era of the Civil War

War broke out between the north and south after all attempts to avert it failed. The United States had acquired vast new territories to the west as a result of its 1848 war with Mexico, and the question of whether slavery would be legal in these territories had been resolved temporarily in a series of hotly debated compromises.[249] Which would prevail: a system of free wage labor, as desired by the northern industrial states, or a system of slave labor, as desired by the southern slave-owning states? The Supreme Court's 1857 decision in the case of *Dred Scott v. Sanford* created an impasse over which there could be no compromise. Slaves were property, said Chief Justice Roger B. Taney, and since the Constitution protected property, slave ownership was to be protected in any state of the union—north, south, east, or west. The showdown came in 1860, when Lincoln's election forced a split in the union. By default, the war begun to repair the split became the war to end human bondage. Those who had so long fought to end slavery welcomed its ultimate abolition, but deeply mourned the grim measure of loss and despair exacted by the war on all sections of the country.

Early battles brought scores of wounded soldiers into Washington, DC and St. Louis. The military was unprepared to cope with the resulting problems of poor hygiene, crude camp sanitation, treatment of infection and disease, transport of the wounded, hospitalization, and a lack of linens and dressing supplies. Army officers were initially resistant to accepting help from the Women's Central Association of Relief, organized in New York City with the help of Dr. Elizabeth Blackwell. Henry Whitney Bellows, minister of the First Congregational Church of New York City (now the Unitarian Church of All Souls), began working with the Committee. The women sent Bellows with a group of civic-minded men to lobby for military cooperation. Their efforts led the government to charter the U.S. Sanitary Commission, which took responsibility for organizing the collection of donated medicines, bandages, food, blankets, and other much needed amenities for the ill-supplied soldiers in the Union Army.[250] The Commission also gave advice to both civilian and Army personnel on public health and medical treatment. [251] It soon assumed the additional task of attending tens of thousands of the wounded and evacuating them out of Washington, DC. Bellows was assisted in the work of the Commission by a number of Unitarians and Universalists, many of whom had been active in the cause of abolition and other reforms prior to the war. This work was surely another kind of community ministry.

William Greenleaf Eliot of the First Unitarian Church of St. Louis headed up the Sanitary Commission in the West. St. Louis had quickly become a focal point of activity in the war. The costly Union victory at Wilson's Mills, Missouri, in 1861 brought a flood of wounded soldiers into St. Louis, where it was necessary to lease and furnish four large buildings as hospitals equipped with thousands of beds. Appeals published under Eliot's name brought in fifty thousand cases of clothing, comforts, and food items, along with hundreds of thousands of dollars from across the country.[252] Thomas Starr King utilized his oratorical gifts to raise 1.5 million dollars in mining towns across the state of California to support the work of the Commission. As a result of Starr King's efforts, the money collected from citizens in California (many in mining communities) equaled twenty-five percent of the total funds collected to support the Commission. Robert Collyer, minister at large at the First Unitarian Church in Chicago, was also called to service into the Sanitary Commission. He considered this work another ministry-at-large. Also in Chicago, Mary Livermore, who had been volunteering in the cholera epidemic, headed up the Northwestern Branch of the Sanitary Commission. Livermore, as we have seen, was a Universalist lay woman and writer who had become involved in anti-slavery work with her husband Daniel. Called upon to serve the Commission, she recruited volunteers for the Union hospitals, wrote letters "by the thousands" for soldiers, and raised large sums of money for the work of the Commission. The Northwestern Sanitary Fair in Chicago, for which Livermore and Jane Hoge were responsible, opened with a procession three miles long of farmers' wagons loaded with food and clothing. The fair, one of many held in large northern cities, lasted fourteen days, its star exhibit being a manuscript of the Emancipation Proclamation.[253] In addition, Livermore personally organized over 3,000 local aid societies, which helped her gain experience for the public speaking she would do in subsequent years on behalf of woman suffrage and other reforms.

Both Julia Ward and Samuel Gridley Howe had worked in the anti-slavery cause in the 1850s, and during the war they joined in the work of the Sanitary Commission. In Washington, DC in 1861, they witnessed a Union army review become dispersed under Confederate attack. It was during this episode that James Freeman Clarke suggested to Julia that she write better lyrics for the popular patriotic song, "John Brown's Body." This was a gruesome marching song honoring the fallen martyr: "John Brown's body lies a moldering in the grave, but his soul goes marching on!" That night Julia got up from her bed and quietly penciled out the words to "The Battle Hymn of the Republic." The song was published in *The Atlantic* in February 1862. It soon swept the North and became the mobilizing song of the Union in the war.[254] Having written this song in war, Julia Ward Howe would later turn her efforts toward peace.

The war exacted labor of a different sort among community ministers, and in the process, left no one unchanged. Thomas Starr King campaigned up and down the state of California to raise money for the Sanitary Commission and, at the same time, urged Californians to stay in the Union. A powerful speaker, Starr King drew huge crowds and was able to persuade state lawmakers to resist pressure from secessionists. Unfortunately, he became exhausted from overwork, contracted diphtheria, and died from pneumonia in March, 1864 at age forty. Lincoln credited Starr King with saving California for the Union, and in 1913, he was voted one of California's two greatest heroes. In 1931 a bronze statue of Starr King, done by artist Haig Patigian, was donated by the state of California to the National Statuary Collection, housed in the United States Capitol in Washington, DC. The statue is an important civic monument to what we recognize as Starr King's sacred work of ministry.[255] Only recently, in September 2006, the California legislature voted to remove the statue and replace it with a statue of Ronald Reagan. The Thomas Starr King statue was to be relocated in the State Capitol building.[256]

Thomas Wentworth Higginson, a minister and reformer who had worked intensely on behalf of temperance and abolition, was offered command of the First South Carolina volunteers, the first Union regiment of freed slaves permitted to serve in the war. Uncompromising in his beliefs, Higginson had spent the 1850s refusing compliance with the Fugitive Slave Law. It will be remembered that a U.S. Marshal met with mob resistance in 1854 when he tried to investigate Higginson for his part in the attempted escape of captured slave Anthony Burns in Boston. Higginson claimed that leading the black regiment during the war helped him reconcile his disillusionment with the government and restore his faith in America.[257]

Sallie Holley, who had written for The Liberator before and during the war, continued after the war to lecture and work through the American Anti-Slavery Society for the rights of freed blacks. Slavery had ended, but rights of citizenship and the franchise, granted to free blacks by the Fourteenth and Fifteenth Amendments, were not well enforced.[258] Holley and many others worked to help freedmen and freedwomen act on their right to vote. In 1870, Holley went with her friend and life partner, Caroline Putnam, to Lottsburgh, Virginia, where they built a schoolhouse staffed with black teachers.[259] In the face of much white opposition, the Holley School brought education to many poor black children in Lottsburgh, a significant legacy of its founder and namesake, Sallie Holley.

After the war, Robert Collyer returned to his ministry-at-large with the First Unitarian Church of Chicago. He was almost immediately recruited, however, into parish ministry at the new Second Unitarian (Unity) Church on Chicago's North Side. At this point, it seems his ministry-at-large came to an end. Yet, his egalitarian spirit lived on in his parish work. When his new church sought to draw up a constitution and a "platform of faith," they found it impossible to agree on anything. This state of confusion was a sign of things to come among Unitarians in post-Civil War congregational life. One of the founders wrote, "Our belief was too inclusive to be imprisoned in words and we gave it up. The one point on which we agreed was that all might differ." Lyttle writes that this "suited their minister, whose personal and pulpit faith was a warmhearted, non-doctrinal, practical Christianity."[260] Sadly, the church building burned to the ground in the Great Chicago Fire of 1871. Collyer stayed with the congregation for a few more years before finally moving back to New York.

Dorothea Dix was named Superintendent of the United States Army Nurses during the war. In this work, she organized first aid stations, recruited nurses, and upbraided resistant doctors for their neglect of sanitation. Male physicians and army officers resisted the intrusions of such women at first. It was argued that exposure to wounded soldiers would offend women's delicate sensibilities or provoke improprieties. It was also believed that women would simply get in the way. Eventually doctors and military personnel welcomed the help of the hundreds of women who nursed the wounded. Indeed wounded soldiers referred to Dix as an "angel of mercy," a common testimony that overcame the male cultural and medical prejudice against women who brought nursing care to the front.

In this desperate arena, Dorothea Dix had an important counterpart in Clara Barton. Born twenty years after Dix into a Universalist family, Clarissa Barton approached life with a desire to be of use. As a young girl, she nursed her younger brother through a two-year illness. As a teenager she was inspired to found a school for poor urban children in Bordentown, New Jersey. Despite her shyness, she was a popular teacher, earning the lifelong respect of her students because of her integrity, patience, and sense of fun. When the school grew to 600 pupils and the townspeople voted to hire a man at the head of it, Barton resigned in protest. She moved to Washington, DC, where she secured a clerkship in the Patent Office, becoming perhaps the first woman civil servant in the American government.

Barton left Washington when a change in government leadership interrupted her position, but when Lincoln was elected in 1860, she was called back to the Patent Office. When the Civil War broke out, she soon found ways to be of service to the soldiers stationed or hospitalized in Washington. At first she befriended homesick Massachusetts soldiers. Later, when she became aware of the lack of first aid facilities for the soldiers, she advertised in the *Worcester Spy* for supplies for the wounded.[261] From her base in Washington, she worked with women's relief agencies, instructing them about what to send and how to pack it. Soon she was personally delivering bandages, medicines, and food by mule-drawn wagon to the battlefield, working among the wounded for days on end without sleep.

Like Dix, Barton assumed administrative functions with a pragmatic intelligence that was inventive, resourceful, and deeply humane. Unfortunately, however, the two women did not work as allies. Having left the battlefield for a time to recuperate from a bout of illness and depression, Barton met with disappointment when she learned her place at the front had been taken over by Dix's nurses. This seems to have sparked an unfortunate case of resentment where there could have been consolidation and even sisterhood. Avoiding Dix altogether, Barton continued to appear at military engagements with much needed supplies. She brought candles to surgeons who were working in near-total darkness and prepared soup and coffee for thousands of men, sometimes under fire. Respect for her grew, as is evident in one surgeon's remark: "If heaven ever sent out a holy angel, she must be one, her assistance was so timely." Thousands of soldiers remembered her as the "Angel of the Battlefield."[262] In the face of deep human need, under the most desperate of circumstances, Clara Barton found ways to respond again and again. Her service to the soldiers and to health care in general, would continue after the war when she established an office at Annapolis for collecting information about missing men. Letters had come in from distraught relatives in search of their missing fathers, husbands, sons, and brothers. Barton drew up lists of the names for distribution to newspapers throughout the North. She also directed an effort to mark the graves of almost 13,000 men who had died at Andersonville Prison. Congress voted the next year to reimburse her $15,000 for her expenses in this work.

Barton is best known for her work to organize an American counterpart to the International Committee of the Red Cross, first formed in Geneva, Switzerland in 1863[263] and given official status when eleven governments ratified the Geneva Treaty in 1864. This treaty gave protection to wounded soldiers in war as neutrals under the sign of the emblem of a red cross on a white background. When the U.S. government resisted ratification of the Geneva Treaty, Barton determined to bring her country into alignment with the ideals set forth in the treaty.[264] After serving on behalf of the International Red Cross Committee in 1871, during the Franco-Prussian War, she initiated a ten-year struggle to organize the American Red Cross Society, in the face of significant government apathy. In addition, she lobbied tirelessly, often feeling deeply discouraged, to persuade the White House, the State Department, and the Congress to ratify the Geneva Treaty. A promise to recommend American affiliation with the International Red Cross came from President James Garfield before he was assassinated, and the American Red Cross was formed in May 1881. Barton presided as its president until 1904. In 1882, President Chester Arthur signed the Geneva Treaty. Significantly, Barton's 1905 letter to an

Ohio inquirer affirmed that her Universalism had inspired what was indeed a life of community ministry. "Your belief that I am a Universalist is as correct as your belief in being one yourself, a belief in which all who are privileged to possess it rejoice."[265]

Mary Livermore's leadership in the Sanitary Commission in Chicago raised her awareness that women would have little protection or power unless they were able to vote. After founding and editing the woman suffrage journal the *Agitator*, she was invited to come to Boston as editor of the new *Woman's Journal*. This is where she was when long-time abolitionist James Redpath invited her to devote herself to lecturing on behalf of women's rights. Unlike Samuel Howe, who had resisted Julia Howe's public activities, Daniel Livermore offered his wife Mary her most insistent source of encouragement. Mary remembered him saying to her: "It is simply preposterous for you to continue baking and brewing, making and mending, sweeping, dusting, and laundering, when work of a better and higher order seeks you."[266]

Mary lectured publicly on a range of reform topics for the next thirty years, while Daniel traveled with her and did much of the library research for her talks. Known as "Queen of the Platform," her speaking popularity soon eclipsed her reputation as an editor. Her most popular lecture, delivered more than 800 times, was "What Shall We Do with Our Daughters?" in which she called for efforts to prepare the next generation of young women to assume places of leadership in the world. This talk resulted from her reading Fuller's *Woman in the Nineteenth Century*. What she advocated was protection of physical health, a range of training and employment options, and moral and religious instruction to prepare young girls for the new age.[267] In 1875, she became president of both the American Woman Suffrage Association and the Massachusetts Women's Christian Temperance Union. Charles Howe writes that both Mary and Daniel acted consciously out of their shared commitment to Universalism; its principles were central to their work. For Mary, this had been a remarkable journey of transformation. Here she found release for herself and others to engage their inner source of well-being and to claim their rights as full citizens of the world. It had been a remarkable transformation for Daniel as well, one in which he set a new example of a husband acting in support of his wife.[268]

In 1860, Frances Ellen Watkins married Fenton Harper and gave birth to their one child, a daughter. As we know, Frances had devoted herself to writing and lecturing for the anti-slavery cause before the war and had supported John Brown during his trial. After the war, with her husband having died in 1864, Frances Watkins Harper directed her writing and speaking energies toward advancing her race, gaining rights for all women (especially the right to vote) and for children, and advocating for temperance. In 1873, she became Superintendent of the Colored Section of the Philadelphia and Pennsylvania Women's Christian Temperance Union. In 1894, she helped found the National Association of Colored Women, serving as its vice-president from 1895 to 1911. She supported herself through publication of her books, which sold a remarkable 50,000 copies. In one 1892 novel, the title character *Iola Leroy* embraces her black roots in spite of her ability to pass for white. Frances Harper depicted her female characters as liberated women, which was in keeping with how she seems to have viewed herself.

Harper's liberation was not without purposes beyond herself. Always she was deeply committed to improving the plight of African Americans, and joined with Ida B. Wells, a prominent African American journalist of the day, in writing and lecturing against lynching.[269] When she settled in Philadelphia with her daughter in 1870, she joined the First Unitarian Church. Frances Harper had become interested in the Unitarians because of their support for abolition and the Underground Railroad before the Civil War, and because her Christology was Unitarian.[270] Nonetheless, she continued her associations with churches in the black community near her home in north Philadelphia, and participated in their efforts to feed the poor and prevent juvenile delinquency. She also taught Sunday school at the Mother Bethel African Methodist Episcopal Church, which shares with the First Unitarian Church a claim to her membership.

Henry Whitney Bellows' work in the Sanitary Commission may be credited as a major factor in the success of the Union cause in the Civil War. In the performance of his work with the Commission, Bellows traveled throughout the Midwest, stopping often to assist the western Unitarian churches. These contacts brought to his attention the need for a national organization that would unify Unitarians from east and west. Bellows saw that creedal confusion and division, already evident in the Second Unitarian Church in Chicago, was threatening the stability of Unitarianism nationwide. The emergence of Transcendentalism and scientific rationalism had sparked significant controversy among Unitarian churches in the years before the Civil War. Bellows had spoken about it in 1859 in *The Suspense of Faith: An Address to the Alumni of the Divinity School of Harvard University*. This address exposed "an undeniable apathy in the denominational life of the body."[271] Meanwhile, he saw that the western churches had formed their own organization in 1852, the Western Unitarian Conference, where many had voiced disdain for the radical "unchristian" views of Theodore Parker. Bellows felt there needed to be a national organization that would signify a common principle of faith to unify all the churches and overcome the "great and painful indefiniteness of opinion among thinking men of all sects." At the same time, he feared that the question of establishing a creedal basis of organization would jeopardize any hope of unity. Thus, Bellows believed it would be in the best interests of the body, especially in western communities where converts were likely to come out of orthodox Christian churches, if a statement of unity identified the Unitarian movement as Christian.[272]

Upon Bellows' invitation, 600 ministers and lay leaders representing churches from east and west came to New York City, where Bellows was minister of the All Souls Unitarian Church. Assisting Bellows in this effort was James Freeman Clarke, whose well-known broad sympathies helped inspire a mood of reconciliation. This National Conference of Unitarian Churches established a denominational constitution, with a preamble that described its members as "disciples of the Lord Jesus Christ, dedicated to the advancement of his Kingdom." Bellows was targeted by some for directing the conference toward his own views (he was a traditional Christian Unitarian and critical of Parker), yet the conference established no creedal test of membership, and the statement in the preamble was widely approved ten to one by the churches represented. Some of the Radicals broke with the National Conference in the following year and established the Free Religious Association. This association was run only for individuals, however; it was never joined by whole congregations.[273] With credit to Henry Whitney Bellows, the National Conference served as a bridge for western and eastern churches, manifesting a diversity of religious views. It was probably critical to the survival of Unitarianism as a viable religious body at one of the most fragmented periods in its history. The AUA continued its primary purpose of soliciting support from churches for its administrative and missionary functions within the denomination.

Ironically, the Christian identification that Bellows sought to preserve for the sake of the western churches would soon be confronted by a revolt from within the western constituency itself. In 1875, Unitarian minister Jenkin Lloyd Jones became Secretary of the Western Unitarian Conference (WUC). As has been mentioned, the Western Unitarian Conference was formed in 1852, its first meeting held in St. Louis under the leadership of William Greenleaf Eliot and Mordecai De Lange. As Secretary of the Western Conference in 1877 and missionary secretary in 1880, the Rev. Jones sought to establish the Conference on a creedless ethical basis with no reliance on Christological or even theological language. A westerner all his life and a veteran of the Union Army, Jones had worked his way through Meadville Theological School and had begun his ministry at a church at Janesville, Wisconsin. Later he became minister of All Souls Unitarian Church in Chicago. He founded the periodical *Unity* to help spread his ideas. Jones' ethical Unitarianism articulated within the WUC a view quite distinct from the traditional theological position of the New England-based American Unitarian Association.[274]

Not everyone in the Western Conference agreed with Jones. His radicalism was countered in the person of Jabez T. Sunderland, a former Baptist, born in Yorkshire, England and raised in western New York State. Sunderland subscribed to the view that the Unitarian denomination needed to maintain its historic connection with Christianity. By this he meant "pure Christianity" unadulterated by centuries of "corrupt accretions."[275] When Sunderland became Secretary of the WUC in 1884, he sought to establish the conference on a more explicitly Christian basis, in keeping with the position of the New England-based American Unitarian Association. In a famous pamphlet, *The Issue in the West* (1886), he argued that Unitarianism in the west was doomed if it did not stand for something more than "generally accepted ethical principles." At the 1886 Cincinnati meeting of the WUC, he proposed a resolution that the Conference express its purpose as "the promotion of a religion of love to God and love to man." This resolution was rejected by the delegates in favor of a non-theistic resolution offered by William Channing Gannett, a member of the *Unity* editorial board. The controversy continued until Sunderland proposed a compromise in 1892. Added to Gannett's statement, "Things Most Commonly Believed," would be a clause describing the purpose of the WUC to "promulgate a religion in harmony with the foregoing preamble and statement." Acceptance of this amendment marked the end of the Western controversy.[276]

Coming out of the West, Jones and Sunderland articulated two intensely felt ideas that collided within Unitarianism nationwide. The faithful everywhere had become mired in questions of religious meaning. Would divine revelation come from the Bible or from nature? Would there be reliance on divine revelation at all? Would a theistic formulation be used as a test for membership? Standing in opposition, their separate ministries helped bring about an eventual reconciliation and strengthened a non-creedal Unitarian identity. Jones went on to play a central role in the 1893 World Parliament of Religions, held as part of the World's Columbian Exposition in Chicago. Jones viewed this historic gathering as a step toward his dream of a universal church for humankind.[277] Sunderland traveled to India to assist in the progress of the recently organized indigenous Unitarian church in the Khasi Hills of Northeast India. This began a long association that led to his outspoken criticism of British rule in India, for which he was praised by *Time* magazine. When he died in 1934, his funeral was an international event at which he was spoken of as a Maharishi, one whom all Indians could admire with pride and awe.[278]

PART III

After the War
From "Gilded Age" to Social Gospel

The Civil War propelled the nation into a full-blown industrial economy that produced desirable goods and services for an expanding urban middle class. It was a promising time of opportunity for women to pursue the franchise, education, and ministry – especially as community builders in the Midwest. It was, on the other hand, a time of receding hopes for African Americans, farmers, and hordes of immigrant laborers. By century's end, community ministry was synonymous with the Social Gospel impulse, aimed at the practical application of Christian principles to effect progressive social change.

CHAPTER NINE

Mid-Century Continuities
The Theological Schools

At the same time that Henry Whitney Bellows and James Freeman Clarke urged institutional structuring among Unitarians, Universalists sought to secure firmer denominational footing through the founding and sustaining of their theological schools. David Robinson ranks Thomas Jefferson Sawyer among "the greatest of the pioneer educators of nineteenth-century Universalism."[279] Sawyer promoted the establishment of two Universalist colleges and their associated seminaries: Tufts College and Crane Theological School, in Medford, Massachusetts, and St. Lawrence University and Canton Theological School in Canton, New York. Sawyer had become a Universalist and begun preaching in 1829, after graduating from Middlebury College. He was ordained by the Universalist General Convention at Winchester, New Hampshire, where he had studied theology under William Balch. Charles Howe writes: "Consciousness of his own inadequate preparation inspired him to become a champion of theological education for others entering the Universalist ministry."[280] Sawyer was successful as a parish minister, rejuvenating a declining church (where Horace Greeley was a parishioner), but his passions overflowed into larger denominational work. In 1831, he founded *The*

Christian Messenger, which he edited from 1831 to 1845. This weekly Universalist newspaper merged with other papers, and became in 1848 *The Christian Ambassador*. In 1834, Sawyer was the impetus behind the formation of the Universalist Historical Society. In 1847, he issued a call for an Educational Convention in New York City, where it was decided by unanimous vote that "Universalists need a well endowed College."[281] The college was established in 1852 as Tufts University in Medford, Massachusetts. Tufts had no divinity school at first, which was a disappointment to Sawyer.

Sawyer turned to the New York Universalist Education Society to establish a Universalist college in that state. The village of Canton, in northern New York, offered the highest bid, which led to the chartering in 1854 of the St. Lawrence University and Canton Theological School. The charter provided that the University would be nonsectarian, and the theology school would be "especially intended and organized for preparation and training persons for the ministry of the Universalist Church."[282] Sawyer turned down the offer of the presidency of the University. The reasons reported were that the location was too remote, and that the school was unable to pay a sufficient salary. It is probable that both reasons were true. Sawyer returned to parish ministry and other pursuits, and the St. Lawrence presidency was given to Ebenezer Fisher.

Ebenezer Fisher had grown up the son of a Baptist mother. He refused entreaties from the family to become a Baptist minister, as he had personally come to doubt the doctrine of eternal damnation. Friends introduced him to the writings of Hosea Ballou and Thomas Whittemore, which led him to embrace Universalism. He was ordained to the Universalist ministry in 1841, and achieved notice for his contributions to the *Universalist Quarterly* and *The Trumpet*. On the basis of his reputation, rather than his educational credentials, he was offered the presidency of the school at Canton. In the first few years, he was both the president of the school and its sole faculty member. The school operated with few financial resources, and Fisher struggled to bring in endowment monies that would support additional faculty. Students came to

Fisher with little money of their own and little prior training. Fisher's greatest legacy is the manner in which he nurtured students' theological development and brought them into productive ministries. In 1862, Lombard College awarded him a Doctor of Divinity degree, the only degree he ever held. Fisher served as president of the school until he died in 1879.[283]

Meanwhile, in 1869, the Crane Theological School was added to Tufts University in Medford. When Thomas Jefferson Sawyer was offered the presidency of Crane, he happily accepted the position, serving in it until he retired in 1892. Sawyer was a Biblical Christian Universalist in the Restorationist mode. He saw Christianity as a revealed religion and disdained Transcendentalism. In his Installation Address at the school, he proclaimed the school would teach Christian theology, not natural theology; it would "hold fast the traditional faith of our fathers, firm as the rocks that bound her coast," rather than "float out into a limitless sea of wild and cheerless conjecture."[284] For Sawyer, Christianity was the only full and perfect religion of the world, "revealed by God through his Son, Jesus Christ, whose divine mission was fully attested by prophesy and miracle."

At the same time that Sawyer was affirming the Christian Universalist foundation at Crane Theological School, conservative Unitarians maintained the Christian Unitarian view at Harvard Divinity School, consistent with the ideas of William Ellery Channing, Henry Ware, Jr., and the early Unitarian moralists. The faculty in this period reflected the 1853 pronouncement of Rev. Samuel Kirkland Lothrop, minister of the Brattle Street Church: "We desire a denominational capacity to assert our profound belief in the Divine Origin, the Divine authority, the Divine sanctions, of the religion of Jesus Christ. This is the basis of our associated action."[285] They persisted in resisting the influence of Transcendentalism in the school curriculum. Student requests that Emerson be invited to speak were refused until 1872, when he was permitted to come and give a reading.

From 1840 to 1880, the Harvard Divinity School reportedly did not grow, and morale declined. Francis Greenwood Peabody, who graduated in 1872, described his student years as "a disheartening experience of uninspiring study and retarded thought." He could not remember "attaining in seven years of Harvard classrooms anything that could be fairly described as an idea."[286] In 1880, under the presidency of Dr. Charles Eliot (father of Samuel Atkins Eliot, who would become president of the AUA in 1900), the school became "unsectarian"—no longer defined as a Unitarian school for Unitarian faculty and students. This change reflected a significant broadening of the constituency being served by the school, both within and beyond the Unitarian denomination. Five new professors were hired, one of whom was Francis Greenwood Peabody. He would initiate a "scientific" method of study and a popular course, the Practical Ethics of Social Reform. Levering Reynolds describes Peabody as "the first teacher in the United States to demand and create a place for systematic Christian ethics as a university discipline in liberal education."[287] His work pioneered a new era in Unitarian theological education, as well as in Christian theological education more generally. More will be said about Peabody in the chapter on the Social Gospel.

The importance of establishing proper institutions of theological training carried over to the far West, where Unitarians opened the Pacific Unitarian School for the Ministry, incorporated in 1906. The school's founders wanted a liberal theological school in the West that could train ministers who would be working in the West, focused on the practical realities of church life, and intent on serving the common good. The first dean, and soon the president, was Earl Morse Wilbur, a Unitarian minister who had come to his Unitarian beliefs somewhat cautiously. Having completed his course of ministerial study at Harvard, Wilbur was turned down for licensing by the Nebraska Congregational Association due to his unsatisfactory views on the divinity of Christ. This opened the way for him to serve sequentially as assistant parish minister in two Unitarian churches. Wilbur wrote histories of the churches he served and pursued additional study at Oxford and Berlin. This marked him as a man of scholarly potential. Samuel A. Eliot, president of the AUA from 1900 to 1927, asked Wilbur to help organize the new Pacific Unitarian School, which he did. Wilbur served the school in various capacities—as dean, president, and professor—until 1934. In those years and after, he produced a prodigious amount of scholarship, the most valuable of which was his two-volume investigation into the development of Unitarian beliefs within Christianity.[288] This life-long work, the first volume of which was dedicated to Wilbur's late son, affirmed the "principles of Freedom in thought, Reason in conduct, and Tolerance in judgment . . . crowned by uprightness of character."[289]

The principal theological schools of the Universalists and Unitarians reflected larger developments within their respective movements. It is worth noting that, at least until 1880, they all maintained a commitment to a liberal Christian curriculum. The ministers who served these schools as presidents, deans, professors, and scholars were community ministers who devoted themselves to the training of ministerial students in developing their spiritual gifts and working in the churches. Their pioneering efforts toward liberal theological education played a vital role of institutional support, necessary for articulation of the faith and the survival of each denomination. Over time, their teachings would reflect a broader theological worldview, as needed to serve the modern century.

CHAPTER TEN

Suffrage Pioneers as
Lay Community Ministers

I n the later decades of the nineteenth century, women in greater
numbers began to assume leadership roles traditionally
reserved for men. Much of women's activism was encouraged
by their earlier work as advocates for the abolition of slavery
and their efforts in support of troops during the Civil War. The
U.S. Sanitary Commission had a women's branch that aided nurses
in their work with the sick and wounded, and later assisted in
locating the family members of the newly freed men and women.[290]
The latter effort supplemented the work of the Freedmen's Bureau,
which also sought to locate family members lost to sale in slavery.
These experiences encouraged Unitarian and Universalist women
to engage in organized religious and reform activities after the war.

The first national churchwomen's organization began in
response to a request to assist in raising funds for the Universalist
centennial celebration in 1870. The Woman's Centenary Aid
Association formed in a basement Sunday school room, while
the men were gathered for the General Convention in Buffalo in
September 1869. After raising $35,000 during the next year, they
decided to continue as the Woman's Centenary Association, despite

the expectation of male leaders that they would disband. One of their initial goals was to explain and spread Universalism by publishing and widely distributing educational materials.[291]

At the 1877 meeting of the Western Unitarian Conference, women formed their own organization,[292] and the next year, they were encouraged by the WUC Board to undertake "the study and dissemination of the principles of free thought and religious culture." They were also charged to engage in "the practical assistance of all worthy schemes and enterprises intended for the spread and upholding of these principles." With these two related goals in mind, they set about raising money and using it to support missionary efforts, such as collecting books for Sunday schools and church libraries and promoting the formation of Unity Clubs for the ethical training of young people.[293]

In the area of late nineteenth-century social reform, it should be no surprise that many Unitarian and Universalist women, as well as men, were active in campaigns to expand women's rights, especially to secure women's right to vote. They recognized that women would not be able to act as whole persons unless they were free to assert protections for themselves via the franchise. In the aftermath of the Civil War, proponents of suffrage for newly freed black men championed the Fifteenth Amendment. Many who were fighting for woman suffrage believed this amendment should apply to women as well. Woman suffrage supporters divided on this issue, leading to a split in the suffrage movement and the formation in 1869 of two organizations. The National Woman Suffrage Association (NWSA) insisted that women should get the vote along with newly freed black men; the American Woman Suffrage Association (AWSA) was willing that women wait to insure no further delay in black male suffrage. Over the next twenty years, the AWSA attracted the larger more moderate membership and the NWSA appealed to a smaller more radical population. The two groups differed in strategy. The AWSA aimed to gain support for woman suffrage on a state-by-state basis through amendments to state constitutions. The NWSA preferred to pursue passage of a single amendment to the federal Constitution.[294]

Lucy Stone led the founding of the American Woman Suffrage Association in 1869. In spite of her parents' opposition, Stone had saved money for ten years as a schoolteacher in order to attend Oberlin College beginning in 1843.[295] Her experiences at college profoundly affected her development. Here her reform impulses were nurtured academically and at the same time given a progressive religious grounding. While a student, Stone learned that women were not allowed to enroll in public speaking courses; she thereupon organized a woman's rhetoric and debating club.[296] It was also at Oberlin that Stone turned away from the hell-fire sermons of resident minister Charles Finney and declared herself a Unitarian. She taught school to a class of fugitive slaves and freedmen and women to earn money; in the process she learned from her pupils what it meant to live in slavery.

From this time on, Stone embraced abolition, and after graduating in 1847, she became a lecturer on abolition and women's rights. Soon she was calling for the first National Women's Rights Convention, held in Worcester, Massachusetts, in 1850. Traveling by train, stagecoach, and horse-drawn carriage, Stone spoke before audiences everywhere and addressed every state legislature in the country. Wherever she traveled, she organized small women's rights education and action committees and instructed women in how to petition their state legislatures and local governments. Stone's commitment to improving the status of women even extended to her wedding in 1855, when she and her future husband Henry Blackwell read aloud a protest of women's lack of property rights in marriage. It is worth noting that Stone kept her own last name, a radical decision at the time. Further, the ceremony was conducted by the Unitarian minister and reformer Thomas Wentworth Higginson.

Known as "the morning star of the woman's movement" for her early activism, Lucy Stone had written to her mother in 1846, "I know, Mother, you feel badly about the plans I have proposed to myself. . . . I surely would not be a public speaker if I sought a life of ease . . . nor would I do it for the sake of honor . . . [or] wealth. . . . If I would be true to myself, true to my Heavenly Father, I must be actuated by high and holy principles, and pursue that course of conduct which, to me, appears best calculated to promote the highest good of the world." Her letter further stated, "I expect to plead not for the slave only, but for suffering humanity everywhere. Especially do I mean to labor for the elevation of my sex." Lucy Stone and Henry Blackwell founded *The Woman's Journal*, a weekly paper in which they published the positions and activities of the AWSA and later the suffrage movement as a whole. They found an ally in the Universalist Mary Livermore, who edited *The Woman's Journal* with them for a time, and subsequently became one of the most effective and popular lecturers on suffrage. In 1875 Livermore was named president of the American Woman Suffrage Association. In later years, Lucy and Henry were joined in their suffrage work by their daughter Alice Stone Blackwell.

As a sympathetic contemporary of Lucy Stone and Mary Livermore, Julia Ward Howe also turned to suffrage work. Having campaigned for abolition with her husband Samuel before the war, Julia founded the New England Woman's Club after the war. She also was a founding member of the New England Woman Suffrage Association and served as its president during two lengthy terms: 1868–1877 and 1893–1911. She worked with Lucy Stone in 1869 to found the American Woman Suffrage Association. Additionally, she edited and contributed to the *Woman's Journal* from the time of its founding. Her work on behalf of women's rights brought about what she called "the addition of a new continent to the map of the world."[297] She recalled, "During the first two thirds of my life, I looked to the masculine idea of character as the only true one. . . . The new domain now made clear to me was that of true womanhood—woman no longer in ancillary relation to her opposite, man." Rather, woman was a "free agent, fully sharing with man every human right and every human responsibility."[298]

Having witnessed firsthand the devastation caused by the Civil War, Julia was compelled into action by reading about similar carnage in the Franco-Prussian War in 1871. The "appeal to womanhood throughout the world" she wrote that day was translated into five European languages, widely distributed, and led to her extensive correspondence with women leaders in a number of countries:

> As men have so often forsaken the plow and the anvil at the summons of war, let women now leave all that may be left of home for a great and earnest day of counsel. Let them meet first, as women, to bewail and commemorate the dead. Let them solemnly take counsel with each other as the means whereby the great human family can live in peace.[299]

Although her goal of holding a woman's peace congress never came to fruition, the Mother's Peace Day she proposed was observed the second Sunday in June for many years in a number of cities in the northeastern United States and several cities in Europe. Unfortunately, the day became sentimentalized in later years with a purpose quite removed from its original intent.[300]

Julia had long borne her husband's disdain for her work, which he thought was not proper for a woman. Samuel softened his views as the two worked together toward abolition and in the Sanitary Commission, and eventually they were reconciled. After Samuel died in 1876, Julia preached frequently at their Unitarian church, the Church of the Disciples, where James Freeman Clarke was the minister. In 1893, Julia gave a lecture entitled "What is Religion?" at the World Parliament of Religions. Julia Ward Howe survived her husband by thirty-four years, enlivened in her last years by preaching and writing, and by her valuable work for woman suffrage. In response to a younger woman who, with many others, sought her advice, Howe is known to have said, "Study Greek, my dear; it's better than a diamond necklace."[301]

Susan B. Anthony came to suffrage work in 1849 after having moved from eastern New York to a small farm near Rochester, New York. Anthony's family had relocated there earlier, but Susan arrived only after teaching for ten years to pay off the debt incurred when the family business failed in 1838.[302] The Rochester farm turned out to be the local meeting place for anti-slavery activists, where the likes of William Lloyd Garrison, Wendell Phillips, Samuel May, Sallie Holley, and Frederick Douglass appeared. Here in upstate New York, Anthony's family left the regional Society of Friends, which had forsaken involvement in the abolitionist movement. They now joined the First Unitarian Church of Rochester, which was committed to ending slavery. Anthony began active participation in the church the year after her family started attending and remained active for more than fifty years.[303] Anthony's support for abolition evolved into support for women's rights, including the right to vote.

In 1853, Anthony joined Lucy Stone, Antoinette Brown Blackwell, Elizabeth Cady Stanton and others to form the National Women's Rights Society. Anthony partnered with Stanton for the remainder of her life, usually traveling and delivering the speeches that Stanton, unable to travel because of her children, would write.[304] During the 1850s, Anthony organized and ran door-to-door petition campaigns across New York State, demanding that women gain rights to child custody, property, earnings, and the ballot.[305] These campaigns sometimes met with hostile mobs, and in such situations, the formal speeches were abandoned in favor of Anthony's more spontaneous and reportedly powerful delivery. In 1869, she founded with Stanton the National Woman Suffrage Association (NWSA). Their immediate goal was that black and white women would gain suffrage along with black men in the wording of the Fifteenth Amendment. This campaign unfortunately led them into using some elitist and racist rhetoric, suggesting that educated white women had a greater claim to the franchise than illiterate black men. It was this issue, we know, that forced a split in the suffrage movement, leading to the formation of two groups, the National and the American suffrage associations. When it was clear that women would be passed over at this juncture, Anthony and Stanton carried on with their supporters for another twenty years, traveling, organizing, lecturing, raising money, lobbying, and holding conventions under the banner of the NWSA. Anthony underwent federal arrest for voting in the 1872 presidential election. At her highly publicized trial, the judge openly ordered the jury to find her guilty. When asked if she had anything to say, she berated the judge for "trampling every principle of our government. Robbed of the fundamental privilege of citizenship, I am degraded from the status of a citizen to that of a subject, and not only myself individually, but all of my sex." Fined $100, she proclaimed, "I shall never pay a dollar of your unlawful fine. Resistance to tyranny is obedience to God."[306] Facing the pressure of massive publicity, the judge ordered that Anthony would not be jailed, even though she never paid the fine.

In the 1880s, Anthony helped write the first four volumes of the *History of Woman Suffrage*. Since Anthony relied on materials from her experience in the NWSA, these volumes offered little on the work of the counterpart organization, the American Woman Suffrage Association (AWSA). While the NWSA used multiple strategies to pursue an array of reforms and a federal suffrage amendment, the more numerous AWSA maintained an exclusive focus on getting the vote and winning support for it on a state-by-state basis. This latter path had become more widely accepted as the way to achieve success. Moreover, the AWSA made an alliance with the ubiquitous Women's Christian Temperance Union (WCTU), thereby gaining an army of supporters among more conservative elements of the general public.

Alice Stone Blackwell of the AWSA is usually credited with facilitating the 1890 merger between the AWSA and the NWSA.[307] But it was Anthony in the NWSA who at the same time courted the support of the WCTU. She also developed an abiding friendship with the warm-hearted Methodist minister Anna Howard Shaw of the AWSA, much to the consternation of others in the NWSA.[308] Anthony long wished to see a single movement and understood as well the pragmatic worth of an alliance with the WCTU. When Frances Willard, head of the WCTU proclaimed support for suffrage in 1876, Anthony wrote to her, "I wish I could see you and make you feel my gladness."[309] At the suggestion of the AWSA, Anthony met secretly with Stone in 1888 to discuss the matter of a merger. In the absence of a key opposition member at NWSA, Anthony pushed through a vote on the motion to merge.[310] The two suffrage associations combined in February 1890 to form the National American Woman Suffrage Association (NAWSA).

Upon Anthony's urging, Stanton was elected the first president of the new association. Anthony was made vice president, Lucy Stone was chosen chair of the executive committee, and Alice Stone Blackwell was made one of the secretaries. In later years, when Stanton caused an uproar over publication of her *Woman's Bible*, Anthony sought to steer the fold toward a middle course.[311] "I want our platform to be kept broad enough for the infidel, the atheist, the Mohammedan, or the Christian. . . . These are the broad principles I want you to stand upon." All things considered, it is with good reason that the Nineteenth Amendment was named the Susan B. Anthony Amendment when it was ratified in 1920. Its achievement was not hers alone, of course, as she would have been the first to agree.

Mary Livermore, Lucy Stone, Julia Ward Howe, and Susan B. Anthony were Universalist and Unitarian suffrage pioneers for whom the suffrage campaign was a lay community ministry. Many others of their generation participated in this work, and when all were gone, their successors brought the torch forward into the next generation. Painfully, alliances with African American women such as Unitarian Frances Ellen Watkins Harper, once welcomed in the years immediately following the Civil War, were questioned by century's end. The suffrage strategy focused on gaining support in every state legislature, and women in the NAWSA generally believed that the presence of African American women in the suffrage movement threatened white male support in southern states. Black women diplomatically formed their own suffrage organizations, accepting with grace the humiliation of being asked to march at the end of the line in suffrage parades. As with the split in the movement over the Fifteenth Amendment, this request was yet another regrettable accommodation to the reality of race politics in America.

The power that nineteenth-century suffrage pioneers held in life is evident in the remarkable outpouring of public grief shown at their deaths. When Lucy Stone died in 1893, some 1100 mourners filled the Church of the Disciples (Unitarian) in Boston.[312] When Julia Ward Howe died in 1910, memorial services were conducted at the Church of the Disciples and at Boston's Symphony Hall. The crowds were so great that hundreds had to be turned away, and the four thousand who were present sang "The Battle Hymn of the Republic" in her honor.[313] Finally, after the death of Susan B. Anthony in 1906, 10,000 mourners filed past her simple casket displayed at the Central Presbyterian Church, chosen over her own Unitarian church because of the need for space.[314] The next generation of leaders, younger women less burdened by the hardships of old, adopted new tactics for a new age. These "New Women" spoke publicly on street corners; they staged a huge suffrage parade to disrupt Woodrow Wilson's inauguration; and they lobbied the male-dominated halls of Congress, as well as the state legislatures, to gain passage and ratification of the Nineteenth Amendment. The success of these younger women was made possible by the perseverance of those who had come before.

Ordained Women Move Ministry Beyond Congregations

O f very great significance to the latter half of the nine-teenth century was the ever-growing number of college-educated Unitarian and Universalist women inspired to embrace the work of ordained ministry. For women, parish ministry was almost always coupled with community ministry because they noticed the necessary connections between the congregation and the community. They tended to see ministry broadly, integrating into one seamless whole the life of the congregation and the life of the larger community. By 1920, the Universalists had ordained eighty-eight women; the Unitarians forty-two.[315] Indeed the period from 1860 to 1910 can rightly be called the "woman's hour" in ministry, just as it marked a highpoint in women's professionalization in other fields. In the second decade of the twentieth century, this trend would be eclipsed, and by the 1930s, there would be "a tremendous prejudice against women ministers."[316] From the 1930s to the 1960s, Unitarian and Universalist theological schools typically encouraged women to become trained as parish assistants rather than as ministers; it was "practically impossible to get any woman minister a hearing at any salary whatever."[317] This chapter focuses on that brief late-nineteenth century window of promise for women in ministry.

By any standard Antoinette Brown Blackwell, who became a close friend of Lucy Stone while they were roommates at Oberlin College, was a path breaker. Raised in a liberal Congregationalist family, she decided at a young age to become a minister. The main obstacle she would face in achieving that goal was the prevailing attitude that ministry was an inappropriate domain of work for women.[318] Indeed, when she completed her theological studies at Oberlin, she was not granted a degree. After hearing her preach, however, the members of the Congregational Church of South Butler, New York called her to preach to them for one year. In 1853, she was ordained with the assistance of a Methodist minister in what Congregationalists considered a "renegade ordination." Having gained this trust, she began her ministry with enthusiasm and resolve. Sadly, she soon faced a discouraging reception. At the 1853 World Temperance Convention, which she attended as a delegate of her church, she was shouted down several times by the male ministers when she tried to speak. Further, she encountered criticism from the women of the South Butler parish, who wanted a father figure in their minister. Finally, when a baby died without having been baptized, Antoinette Brown could not accept the church's position on infant damnation. Only ten months after it started, her work as a Congregationalist parish minister came to an abrupt end.

Antoinette Brown's life from that point moved toward community ministry. She lectured on abolition, temperance, and women's rights and wrote a number of books. In her role as public lecturer, she met and married Charles Blackwell, whose brother Henry married her friend Lucy Stone and who would influence her religious views in the direction of Unitarianism. This ultimately led to her being recognized as a minister by the American Unitarian Association in 1878, and to her founding in 1907 of the Unitarian Society in Elizabeth, New Jersey.

She continued to lecture and write the rest of her life, completing a total of seven books. In *The Physical Basis of Immortality*

(1876), she struggled with Darwin's theory of evolution and attempted to discover "whether there is a Rational Mind behind creation, and what the implications of these theories are for social justice."[319] Other books include *The Sexes throughout History* (1869) and *The Philosophy of Individuality; or The One and the Many* (1893). Ideas about gender and evolution held political implications among Brown's contemporaries. Charles Darwin had written that women evolved to a lower level on the scale of human civilization than men, chiefly because of their "greater tenderness." Men, on the other hand, attained higher eminence than women in anything requiring "deep thought, reason, or imagination."[320] Antoinette Brown Blackwell accepted that women developed with different capacities, but she condemned the argument that women were mentally inferior to men. "Women's thoughts are impelled by their feelings. Hence the sharp sightedness [and] warmer prejudices." Indeed, she argued, women should be educated alongside men to provide balance between "men's cold calculation" and "women's penetrating insight."[321] Brown Blackwell's significant involvement in the gender-based scientific discourse of her day gave intellectual weight to her work on behalf of woman suffrage. In 1920, at age 95, she became the only surviving delegate to the 1850 National Women's Rights Convention to vote.

While a student at Antioch College, Olympia Brown (no relation to Antoinette) invited Antoinette Brown to lecture and preach. Olympia wrote, "It was the first time I had heard a woman preach, and the sense of victory lifted me up."[322] Olympia applied to the theological school at Meadville, but was turned down because the trustees thought it would be "too great an experiment" to admit a woman. Instead, Brown studied at St. Lawrence University in Canton, New York, where she overcame the skepticism of the school's president, Ebenezer Fisher. Fisher had written discouragingly that he "did not think women were called to the ministry." Nonetheless, he would "leave that between you and the Great Head of the Church."[323] Brown thought that was exactly where it should be left and took "his discouragement" as "her encouragement." After graduating in 1863, Brown convinced the reluctant ministers of the Northern Association of the New York State Convention to ordain her a Universalist minister in June 1863.[324] Fisher reluctantly attended, upon the encouragement of his wife.[325] The Rev. Brown became the first well-known woman minister, combining parish ministry in New England and Wisconsin with travel and organizing for woman suffrage over the next twenty-five years. In 1867, she was granted a generous four-month leave by her Weymouth, Massachusetts congregation and undertook a lecture tour with Lucy Stone, Susan Anthony, and other suffrage leaders, in Kansas. Their goal was to urge passage of a state-wide measure for woman suffrage there. In spite of summer heat and hostile townspeople, Brown delivered over 300 lively lectures.[326] Although the measure failed, with only one-third of the all-male voters approving the amendment, Anthony nonetheless believed Brown's work was an important triumph, laying the groundwork for future woman suffrage campaigns in the west. Like Mary Livermore, Brown was assisted in her travel and work by her husband, John Henry Willis. He was, she claimed, "entirely in sympathy with my work." When he died unexpectedly in 1893, she wrote, "Endless sorrow has fallen on my heart. He was one of the truest and best men that ever lived."[327]

With her children almost grown, Brown left parish ministry at the age of 53 and followed a call to pursue full-time community ministry as an organizer and lecturer for suffrage. In these years, she led the Wisconsin Suffrage Association and served for a period as vice-president of the National Woman Suffrage Association. Like Anthony and Stanton, she supported a broad range of reforms for women, especially in higher education. When the radical National Woman's Party was formed in 1913 under the leadership of Alice Paul and Lucy Burns, Brown welcomed the invitation to be a charter member. "I belonged to this party before I was born," she declared, and readily participated in its militant demonstrations. Perhaps no act better captures her passionate spirit than the day the eighty-year old Brown burned copies of President Wilson's speeches in front of the White House to protest his opposition to woman suffrage. Like Antoinette Brown Blackwell, Olympia Brown was one of the few original suffragists still alive when the Nineteenth Amendment was ratified in 1920. With this work successfully completed, she turned in the last years of her life to promoting world peace. In the wake of the slaughter we know as World War I, Brown joined Jane Addams and others in the founding of the Women's International League for Peace and Freedom. Brown died in 1926. A plaque displayed in her honor at St. Lawrence University aptly reads: "Preacher of Universalism, Pioneer and Champion of Women's Citizenship Rights, Forerunner of the New Era, The Flame of Her Spirit Still Burns Today." [328]

Augusta Jane Chapin was the second well-known female Universalist minister, ordained in Lansing, Michigan, in December 1863. Born in 1836 in Lakeville, New York, Chapin had had a defining experience during her student years in Olivet, Michigan. At Olivet College, she had come up against the rigorous Congregationalist training of the school and, after months of isolated study, emerged at the age of 17 convinced of the universality of salvation for all souls. From that moment, she knew she would devote her life to preaching the doctrine of Universalism. [329] To fulfill her ministry, Chapin frequently relocated, serving as minister in towns and cities in Michigan, Wisconsin, Pennsylvania, California, Nebraska, Massachusetts, and New York. Her considerable accomplishments as a minister included building up several congregations and even rebuilding a church after it had burned in Iowa City. She proved an intelligent and articulate minister, setting a standard of excellence for subsequent Iowa women ministers. Her work further engaged the Iowa City church in providing aid to people living in poverty through the establishment of a Ladies Social Union.

Chapin also lectured for a time at Lombard College and delivered an address at Lombard's first commencement in 1856 on the importance of a liberal education for women. [330] Chapin participated in both temperance and woman suffrage movements, and was a charter member of the American Woman Suffrage Association. She made twelve summer study trips to Europe in the company of literary groups. She also served on the revising committee to assemble Elizabeth Cady Stanton's *The Woman's Bible*, which provided critical commentary on biblical passages that denigrated women. In 1893, Chapin was appointed chair of the Women's Committee of the World Parliament of Religions. She spoke at the opening session, pointing out that a woman like herself would not have been invited to speak, nor have been prepared to speak, at such a gathering only one generation earlier. She also spoke at the closing session, declaring that the Parliament had been "the fulfillment of a dream, a long-cherished prophecy."[331] Perhaps the most significant moment of recognition came for her when Lombard University conferred upon her an honorary doctorate of divinity at the Parliament. Her Universalist ministry offered an expansive vision of love to the world at large. When she died in 1905, the *Universalist Leader* commemorated her as "one who by her ability and consecration and broad-minded sympathies with every good cause, commanded universal respect and won enduring friendships."[332]

Then there was Celia Burleigh, who in 1871 became the first woman ordained to Unitarian ministry. Born in 1826 in Cazenovia, New York, Celia's early life seems to have been somewhat troubled. Indeed, her biographer Dennis Landis suggests that some period of personal suffering "instilled in her a sense of inner strength and grace of character."[333] Working much of her life as an editor, she overcame the trauma of two divorces (at a time when divorce was rare) and had the good fortune to marry William Henry Burleigh in 1865. Burleigh had become a Unitarian through his contact as an abolitionist editor with the Rev. Samuel J. May. With her husband's encouragement, Celia became active in lecturing and reform work, playing a prominent role in woman suffrage conventions, and speaking eloquently on behalf of divorce reform and the need for education for both sexes. William had encouraged Celia to pursue ministry, and only months after he died in 1871, she accepted an opportunity to preach for eight weeks for the First Ecclesiastical Society of Brooklyn, Connecticut. Soon she was called to serve as minister for one year to this congregation, who had found the human quality of her preaching effective and appealing. In an almost sacramental way, Celia Burleigh understood that women would bring to ministry the kind of service they traditionally brought to the home. "In the work of ministry," she said, "[a woman] will be carrying into a broader field the priestly office which she has always exercised in the family."[334] Sadly, Celia grew ill soon after this and died of breast cancer in 1875. Her untimely death extinguished all too soon the brief shining light of her work.

What becomes apparent in these stories is the extent to which the lives of many nineteenth-century Unitarian and Universalist women ministers drew on the roots and sustaining landscape of the American Midwest. Here in the heartland states of Michigan, Illinois, Iowa, and Missouri, the hardships and desolation of wilderness living offered ample opportunity for ministries aimed at building community. Florence Ellen Kollock's birth in a remote Wisconsin log house in 1848 is a poignant illustration of such hardship and desolation. An early influence on Kollock's life was her Universalist father, who believed in equal rights and education for women. When she later discovered that Universalist women were ministers, there was no question in her mind but that she would take that path. She wrote to Mary Livermore, who advised her to enroll at the Canton Theological School at St. Lawrence University. After completing her course of study, Florence graduated with high honors and was ordained in Waverly, Iowa, in February 1877. Augusta Chapin preached the ordination sermon, evidence of the connections maintained among western women ministers.

Florence Kollock engaged congregations in serving people beyond their church walls. In Englewood, Illinois, she set up the State Street Mission in her suburban church to serve inner-city families and children. While on a sabbatical leave in England, she studied the methods employed in the Social Settlements of Toynbee Hall. In the United States she sought to apply these methods when she served as associate minister of the Everyday Church in the slums of Boston's South End. At this experimental religious settlement, she was challenged to address conditions of poverty and deprivation in both practical and spiritual ways. While working at the Every Day Church, Kollock spent her Sundays preaching all over New England to raise money for support of the Church's settlement-style ministry to the community. Kollock also established a reputation for helping congregations overcome financial, organizational, and membership difficulties. She accepted a call to a failing congregation in Pasadena, California, and was instrumental in bringing that church out of debt. The church's financial secretary wrote about her, "She, a *woman*, showed our prosperous businessmen how to do church business successfully."[335] Finally, Florence did important work with women's organizations and was frequently chosen as spokeswoman for her denomination. In 1893 she spoke at the World Congress of Representative Women, another of the important conferences held at the World's Columbian Exposition in Chicago.

In 1896, at the age of 48, Florence married Joseph Henry Crooker, a Unitarian minister she had met ten years earlier at the Congress of Liberal Religions. Their marriage resulted in a blended dual-denominational ministry. For instance, while Joseph served as minister to the Unitarian church in Ann Arbor, Michigan, Florence served as a commissioned missionary for the Unitarians and the Universalists throughout the state. Then, having late in life accepted a call to serve St. Paul's Church in Jamaica Plain, Massachusetts, she was inexplicably dismissed six years later due to the objections of some in her parish to the *idea* of a woman minister. After all her work in the Midwest, where she had achieved success and acclaim, this was an unexpected and stinging blow. Sadly, Florence and Joseph burned all their manuscripts and personal journals before leaving their home in Lexington, Massachusetts, in 1921. This may have been an attempt to simplify the process of moving; it may also have been a bitter farewell to unfinished work. Whatever was contained in these unpublished writings was forever lost to future generations. Florence Kollock Crooker should be remembered for what she did to strengthen churches and bring social reform into the church context.[336] Her remarkable ministry linked the success of the church to its preparedness for meeting the needs of the community.

Born in 1848, Celia Parker Woolley grew up as the daughter of abolitionist parents in Coldwater, Michigan, a stop on the Underground Railroad. By 1867, Celia had graduated from the Coldwater Female Seminary, and in 1868 she married Dr. J. H. Woolley, a dentist who would become a supportive partner in her life. The two shared an interest in liberal religion and moved in 1876 to Chicago. There they became active in the All Souls Unitarian Church, where Jenkin Lloyd Jones was minister, and in the Western Unitarian Conference. Celia was a leader in the Western Conference and in the Women's Western Unitarian Conference. In 1893, she accepted an invitation to serve the pulpit of the Unitarian Society of Geneva, Illinois and was ordained in 1894. In 1898, she returned to Chicago and to the writing that had been her life-long passion. In addition to producing several novels and an autobiographical memoir, Woolley published articles for over 34 years in *Unity*, a Unitarian publication voicing the ideas of a creedless ethical religion. Always she challenged readers to consider the importance of social, political, and racial justice, especially in light of each person's relationship to the divine.[337]

Woolley met African American lecturer, musician, and clubwoman Fannie Barrier Williams at All Souls Church. When Woolley and some others invited Williams to join the exclusive Chicago Woman's Club, there was consternation among other members who claimed that the membership of a black woman would "defile" the organization.[338] Williams had grown up in Brockport, New York in one of the few black families in town. Her parents were well respected in the community, and she and her siblings associated freely with their white classmates at school. Since that time, she had experienced the humiliation of racial prejudice while working as a teacher in the South and as a student at Boston's New England Conservatory of Music. In Chicago, this latest rebuff from a vocal minority in the Woman's Club made her realize that a black woman's place in American society, whether north or south, was "always at risk of being compromised." In 1894, after a year of heated debate, a decisive majority in the Woman's Club voted her in.[339]

To battle this vulnerability, Williams became highly involved in speaking out and establishing clubs for black women "to uplift their spirits and develop their competencies for homemaking and motherhood as well as employment."[340] She helped found the National League of Colored Women in 1893 and watched it join with other groups to form the National Association of Colored Women in 1896. In 1893, Williams gave two controversial speeches. First, she argued before the World Congress of Representative Women that black women were eager to gain educational skills. In the second speech, she criticized Christians at the World Parliament of Religions for bringing Africans to America as slaves and preaching to them a "false demoralizing Gospel" to make them docile and dependent. Asking, "What can religion further do to advance the condition of the colored people?" she insisted there should be "less theology and more human brotherhood." Because slavery had so devastated "family instincts," she argued, ministers should do less preaching and knock on every cabin door, teaching Southern black families the "blessed meanings of marriage, motherhood and family."[341] Williams was an African American woman who moved in circles of high-status white society. It is probable that her light skin and cultured manner facilitated a measure of acceptance. Plainly she did not allow these marks of privilege in her own life to blind her to the barriers faced by most of her African American sisters.

Woolley and Williams remained friends for forty years, their lives intimately connected as together they established the Frederick Douglass Center, Chicago's first interracial social center. The Frederick Douglass Center offered community services similar to those at Hull House, including educational and cultural programs for people living in the neighborhood. (Hull House is described in a later chapter of this history.) In addition, Woolley regularly brought in religious speakers who raised questions about the meaning of being human and the manner of relating to the divine. Both Woolley and Williams remained committed to a ministry of racial justice in civic life, working out of the Douglass Center for the rest of their lives. In 1909 they both became founding members of the

National Association for the Advancement of Colored People (NAACP). Woolley also helped found the Chicago Urban League, patterned after the one established in New York City in 1910, to assist rural black families with housing and employment upon arrival in the city. Williams helped establish Chicago's Phyllis Wheatley Home, where young black women new to Chicago could stay and be protected while they looked for employment. As friends for life, and as colleagues in reform, Woolley and Williams lived out a rare interracial partnership of community ministry in a society that was largely oblivious to the vision they shared.

Caroline Bartlett Crane was born in Hudson, Wisconsin, in 1858. Early in her life she began to question the theological concept of eternal damnation and the Christian emphasis on the crucifixion. When she heard an Iowa Unitarian minister preach, she felt reassured about her views and decided to become a Unitarian minister herself, in spite of her father's objections. In the fall of 1887, Crane officially became a minister and soon established a pattern of success in building up congregations in Sioux Falls, South Dakota and Kalamazoo, Michigan. In the latter case, a new facility was erected in 1894 and named the People's Church in recognition of its mission to reach out to the community. It was here that Crane established a kindergarten for children and special classes for women in the African American neighborhood where the church was situated. After her marriage on New Year's Eve in 1896 to Dr. Augustus Warren Crane, she moved to Grand Rapids, where she worked toward urban sanitation. By 1916, she had become a sought-after speaker on behalf of public sanitation.[342] She espoused a kind of practical religion which, together with science, would lead to municipal reforms.

Crane's practical religion fit with what was undertaken by the women in the Iowa Sisterhood. The Sisterhood was made up of liberal women ministers who served churches in Iowa and the surrounding states from about 1880 to 1910. As a Sisterhood, they "promoted the cause of liberal religion in the Midwest and insisted on the contribution to be made to that cause by women in the ministry."[343] Out on the far-flung prairies, the Sisterhood provided a valuable network of support for each other and for their communities. In some of the most isolated towns of the Midwest, they determined to revive dying churches and build up new ones. They developed what Helene Knox describes as "full-service churches that provided a wide range of social, educational, and service opportunities."[344] Celia Parker Woolley, for instance, preached that the "Ideal Unitarian Church" should be "a working church." It should be, she said, a "religious workshop with club and classrooms, library, parlors, and complete domestic arrangements to further the social life of the church."[345] Likewise the Rev. Mary Safford, who served the church at Humboldt, Iowa and was widely revered across the state, urged: "If you have money to give, give it gladly, [if not], give time, give thought, give work, anything you have the power to give that will help make [this church] a beacon of light to storm tossed souls."[346] Eleanor Gordon, a close friend of Safford and a Unitarian minister for thirty-three years, believed that the purpose of religion was to make truth, goodness and beauty the supreme things in the world. This was possible, she believed, only by making religion applicable in all aspects of life. Religion could not be separated from the practical realities of living.[347] Women ministers in the Iowa Sisterhood, writes Knox, "determined that Unitarian churches put their professed principles into practice through concrete actions promoting social reform."[348]

Marion Murdoch and Florence Buck were two women whose life partnership was recognized and respected by their colleagues in ministry. Marion Murdoch was born in 1848 and grew up in Iowa, the daughter of a Scots-Irish Presbyterian father and a Universalist mother. In 1885, she became the first woman to receive a bachelor of divinity degree from Meadville Theological School. Murdoch's ordination to Unitarian ministry took place at the Unity Church of Humboldt, Iowa. She remained in service there for five years, before she went to Kalamazoo, Michigan, to work with Caroline Bartlett Crane. In both places of ministry, Murdoch was praised for her effectiveness and for being "scholarly, deep and original in thought."[349] Florence Buck was born in 1869 in Kalamazoo. While working there as a teacher, she met Murdoch, whose influence led her to become a Unitarian and to enroll at Meadville Theological School. Following Buck's graduation, she and Murdoch geographically paired their ministries to the extent that was possible, and even co-ministered at the Unity Church in Cleveland, Ohio. Buck's ministry incorporated her past training in science, conveying her view that the insights of science were revelations of God in nature and should not be seen as a threat to religion. Her ministry also reflected the impact of the Social Gospel Movement of the late nineteenth century, stressing the practical application of religious principles in people's lives.[350] This was Adin Ballou's Practical Christianity revived more broadly for a later generation of Americans.

While serving in Cleveland, Buck and Murdoch established two kindergartens, one in the Unity Church and another in a poor section of town. These kindergartens utilized the new educational methods that stressed the process of discovery as children grew. Thus, Buck's community ministry would be most visibly experienced in religious education work and religious education writing. In 1912, she was offered the job of Associate Secretary of the AUA Department of Religious Education. From this time until 1925, she edited the *Beacon* (a newsletter for children), wrote for the *Christian Register,* and was author of the books, *The Story of Jesus* (1917) and *Religious Education for Democracy* (1919). Always she used the *Beacon* to encourage young girls to develop to their full potential. In 1925, she became the first woman named Executive Secretary of the AUA Department of Religious Education.[351] As for Murdoch, her parish ministry was coupled with the teaching of art, literature, and public speaking. She was well known as a compelling speaker who lectured passionately on subjects of social reform. After Buck died in 1925, Murdoch moved to California and lived with her sister until her own death in 1943.

This section concludes with Eliza Jane Read Sunderland, whose lay ministry was integral to the work of religious teaching, as well as preaching with her ordained husband, Jabez Sunderland. As a college graduate, scholar, and teacher of world religions, she offered a religious and educational ministry that touched the lives of hundreds of adult students. Born in Abington, Illinois, in 1839, Eliza graduated from Mount Holyoke Seminary in 1865. In 1871, she married Jabez Sunderland, whose ministry is described in the section on community ministry in the era of the Civil War. The couple left their Baptist backgrounds behind, both becoming Unitarians in 1872.[352] Over the course of their marriage, Eliza would bear and raise three children, teach high school, and in 1892, obtain a Ph.D. in philosophy and psychology from the University of Michigan. Barred from teaching at the university due to her sex, she taught non-credit classes in critical study of the Bible for 17 years, with adult attendance averaging well over 100 at her lectures.

During these years, Sunderland also preached in her husband's pulpit and in other Unitarian and Universalist churches. In spite of sharing her husband's theistic view in the Western Unitarian controversy, she believed that Unitarians and Universalists should be united. "If you direct your appeal to one creed or religion you will have but a limited audience. If you direct your appeal to the heart and the conscience, no walls can contain your audience."[353] At the World Parliament of Religions and the World Congress of Representative Women in 1893, she spoke on behalf of Unitarian women, claiming "the study of all religions is necessary to the intelligent comprehension of any one religion."[354] Like ordained ministers Antoinette Brown Blackwell, Olympia Brown, Celia Burleigh, and others, Eliza Sunderland addressed audiences in public venues, becoming one of Michigan's most widely recognized advocates for woman suffrage and educational opportunities for women. Like them, she was also inspired to preach to congregations her message of liberal religious purpose. In sum, the work undertaken by Eliza Sunderland represents an important form of lay community ministry. She was a Unitarian woman with college and graduate degrees who adopted a quasi-professional role in a religious venue and integrated her deeply-informed theological views into an educationally egalitarian perspective.

As ordained ministers, Unitarian and Universalist women dramatically impacted their respective denominations and the communities they served, both inside and outside the parish. At a time when women were attending colleges in greater numbers than ever before, these women experienced their professional call in religious terms. For some, success was facilitated with the help of a supportive partner or husband; for all it was greatly enabled by the links they forged with each other. Indeed, when Unitarians were avoiding Universalists because they were too uneducated and emotional, and Universalists were avoiding Unitarians because they were too unbiblical and intellectual, these Unitarian and Universalist women found common cause in the service of benevolent liberal religion.[355] Again and again, they saw truth in broad terms and, out of private conviction, claimed public space on behalf of critical social and political needs. Much of their work was performed in the Midwest, where, as Celia Woolley observed, the women ministers were "made to feel more at home than in the convention-loving East."[356] It was here that members of the Iowa Sisterhood introduced the idea that churches should have kitchens, thereby enlarging the role of the church to fulfill a more community-conscious ministry. Finally, it is a remarkable feature of their like-minded commitment to inter-religious understanding that so many of them played an active role in the 1893 World Parliament of Religions and World Congress of Representative Women. From behind and beyond their pulpits, they dared to extend the "priestly office of the home" to a larger and intentionally inclusive arena of care.

CHAPTER TWELVE

African Americans
and Community Ministry

A frican American ministers have been few in number and a long time coming within Unitarian and Universalist circles. Their absence has been rooted in a complex of social, economic, and cultural factors explained perceptively by African American Unitarian Universalist historian Mark Morrison-Reed. "A cultural and economic chasm exists between blacks and liberal religionists," explains Morrison-Reed, which largely accounts for the division between African Americans and liberal religion. "Black religion is a religion of the disinherited, and Unitarianism is a religion of the middle class." For blacks, a history of enslavement and oppression made necessary a religion focused on physical liberation and salvation; for middle-class liberals, a history of individualism and material privilege made possible a religion focused on intellectual freedom and rationality.[357] Thus, a majority of African Americans belonged to Baptist or African Methodist Episcopal (AME) congregations and did not seek out associations with Unitarian or Universalist people.

These separate experiences speak to the obvious fact of racism, a societal presumption that allowed American blacks to be

enslaved for 300 years and systematically exiled from white society for a century beyond that. Both Unitarians and Universalists
were well represented in anti-slavery circles, with figures such
as Benjamin Rush, Samuel J. May, Lydia Maria Child, Theodore
Parker, and Thomas Wentworth Higginson among the ranks of
white abolitionists. After the Thirteenth Amendment ended slavery, black freedom exposed deeper layers of white prejudice. The
turn of the century was an especially difficult time, in which any
hint of black upward mobility was ruthlessly crushed. Disfranchisement measures, Jim Crow laws, and lynch mob rule rigidly
exiled blacks in the South from participation in white civic life. For
blacks who journeyed north with the Great Black Migration of the
early twentieth century, rude prejudice and de facto segregation
prevented integration in every conceivable social institution. As
we will see in the stories that follow, white Unitarians and Universalists were not exempt from manifesting the dominant racial attitudes of their time. This factor, as much as historical precedent,
limited the ability of African Americans to feel at home in liberal
religious circles.

Against this backdrop, the effort of Universalist minister Joseph
Jordan to run a school as part of his church was as necessary as
it was brave. Jordan was a black man born free in West Norfolk,
Virginia in 1842. For a time he worked as an oysterman, then a
grocer, and eventually as an accomplished carpenter. Success as a
carpenter did not satisfy his sense of religious purpose, however,
and at the age of 38, he was ordained a Baptist minister. What
bothered Jordan was the belief among most blacks in the South
that their white oppressors were likely to meet with just punishment in hell. When he read Thomas Whittemore's *The Plain Guide
to Universalism* in 1840, he found himself drawn to this unusual
religion whereby God's love was ultimately extended to all.[358]

Jordan sought out a teacher and mentor in Edwin C. Sweetser,
minister of the Universalist Church of the Messiah in Philadelphia.
After studying with him for a time, Jordan returned to Norfolk,
where he began preaching the Universalist faith in a rented room.
This led to his being licensed as a Universalist minister and estab-

lishing a church and a school that operated on Universalist principles. Jordan's view was that religion and education served each other and that both were necessary to empower spiritual growth, dignity, and self-respect. Thus, he ministered to the church and also ran a day school for community children during the week. The support of many outside donors, including the Universalist Woman's Centenary Association, made it possible to complete a new building needed to accommodate the 100 students being taught by Jordan and his assistants.[359]

Among those who helped in this ministry was Thomas E. Wise, another African American minister from Virginia. Wise had studied at Howard University and, like Jordan, had left an orthodox faith to become a Universalist. Soon he became Jordan's associate at the Norfolk church and school, serving tirelessly as organizer and as academic principal.[360] Then Wise was recruited by the neighboring community in Suffolk to establish a similar church and school. He did this, dividing his time from 1894 to 1901 between the two schools and generally exhausting himself. At the same time, however, he was successful in spreading Universalist belief, helping to dispel community suspicion toward this unusual faith. When Jordan died unexpectedly in 1901, Wise moved to Suffolk, continuing to run both schools simultaneously.[361]

The attitude of the Universalist leadership toward Wise seems to have been somewhat mixed. During the early years of his work in the Virginia mission schools, he was granted a license to preach. Universalist missionary Quillen Hamilton Shinn was instrumental in raising over $1000 to purchase a lot and construct a two-story building for the mission in Suffolk. The building was dedicated in 1897 as St. Paul's Universalist Mission. Yet, when Wise opened a third mission at Ocean View in 1903, a commission was appointed by the Universalist General Convention to investigate his financial soundness as well as his Universalist views. Rather than offering more support, the commission recommended that Wise run only the Suffolk mission and turn it into a school for practical education, similar to the Tuskegee Institute run by Booker T. Washington. Wise preferred to offer a full curriculum, believing with black intellectual W. E. B. Du Bois that black students should have academic opportunities equal to whites.[362]

This debate speaks to a central question of that day: whether "Negroes" were "suited for" higher levels of learning. For reasons relating to their own prejudices, white philanthropists were generally more willing to support practical as opposed to academic education for black people.[363] In time, Wise became discouraged. We are told that with little support coming from the denomination, he abandoned the effort in 1904 and joined an African Methodist Episcopal congregation. The Norfolk school built lovingly by Joseph Jordan closed in 1906; the Suffolk school begun by Thomas Wise continued under the leadership of a third African American Universalist minister, Joseph Fletcher Jordan (no relation to Joseph Jordan), for whom Shinn undertook fundraising. Financial assistance from the Universalist denomination, along with the continuing interest of the Association of Universalist Women in the mission, kept the school going under Jordan's leadership. This lasted until 1929 when Jordan died.[364] Thereafter follows another remarkable story.

Annie B. Jordan Willis was Joseph Fletcher Jordan's daughter. She had grown up watching her father work, and when he died, she took over the leadership of the Suffolk Normal Training School at age 36. She devoted her life to the students, "drawing forth the character of the kids so they would have a solid sense of who they were."[365] Students from the school went on to pursue a variety of respected careers as surgeons, teachers, electricians, and preachers. Times were tough in the Depression years, and many students could not even afford to pay the tuition of five cents per week. Black churches and Universalist congregations did what they could to support the school and its staff of four. In addition, they donated boxes of clothing, toys at Christmas, and school supplies. Miss Annie, as all knew her, provided a home-cooked meal for her students every day. When public education began to improve for Southern black children in the 1940s, the Suffolk school phased out its elementary grades, retaining only a kindergarten. The building was made into the Jordan Neighborhood House, named after Annie and her father, Joseph Fletcher Jordan. Annie retired in 1974.

The night before she died in 1977, she reminded any who might listen, "Watch out for my children."

Among Unitarians, African American ministers faced an ambivalent paternalism that was sometimes grudgingly supportive and other times harshly critical. In 1860, a certain Rev. Jackson of Bedford, Massachusetts announced his conversion to Unitarianism and appealed to the AUA for support. Those present took a collection, which summoned up a meager $49. The record shows that when he left, no one offered "a word of praise or satisfaction that Unitarianism was now reaching out to the 'coloured.'"[366] A more complex illustration of AUA ambivalence is found in the poignant story of the Rev. Egbert Ethelred Brown. It is a story of the mission that might have been, had it not been for what W. E. B. Du Bois identified as "the problem of the color line." Racial prejudice was visible everywhere in the white industrial world in these years, both in domestic affairs and in far-flung colonial enterprises. What happened between Egbert Ethelred Brown and the AUA brings this larger dynamic closer to home.

Egbert Ethelred Brown was admitted in 1910 to Meadville Theological School, which had accepted six African American students since its founding in 1844.[367] In Brown's day the president of the school was the Rev. Franklin Southworth, a man known for supporting African American students. "I believe that liberal Christianity has a mission to the blacks," he said, "whether it is labeled Unitarian or not, and I want Meadville to help in solving the race problem."[368] What was unique about Brown was that he was the first African American student at Meadville to seek Unitarian ministry. Southworth warned him that as there was "no Unitarian Church in America for colored people and that as white Unitarians required a white minister," he was unable to predict what the future would be for Brown after graduating. Likewise, the AUA told him not to expect that any Unitarian church would hire him upon completion of his degree. Brown persevered nonetheless and found his years at Meadville to be the "most exciting and happiest of his life." In 1912, he became the first African American ordained into Unitarian ministry.

Brown returned to his home in Jamaica and, with some financial assistance from the American Unitarian Association and the British and Foreign Unitarian Association (B&FUA), founded a Unitarian society at Montego Bay. Regrettably, from 1914 to 1920, the support Brown received wavered, apparently due to the perception that his blackness prevented him from securing a congregational following. Here was a dual burden for Brown: facing the prejudicial perceptions of white leaders in the AUA and B&FUA, and at the same time finding limited constituent support from blacks. When the retired Rev. Hilary Bygrave was sent by AUA president Rev. Dr. Samuel Eliot to evaluate Brown's situation, he voiced this concern: "The Rev. E. E. Brown is pronouncedly black, which is somewhat of a handicap to him in his work, since those of his race who are fortunate enough to approach absolute whiteness are too proud to sit under any minister save a white gentleman."[369] Bygrave's report suggested that Brown's eloquence could be better appreciated in Kingston, where the population numbered 70,000. Thus Brown was re-settled there, which meant he had to start over. Brown lamented, "I very soon learned that the men who directed the affairs of the AUA were not like the men at Meadville . . . they were business men." He implied that the AUA was more focused on the financial soundness of his mission and less sympathetic to the spiritual presence, however small, of his ministry.

With renewed dedication, Brown successfully raised money in America to build a church in Kingston on a donated lot. Then with the new church half-completed only eighteen months after Brown's arrival, the AUA and the B&FUA suddenly withdrew their support. Morrison-Reed writes: "What Brown saw as a success, his reluctant benefactors, the American Unitarian Association and the British and Foreign Unitarian Association, perceived as a waste of their resources." Essentially, their three-year time commitment was at an end. Furthermore, the B&FUA believed Brown was not managing their money wisely, and AUA president Samuel Eliot believed that resources should not be expended on ventures unlikely to succeed. He wrote to Brown with apparent sympathy: "I beg you understand that those of us who have known of your work have fully appreciated the spirit in which it was undertaken."[370] Sub-sequently, Brown journeyed to Boston and was successful in secur-ing extended support from the Boston Unitarian ministers, who outvoted Eliot. Despite this show of confidence, Brown felt that the controversy itself turned many of his former supporters in Kingston away from the Unitarian mission. He was led in due course to give it up. The land with the half-completed church on it was returned to the donor. Brown's narrative of these events con-cludes wistfully, "Today the church is an Episcopalian church. It may have been ours."[371]

Finally in 1920 Brown came to New York and established a Unitarian church in Harlem without AUA assistance. Due to the financial strain of his circumstances, Brown supported himself and his family for five years as an elevator operator and then as a speaker for the Socialist Party. After a period of real hardship, he secured the position of office secretary for *The World Tomorrow*, a magazine of the American Socialist Party. Finally, in 1937 the Rev. Dale DeWitt, who was the Regional Director of the AUA, arranged for Brown to get $50.00 a month from the AUA. This continued until 1940, when Brown was eligible for a retirement pension. Meanwhile, unknown to Brown, a benefactor who sought to make a $3000 gift to Brown's church was dissuaded from doing so, being told by an AUA official that Brown's church existed "only on paper" and that the congregation was made up "largely of his household." In neither case was this true. The average membership in Brown's church was thirty people, and its yearly income was $730, of which Brown received only $68.56.

Brown's efforts to secure funding assistance from the AUA and from other Unitarian ministers were viewed with annoyance by the AUA leadership. The Fellowship Committee eventually removed Brown's name from the ministerial rolls, prompted by complaints such as this one: "He actually lives by begging for a cause that is generally recognized as beginning and ending in himself and his family."[372] Insensitivity to Brown's plight reached shocking propor-tions when one letter from Unitarian headquarters blamed the sui-cide of Brown's son in 1929 on Brown's unwillingness "to support his family with some real work."[373] It was an irony that in this same letter, the writer rejoiced in the advertising that brought in higher donations at his own Easter service. Finally, in 1932, a new Fellowship Committee investigated the circumstances of Brown's removal from fellowship. Finding fault on all sides, the committee recommended that Brown's fellowship status be reinstated.[374]

However much AUA opinion held Brown responsible for his financial difficulties, it remains that Brown's church was poor in the same way that most black churches were poor. "Negroes, however intelligent and cultured, are poor," wrote Brown, "because in America they are elevator men and porters." Indeed, from this awareness, Brown brought to his ministry a strong commitment to civic involvement.[375] He was a member of the Harlem Job Committee and the Harlem Tenants League. The Job Committee secured an agreement from the Uptown Chamber of Commerce that its members would hire blacks for one-third of their white-collar jobs. Brown's belief in cooperation over competition led him to challenge Harlem's leading churches to start a cooperative store. He protested the emphasis that most churches gave to heavenly goals, which, he thought, distracted members from addressing the injustices of the present world. He also advocated for the Jamaican Progressive League, occasionally interceding on behalf of Jamaican immigrants. In 1938, he was sent to Jamaica to represent the Progressive League before the West Indies royal commission studying Jamaican independence. Moreover, by 1938, certain Unitarian ministers began to recognize that Brown was a significant Unitarian presence in Harlem. Writing in 1939 to the Department of Unitarian Extension and Church Maintenance, John H. Lathrop, minister of the First Unitarian Congregationalist Society of Brooklyn, wrote: "Mr. Brown carries the Unitarian flag with wide reaching influence throughout the community."[376] From these events followed the kind of AUA support and oversight that Brown had desired for so long.

The change in AUA sentiment resulted from a new generation of leaders backed by incoming AUA president Frederick May Eliot. Eliot brought a more humanitarian emphasis to institutional leadership, an important change consistent with an age of new political realities. Moreover, a change in Brown's style of ministry brought greater stability to the church. In the interest of combining political dialogue with religious worship, Brown's congregation had sponsored forums for the airing of views on civil rights, labor politics, and other matters of social justice. These forums made it difficult to establish a consistent liturgy for worship and often put Brown in the crossfire between Socialists and Communists, West Indian and American black communities, supporters and detractors of Marcus Garvey. Now in the waning years of the Depression, the force of these debates diminished. Brown experimented with introducing services of worship in addition to offering forums, which had a stabilizing effect.[377] Some wondered if a different man might have had more success with planting Unitarianism in Harlem. In 1950, his congregation still numbered only twenty, with competition coming from the integrated Community Church led by his long-time friend and supporter, John Haynes Holmes. Speculation that another might have been more successful seems a useless conjecture, in consideration of the full array of obstacles that undermined Brown's chances for success. Finally, it may fairly be said that AUA preconceptions brought about a self-fulfilling prophecy. In the end, none can deny the sincerity of Brown's determination to bring liberal religion to the black community. The Statement of Purpose of the Harlem Unitarian Church is a testament to his belief in the church as a force in the community:

> This Church is an institution of religion dedicated to the service of humanity. Seeking the truth in freedom, it strives to apply it in love for the cultivation of character, the fostering of fellowship in work and worship, and the establishment of a righteous social order which shall bring abundance of life to man. Knowing not sect, class, nation or race, it welcomes each to the service of all.[378]

The Social Gospel
Allies for Racial and Economic Justice

Northern whites tended to think of racial injustice as a southern problem. The lynching that enforced racial segregation and disfranchisement in the late-nineteenth century south was not occurring in their neighborhoods, as far as they could tell. A 1908 race riot in Springfield, Illinois disrupted northern complacency. This riot erupted when an angry mob of whites learned that a black man, wrongly accused of attacking a white woman, had been safely removed by authorities to another town. The ensuing violence shocked northern middle-class whites. Blacks knew better. In 1905, twenty-nine black leaders and businessmen had formed the Niagara Movement. This all-black organization renounced Booker T. Washington's accommodationist policies and demanded "full manhood suffrage now."[379] After the Springfield episode, some whites who wanted to be part of the solution came together with some blacks to found the National Association for the Advancement of Colored People (NAACP).

In New York City a Unitarian social worker named Mary White Ovington had been vilified by the press for having scheduled a meeting of New York's interracial Cosmopolitan Club in a restaurant restricted to whites. Reporters gleefully exposed her social indiscretion, condemning the event in print as a "miscegenation dinner...loathsome enough to consign the whole fraternity of persons who participated in it to undying infamy."[380] It made Ovington feel as though she had been "smothered in mud." She proposed that a new organization be formed in keeping with William English Walling's plea that some powerful persons "come to the Negro's aid."

Oswald Garrison Villard, president and editor of the *New York Evening Post* and grandson of William Lloyd Garrison, agreed to issue a call for "a conference to discuss the present evils." The conference would convene on February 12, 1909, Lincoln's birthday. Members of the Niagara Movement were invited to join the meeting, and many did. The NAACP was to be an inter-racial organization, dedicated to gaining civil and legal rights for African Americans. In spite of Booker T. Washington's attempts to undermine the success of the new organization, it thrived and had over 6000 members by the time of Washington's death in 1915.[381]

There were sixty signers of the charter, including black writers W. E. B. Du Bois and Ida B. Wells and white progressives Mary White Ovington, William Dean Howells, John Haynes Holmes, Jane Addams, and Jenkin Lloyd Jones. Ovington's relationship to the organization was unique. As a Unitarian laywoman, she drew on the abolitionist roots of her Brooklyn family and her grandmother's personal friendship with William Lloyd Garrison. Furthermore, Ovington had grown up in the Second Unitarian Church of Brooklyn, Connecticut, where the Rev. John White Chadwick "never lost an opportunity in speech or in writing to show his full sympathy with the colored man."[382] At Harvard, Ovington worked as a research assistant in economics and after graduation, she worked in settlements to improve the living conditions of the working poor. For a time, she lived as the only white resident in the settlement at Tuskegee. Her commitment to racial reconciliation defined her very singular lay community ministry. In 1904, she met W. E. B. Du Bois in the south and began a twenty-five year correspondence with him. He once wrote to her, "you are one of the few persons I call Friend." Ovington stayed with the NAACP well into the 1930s, joining Du Bois in editing its magazine *The Crisis*, and steering the organization always toward the goal of integration.[383]

In addition to racism, late nineteenth-century prejudices brought into sharp relief the "Social Darwinism" that justified labor exploitation and poverty. New realities accompanied America's rising industrial order: widespread corruption, dangerous working conditions in mines and factories, low wages, child labor, crowded tenements, and open sewers, to name the most egregious. According to *laissez-faire* ideology, government regulation to address these problems "perpetuated the unfit" and violated the right of private property. With no apparent irony, the Supreme Court asserted the legality of protecting corporations from government intrusion, as though a corporation were a person. Meanwhile labor organizing and strikes were met with fines, injunctions, and even state or federal military action.[384]

David Robinson writes that the violent strikes of the 1890s challenged the complacent optimism of many Christian thinkers and probably constituted the single most important factor contributing to the Social Gospel movement within American Protestantism.[385] The Social Gospel movement stressed the relevance of Christianity to the socioeconomic realm. The Social Gospel message was aimed at offering hope and compassion, rather than contempt, to the nation's beleaguered poor; it supported reforms intended to end corruption and remedy extreme maldistributions in wealth. Among Unitarians there emerged an influential social gospel pioneer: Francis Greenwood Peabody. Peabody came from Boston Unitarian roots and studied at Harvard Divinity School, where he complained of the tedium of old ideas. His study in Germany under Friedrich A. G. Tholuck at the University of Halle convinced him that theology had a role to play in social reform. Tholuck, it should be stated, was widely known and beloved in Protestant churches in Europe and America throughout much of the nineteenth century. His unique blend of rationalist thought and evangelical pietism had influenced other professors at Harvard prior to Peabody's student years.[386] Peabody's early work in parish ministry was cut short by poor health, and with disappointment in himself, he accepted a teaching post at Harvard in 1880. This was the unlikely beginning of his pioneering work in the study of social ethics.

At Harvard, Peabody was part of a new regime of professors hired by the new president, Charles Eliot. This was the moment when Harvard Divinity School became an "unsectarian school" and invited a "scientific" method of study, calling for objectivity in viewing material and subjecting all ideas to impartial scrutiny and the "historical method of approach."[387] Peabody's popular course, the Practical Ethics of Social Reform, examined questions of charity, temperance, labor, prisons, and divorce, among other things. Students popularly referred to the course as "Peabo's drainage, drunkenness, and divorce." Peabody utilized a case method of study, with the aid of social-scientific analysis, to develop what he called "inductive ethics." From his course would eventually develop the Department of Social Ethics at the College.[388]

Peabody wrote an important work, *Jesus Christ and the Social Question*, published for the first time in 1900 and followed soon after by five more editions. Peabody's book recognized the unique problems of the current age, which he saw summed up in the "contradiction between economic progress and spiritual ideals." The "social question is an economic question," he stated, but "it issues from a sense of wrong." The church should not be alienated from the reform impulse; there should be a reunion of religion and social reform.[389] From Tholuck, he argued that Jesus' teaching was so comprehensive that it could speak to every age including his own—"the age of the social question." The essence of Jesus' ethical message lay in its moral energy. Reynolds notes, Peabody related this moral energy to "a new wider range of social problems," wisely taking into account their complexity.[390]

Peabody was not a political or social radical. He did not advocate overthrowing the social order. Jesus had not offered a systematic plan, Peabody pointed out, only a case-by-case demonstration. His goal was not political but personal. This argument gives credence to the theory that the Social Gospel movement was motivated in part by a desire to pre-empt a radical move toward socialism.[391] For his part, Peabody sought change within existing structures, saying that much could be accomplished through service. Robinson argues that Peabody's idea of service was an appeal to the rich and controlling classes to be more responsible in their stewardship of the nation's wealth. In Peabody is seen the ethical individualism of Unitarianism—of "channeling personal development into an ethic of service to others."[392]

John Haynes Holmes lived out the Social Gospel message in his ministry through numerous avenues of reform. He looked to Theodore Parker as the model of a Christian minister, arguing that the minister's proper role was to speak out on social issues. Like Peabody, he believed that the economic injustice of the industrial age was of central concern to Christian ethics; unlike Peabody, he declared that the brotherhood represented in socialism was "the religion of Jesus." He believed that the individualism of Social Darwinians like Herbert Spencer violated what he saw as historically true—that all individuals are in fact social creatures. He wrote, "The problem of life today is no longer the problem of the individual but the problem of the society which environs the individual and determines the conditions of his life." The role of the church, said Holmes, was "to grapple at first hand with the conditions of society."[393]

Holmes was a young Unitarian minister and social activist when he signed the NAACP Charter in 1909. His lifetime of advocacy for social justice would make him perhaps the pre-eminent Unitarian community minister of the early twentieth century, if not always the most popular among his contemporaries. Holmes had graduated from Harvard Divinity School in 1904 and soon gained the favor of AUA president Samuel Atkins Eliot. Eliot recommended Holmes to the powerful pulpit of the Church of the Messiah in New York City, and, in 1907, the church called him to be their minister. Holmes' ministry led him to discover that the Unitarian denomination was "a middle-class institution . . . with high standards of respectability and culture" in which "labor seemed an alien element." He came to believe that "in the struggle between labor and capital, the Unitarian churches had lined up, more or less unwittingly, on the side of capital."[394] This realization is relevant to the conflict John Haynes Holmes later experienced with the AUA leadership. He began preaching on political subjects wherein he declared Socialism to be "the religion of Jesus." In 1908, he organized other young radical ministers to form the Unitarian Fellowship for Social Justice; in the following year, he participated in the founding of the NAACP; later still, he was a founder and chair of the American Civil Liberties Union.

When Jenkin Lloyd Jones died in 1918, the radical Holmes seemed the natural choice to succeed him as director of Chicago's Abraham Lincoln Center, a center of social activism founded in 1905. This invitation was important in that it enabled Holmes to negotiate critical changes at the Church of the Messiah, which he was still serving in New York City. The congregation agreed to drop the name Messiah and change it to the Community Church of New York; they did away with pew rentals, and eliminated the covenant as a requirement for membership. The focus of the church would move from liberal Christianity to social concern for the larger community, in keeping with the new name. Holmes described the re-conceived role of this church as "the logical completion and perfection of the liberal movement in modern religion. It moves from the individual to society as the center of religious life [and] emancipates religion from the power of money." The Community Church of New York became by 1930 a multi-cultural congregation of 1800 members representing thirty-four nationalities from six continents. For Holmes, this was a great satisfaction: "We have rich and poor, black and white ... orthodox and agnostic, theist, atheist, and humanist, Republican, Democrat, Socialist, and Communist. All of this means ... we are a community church, in the true meaning of the phrase."[395]

Ovington and Holmes lived out the early twentieth-century "Progressive Era" reform impulse that drew on the message of the Social Gospel movement. With other middle-class progressives, they sought to ameliorate the social and economic disparities of the late nineteenth-century Gilded Age. Like Peabody, they saw that the nineteenth-century idealization of *laissez-faire* government was destructive of both the material and spiritual conditions of life. They saw beyond the categories that divided society and institutions. In reaching out to heal the hatreds of race in American society, they went beyond where most white Progressive Era reformers and Social Gospel ministers would go. Finally, drawing on their Unitarian roots, they affirmed the secular world as the proper sphere of religious influence.

Jane Addams, a contemporary of Peabody, Ovington, and Holmes, and a personal friend of Jenkin Lloyd Jones, has often been called the quintessential embodiment of progressive reform. In 1889, Addams founded Hull House, a settlement house on Chicago's south side. It is worth knowing that the inspiration for this work had come about after much personal struggle. From the time of her graduation from Rockford College in 1881 and her father's death in the same year, Addams experienced a period of illness and uncertainty. She had longed to become a physician, but was forced to set that dream aside as she healed from a childhood back injury and a bout of depression.[396] She convalesced in Europe during these years and, while in England, visited Toynbee Hall, a settlement house in London. This became the inspiration out of which she was able to resolve the question of the "family claim" that had been haunting her, and pursue a life of social purpose. Indeed she would one day write of the "Subjective Necessity for Social Settlements" wherein she argued that women who had been "smothered and sickened with advantages" would find health and purpose in the "expression of self rather than the repression of self for the sake of society."[397] Better to serve the world in a purposeful way than to be restricted by society's expectations for women.

Addams returned to Chicago, located and purchased a sizeable house that she felt would serve her purpose, and thus began the work that would achieve nationwide significance. Here middle-class men and women lived and delivered services to the immigrants that inhabited the surrounding neighborhood. They offered classes in baby care, nutrition, food preparation, and the English language. They also offered musical concerts and poetry readings to inspire social and cultural uplift. They babysat for the children of poor women who had to work. Hull House was a busy, lively place. Beyond this, it was a social workshop from which the residents studied problems and lobbied for municipal reforms involving sidewalks, housing codes, street maintenance, and sanitation. Out of Hull House came *Hull House Maps and Papers*, a sociological analysis of the working and living conditions endured by the tenement families of Chicago. This study pressured the Illinois legislature to pass labor laws banning sweatshops and child labor.[398]

Jane Addams was inspired and supported in her work at Hull House in part through her connection to the Unitarian All Souls Church, where Jenkin Lloyd Jones had been the minister since 1882. Addams developed a reciprocal relationship with Jones. He came to Hull House to lecture about various subjects, including the need for labor unions, and to help in giving aid to the poor. In return Addams frequently preached in Jones' pulpit, even performing weddings and funerals. With admiration born of long association, Jones spoke of Addams as the "sage of Hull House."[399] In this sense we may think of Addams' work as a lay community ministry linked with a Unitarian congregation. From Hull House, she launched numerous projects of community benefit, including an Immigrants' Protective League, the Juvenile Protective Association, and a Juvenile Psychopathic Clinic. Her efforts on behalf of children contributed to the creation of the Federal Children's Bureau in 1912 and the passage of a federal child labor law in 1916. Rejecting the rigid ideology of the Chicago socialists, Addams nonetheless advocated a larger government role in addressing the problems of free enterprise. Competition, she claimed, should be replaced by cooperation "for the good of the whole social organism."

The closest Universalist counterpart to Hull House was the Everyday Church, also referred to as the "institutional church." This concept of the church as an institution offering humanitarian services not necessarily religious in nature was pioneered in 1837 when Otis A. Skinner opened an Everyday Church in Boston's

Boylston Hall. Its purpose was "to serve the needs of transients and rootless people who had no church home or even any other home to call their own."[400] It lasted into the 1850s, meeting with limited means the material needs of those who sought its services. In 1894 George L. Perin reinvigorated the same concept at the Shawmut Avenue Universalist Church in Boston. Perin had just returned from Japan, where he had set up the first denominational foreign mission for non-Christians. Back in Boston, he determined to broaden the role of the church to offer a range of services to deteriorating neighborhoods, seven days a week. Perin acquired a sixteen-room house next door to the Shawmut Avenue Church and used the house as a center where people in the neighboring slums could take classes in stenography, dress-making, and cooking. A nursery was provided on site for the children of working mothers, and free legal aid was made available by a lawyer who donated his time. In summer, there were day trips and outings for upwards of 100 children.[401] It was here that Florence Kollock (Crooker) answered a call in mid-career to serve. Like Addams, Kollock had observed the methods being employed at Toynbee Hall to respond to the problems of poverty, crime, and disease. In Boston, Kollock found an opportunity to apply what she had learned, "seeking to offer practical aid as well as fostering spiritual development in the face of overwhelming physical deprivation."[402] She used her Sundays to campaign all over New England to raise funds for support of the Everyday Church. Perin came to rely increasingly on the lay services of volunteers as the Everyday Church grew in popularity. By World War I, the Universalist denomination was operating over twenty such "institutional churches" and non-sectarian centers across the nation.

Perin also founded the Franklin Square House in Boston's South End, a non-profit, non-sectarian rooming house for single working women and students who had few safe affordable housing alternatives in the city. It was so popular that additional wings were added over time, and by World War I, the enlarged facility served 900 young women. Indeed, it is estimated that "by 1922, some 75,000 had used the services of the Franklin Square House, an enduring testimonial to Perin's work and Universalist philan-thropy."[403] In addition to Franklin Square, there was the Bethany Home for Young Women, established by John D. W. Joy, a member of Perin's Shawmut Avenue Universalist Church and forty-nine other investors in 1890. Operating under the auspices of the Massa-chusetts Universalist Convention, the Bethany Home was chartered as a non-denominational refuge for women aged twenty to forty with no means of financial support. In 1898, the name and the charter were revised. The new Bethany Union became a residence for young working women who paid rent on a sliding scale. As with the Franklin Square House, the Bethany Union grew in popularity and size, soon occupying three adjoining buildings. Its operations continued after its move to Newbury Street in 1941, and later it became an independent affiliate of the Unitarian Universalist Asso-ciation.[404] The Everyday Church, with its long-term legacy in resi-dent homes for young working women, contributes an important chapter to the story of Universalist community ministry. In this period when the industrial and commercial marketplace lured thousands to the cities, we recognize the Everyday Church and Hull House as early twentieth-century instances of urban ministry aspiring to address the real material deprivations of urban life.

Addams enjoyed a long and fruitful career. Frequently she worked in association with prominent Unitarians and Universalists in shared arenas of community ministry. We have already seen that in 1909 she joined with Ovington, Jones, and Holmes in signing the charter of the NAACP. She also campaigned with Susan Anthony and Celia Woolley for woman suffrage and served as vice president of NAWSA from 1911 to 1914.

Throughout World War I, Addams joined Holmes and Jones in renouncing war and paid, as did they, a dispiriting price in pub-lic censure as a result. She led a delegation of forty-six American women from the recently formed Woman's Peace Party to the 1915 meeting of the International Congress of Women at The Hague. When the conference was concluded, two delegations of women visited European heads of state to promote mediation by neutrals to end the war.[405] Addams returned home enthusiastic about ending the war through diplomatic means. To her surprise and disappointment, Addams soon discovered she was added to the "traitor list" of the Senate Judiciary Committee for her activism against the war. Partly in response to that experience, Addams joined with Holmes in 1920 in the founding of the American Civil Liberties Union. Further, in 1919, Addams and Unitarian Emily Greene Balch helped found the Women's International League for Peace and Freedom. Finally, in 1931, Addams was the first woman to deliver the Ware Lecture at the General Assembly of the American Unitarian Association. In that same year she was the first woman and the first social worker to be awarded the Nobel Peace Prize. Her story will be a starting point from which to further examine peace ministries in time of war.

PART IV

Twentieth-Century Challenges in Community Ministry

Richard Gilbert observes that events of the twentieth century have left us less optimistic about the prospects for reform than were our Social Gospel pioneers. Nothing can parallel the scope and pace of change in this century in its potential for technological destruction as well as human alienation. These chapters chronicle the work of Unitarian and Universalist community ministers who raised their voices against war, led their respective religious movements through economic malaise, found common ground for merging their gifts of witness and hope, and met the challenges of the civil rights, anti-war, and women's rights movements. The growth of community ministry by century's end was a response to the pain exposed in these long-delayed social eruptions.

The Politics of Peace Ministry

For many who had devoted their lives to improving society, war now seemed a cruel reversal of all they had sought to achieve. World War I, known as "the Great War," proved an unspeakable horror, yet to oppose it was thought to be treasonous. In the end, the trauma to those who survived it was exceeded only by the cost to millions who paid with their lives. Perhaps that is why voices of opposition to war were accorded greater sympathy in later years, when the shock of it all had registered in the public consciousness. At the time, however, there was a heavy price to be paid when progressive individuals advocated peace. John Haynes Holmes, Carolyn Bartlett Crane, Jenkin Lloyd Jones, Emily Greene Balch, Aurelia Henry Reinhardt, and Clarence Skinner were among many who suffered reprisals.

John Haynes Holmes encountered trouble in 1915 when he delivered a series of sermons condemning any action for war as unjustifiable. "Never will I take up arms against a foe. And if, because of cowardice or madness, I do this awful thing, may God in his anger strike me dead, ere I strike dead some brother from another land!"[406] At the Unitarian General Conference in

September 1917, Holmes directed a stunning challenge to the moderator, former President William Howard Taft, and the assembled delegates, with an impassioned denunciation of the war. "This war ...has driven men to the bowels of the earth, the depths of the sea, the vast spaces of the air, for combat. It has marshaled whole populations in the work of death.... Millions of men are dead on the battlefield or in the hospital, more millions are wounded... and still the fight goes on with a determination as wonderful as its cost is frightful."[407] Holmes' emotional speech was cut off as Taft reclaimed the podium and denounced Holmes' "insidious document." The delegates gave Taft a standing ovation.

In truth the American Unitarian Association differed little from the National Catholic War Council, the Federal Council of Churches, and the Jewish Welfare Board in its support of the war. Indeed, the editor of the *Christian Register* claimed that opposition to the war was treasonous and admonished readers that it was their duty as Christians to "vanquish a race that was lusting to take away their sacred freedoms."[408] To be sure, there was political reason for taking so firm a stand. The Espionage Act of 1917 prohibited the publication of disloyal statements, as (broadly) defined by the postmaster general. In May of 1918, the Sedition Act prohibited "disloyal, profane, scurrilous, or abusive language regarding the flag, the American government, or the uniforms of the armed services." Under the Sedition Act, many American Socialists and members of the Industrial Workers of the World (IWW) were fined or went to prison for opposing the draft.[409]

In this atmosphere of compulsory patriotism the directors of the AUA expressed concern that anti-war ministers were creating turmoil in their churches. In April 1918, they passed a resolution in support of the "war for freedom and humanity." Giving financial bite to this sentiment, they stipulated that any society employing a minister opposed to "the vigorous and resolute prosecution of the war cannot be considered eligible for aid from the Association."[410] On the basis of his objection to this decision, Holmes resigned his ministerial fellowship with the AUA and preached his anti-war message around the country. Secret Service agents ominously trailed him wherever he went. It would not be until 1936 that the General Assembly voted to repudiate the 1918 statement denying aid to churches whose ministers had spoken out against the war. With the onset of World War II, the AUA consciously chose not to suppress dissenting pacifists. This reversal of policy was a bittersweet vindication for Holmes, but he did not rejoin the AUA until his retirement in 1949.[411]

In the years before his death in 1918, Jenkin Lloyd Jones had also spoken out against the war. His experience as a Union soldier fighting in Lincoln's army taught him that war was a "shameful material waste." Worse than this was the "moral cost—the murder of the innocent, the degradation, the inebriety, the gambling and sensuality" that followed armies everywhere.[412] Jones had sustained a life-long reputation within Unitarianism for his radical theological defense of an absolutely creedless ethical religion. In 1882 he had reorganized the Fourth Unitarian Society of Chicago as All Souls Church; in 1893 he had played a prominent role in the World Parliament of Religions, believing it was a step toward realizing a universal church for humankind.[413] Now at age 75, Jones accepted an invitation from Henry Ford to sail with his peace party of 100 "representative Americans" to Stockholm in hopes of negotiating a just settlement. When Ford could not go at the last minute, Jones led the mission. His congregation continued to support him, but other colleagues forced him into lonely exile, closing to him their once-friendly pulpits. Celia Woolley, still directing the Frederick Douglass interracial settlement house she co-founded with Fannie Barrier Williams, continued to stand by Jones, assuring him that he would be welcome to preach at the Douglass Center anytime. This loyalty, Jones told Woolley's husband, meant all the more to him when "so many friends had turned their backs." Soon too, the Chicago postmaster began holding up mailings of Jones' pro-peace journal *Unity*. The strain of fighting to get the paper back in the mails, along with his heart condition, probably contributed to Jones' death in September 1918.[414]

Emily Greene Balch was born in 1867 to a prosperous Boston Unitarian family. Balch had grown up in a life of privilege and had obtained a first-rate education, graduating from Bryn Mawr College in 1889 and then studying in Paris. It may have been surprising to her peers, then, when she authored *Public Assistance to the Poor in France*. After further study of economics at Harvard, the University of Chicago, and in Berlin, she joined the faculty at Wellesley College to teach economics and sociology. Most impressive to her students was the breadth of her knowledge and the depth of her compassion for the poor. In addition to her work at the college, she participated in civic efforts to bring about racial justice, an end to child labor, and better pay and conditions for workers. Always an advocate for peace, Balch had followed carefully the work of two peace conferences in 1899 and 1907 at The Hague. With the outbreak of war in 1914, her commitment to peace deepened. She joined Jane Addams as a delegate to the First International Congress of Women at The Hague in 1915. This remarkable gathering of 1500 women was the only international meeting held during the war.[415]

Balch served as an envoy to carry out the plans of the International Congress. She traveled to Russia and to neutral Scandinavian countries and later conferred with British leaders and with President Woodrow Wilson. Upon her return to the United States, Balch campaigned openly against America's entry into the war, even seeking an extended leave from Wellesley College to continue her work for peace. To her surprise, the Board of Trustees at Wellesley terminated her contract, wishing to dissociate the college from her radicalism. Balch then took a position on the editorial staff of the liberal weekly news magazine *The Nation*. As a member of the Woman's Peace Party, the U.S.-based organization she co-founded in 1915 with Jane Addams and others, Balch attended the Second Convention of the International Congress of Women in 1919. With the war over, women from various peace groups had come to the Zurich convention resolved to influence world governments to implement a just and humane peace. Delegates to the convention created the Women's International League for Peace and Freedom (WILPF), and Balch accepted their invitation to become secretary of the new organization.

In the United States, the Woman's Peace Party became thereafter the United States Section of the Women's International League for Peace and Freedom. Professional women like Balch and Addams felt that they could not afford to defer to men in working toward peace, since men had failed to prevent the outbreak of war.[416] Later Balch served on a committee to investigate conditions in Haiti under U.S. occupation and wrote *Occupied Haiti* in response. The reality of Nazi aggression in World War II forced Balch to alter her pacifist views. It was a time for recognizing the need to defend "fundamental human rights, sword in hand."[417] Balch was awarded the Nobel Peace Prize in 1946 for her life-long work on behalf of peace. She donated her portion of the Peace Prize money to the WILPF. In 1960 she received a lifetime achievement award from the American Unitarian Association.[418] Emily Balch died in 1961, one day after celebrating her ninety-fifth birthday.

After serving as parish minister in Kalamazoo, Michigan, from 1889 to 1899, Caroline Bartlett Crane left her pulpit in the hope of becoming pregnant. When it became clear that she would remain childless, Crane found an inner reserve to overcome this unexpected void in her life and embarked on a ministry of her own making. With so many cities bursting with the problems of rapid unplanned growth, Crane created a community ministry in the fields of public health, municipal reform, and woman suffrage. Then, as war enveloped the world of her day, in spite of her aversion to war, Crane felt compelled by her patriotism and love of liberty to serve the Michigan State War Preparedness Board and later the Council of National Defense.[419] In this position, she helped train and place over 900,000 women in over 100 wartime occupations.

It was difficult in this time for Crane to reconcile her hatred of the human slaughter that accompanied war with her work on behalf of the war effort. World War I had presented an unprecedented case of mass killing and material destruction. According to some estimates, about 10,000,000 young men had died in the war, and 20,000,000 more were maimed, crippled, burned, and wounded. Another 13,000,000 civilians died and 10,000,000 had become refugees.[420] When it was over, Crane worked to "convert defense apparatus to peacetime machinery" and at the same time, joined peace reformers to explore the causes of war and find its cure. Ironically, in this effort she became the target of the same kind of criticism that others had known. What made this criticism especially bitter for Crane was that it came from her friends in the Michigan Chapter of the Daughters of the American Revolution, of which she had long been a member. Her name was added to a list of "disloyal Americans" that was circulated among private and public organizations in the state. Crane was disappointed in the DAR for taking this action, which she believed was motivated by a "benighted nationalism." In response, she placed letters in all the major Michigan newspapers and in several national magazines exposing the DAR's practice of blacklisting dissenters. Further, she withdrew her membership from the DAR.[421]

So deep was the animosity toward those who dared question the government's conduct of the war, it is probable that many who might have spoken were silenced or simply wearied by the atmosphere of hysteria. Among the Unitarians who resisted this kind of pressure, it is important to note one other. Aurelia Henry Reinhardt brought to peace work a temperament and consciousness that may have been influenced by her Unitarian and educational background. Born into a Unitarian family in Oakland, California, Aurelia Isabel Henry graduated from the University of California at Berkeley in 1899 with a degree in English literature and from Yale University in 1905 with a Ph.D. in English. In 1906, she married Dr. George Reinhardt at the First Unitarian Church of Berkeley. Only six years later, her husband died, leaving her a widow with two small sons. After teaching for a time, her life changed in 1916 when she assumed the presidency of Mills College in Oakland, a position she would hold for twenty-seven years.[422] Her work in higher education became central to her professional life but did not interfere with her tireless work as a Unitarian lay minister for peace. In 1919, she declared herself an advocate for world peace and broke ranks with the Republican Party in order to back President Woodrow Wilson's plan for the League of Nations.

In 1932 she was invited to deliver the Ware lecture at the May meeting of the AUA, an honor that had gone the year before to Nobel laureate Jane Addams. Her work for peace culminated in 1945 when she served as a delegate to the founding meetings of the United Nations in San Francisco.

Among Universalists, the pre-eminent peace advocate was Clarence Russell Skinner, who would in time also be the pre-eminent leader of the early twentieth-century Universalist Church of America. Skinner's leadership in the UCA will be described in the chapter on institutional leadership. As with Holmes, Crane, Addams, Jones, Balch, and Reinhardt among the Unitarians, Skinner encountered deep criticism for his pacifist views during World War I. With U.S. entry into the war, reports of Skinner's declared pacifism circulated in the Boston newspapers and prompted public censure. The president of Tufts College, where Skinner was Professor of Applied Christianity in the Crane Theological School, was openly angry at Skinner, perhaps because of how his views might stain the reputation of the school. Many members of the faculty shunned him, and some even called for his dismissal. Once when he was speaking in Concord, listeners threw rotten eggs at him. Despite these displays of condemnation, Skinner held firm in his views. Meanwhile his close colleague Dean Lee McCollester and other faculty members supported him out of respect for his integrity and his constitutional right to free speech.[423]

When the war was over, Skinner called for a united world in a hope-filled article entitled "The World Soul." This idea met with criticism even from the Medford Hillside Universalist Church, which he had been serving on a half-time basis, and he was relieved of his position. The congregation's attitude was that he was too socialistic. The accumulation of these experiences led Skinner, finally, to begin his own congregation. In 1920, he established the Community Church of Boston in the hope that he could set forth his views in a free and fully inclusive environment. The story of this church is told in more detail in a later chapter of this work along with a fuller description of the community ministry of Clarence Skinner.

Ministers who advocated for peace during World War I met with a fate common to most pacifists in a time of war—condemnation and rejection. They understood war as the ultimate tragic folly of competitive, narrowly focused, all-too-human leaders impervious to pacifist appeals. It would not be until the cost of that folly was fully assessed that the prospect of war was treated by the American people and their government with less bravado. A series of Neutrality Acts, passed in the late 1930s to preclude war-inducing entanglements, are by implication evidence of national regret.[424] In spite of such measures, the United States was forced to enter the Second World War, which ultimately ushered in a new world order. Unitarian and Universalist ministers, both lay and ordained, would undertake new roles, bringing their merged message of hope, reason, peace, and reconciliation to bear upon the might of the modern age.

CHAPTER FIFTEEN

Ministries of
Institutional Leadership

T he passion for progressive reform in the early decades of the twentieth century included the application of new scientific methods of management in institutional and organizational settings. The idea was to employ advance planning, engineering expertise, and models of efficient production to achieve the most beneficial outcomes. Unitarian and Universalist leaders endeavored to implement such strategies to best serve the purposes of their respective movements.

Among Unitarians, the leadership of strong AUA presidents in the first half of the twentieth century is credited with sustaining denominational stability. Samuel Atkins Eliot II served as president of the AUA from 1900 to 1927. He brought to the office a desire to strengthen the organizational structures of the denomination, running it in conformity with popular scientific principles of efficiency. Eliot's motivation derived from his personal frustration when, as a Unitarian missionary in Seattle in 1888, he had not been able to obtain a building loan from the AUA. "We must have a concentration of responsible authority," he wrote. "The present lack of a system can be amended by the introduction of more precise business methods into the management of the AUA."[425]

Eliot had been serving as secretary of the AUA from 1898 until 1900. At that time, outgoing president Carroll Wright proposed elevating the current secretary to the role of president. Eliot accepted this change, thinking it would empower him to "seize the large opportunities of service which open always before our hesitating fellowship."[426] New bylaws were adopted in 1900 to create an eighteen-member Board of Directors to "have charge of all the business and interests of the Association . . . its funds and operations." In keeping with Eliot's focus on mission, the AUA soon provided $40,000 to aid a total of eighty-nine churches. The downside of this work was that Eliot's emphasis on large-scale efficiency steered money away from smaller societies.[427] We have seen how this pattern affected Ethelred Brown's small Unitarian mission to African Americans in Harlem. The effect was that the smaller churches died and Unitarian membership was increasingly confined to the more educated and well-to-do strata of society.

Indeed, with regard to women ministers, Eliot viewed their vital efforts at building community in the Midwest as too domestic, out of sync with the commanding forces of progress seen in the larger male-run churches. Women, in Eliot's mind, were unsuited to professional life.[428] An unfortunate example of this is found in the experience of Rowena Morse Mann, a woman of outstanding qualifications who was forced out of her ministry while still in her early fifties. Her church was Third Unitarian, situated on Chicago's West Side, a shaky congregation before her arrival in 1911 due to an influx of eastern European immigrants into the neighborhood. Morse's energy and sermon eloquence brought many people from the suburbs back to the church. Parishioners liked her immensely. Further, they benefited financially because she and her husband pledged one quarter of her salary to the church. Regrettably, a race riot occurred nearby, and the suburban people were too frightened to return. When the congregation petitioned the AUA for funds to relocate in Chicago's downtown Loop, Samuel Eliot's response was to deny funding unless the congregation was willing to engage in outreach to the existing community and accept a young new male minister who was nearing graduation from seminary. When the congregation protested that their present minister was preferable to a "man of no ability," all discussion stopped. In the end, no money was given and the congregation collapsed. Rowena Morse Mann was unable to obtain another pulpit; each time she inquired about an opening, it was suddenly closed.[429] Eliot's patriarchal disposition was apparently crucial in erecting nearly insurmountable barriers to women in ministry. From 1906, when Rowena Morse was ordained, until 1917, not one other woman was brought into active Unitarian ministry.[430]

What was gained under Eliot's leadership? Organizationally Eliot put in place a Department of Ministry to help congregations locate suitable (male) candidates to fill their pulpits. A publication agent was appointed in 1901, a first step toward the founding of Beacon Press. Further, Eliot advocated prison and educational reforms that would provide practical inmate education and health care. Finally, he sought to advance toleration of different world religions, believing that individuals of any faith that shared his ethic and commitment to education should be valued. In defense of Eliot's moves to consolidate authority, it may be said that the times shaped Eliot's decisions at least as much as his own temperament did. Elizabeth Curtiss points out that Unitarians had emerged from the nineteenth century "pretty badly battered" by the theological debates of Transcendentalism versus Biblical Theism and the regional governance conflicts of East versus West.[431] Then too, Unitarian membership was down at the turn of the century. Finally, Eliot's time in office was marked by the disorder that accompanied early twentieth-century industrial growth and urbanization, as well as the traumatizing spectacle of world war. In light of these difficulties, his work to strengthen denominational structures may be better understood for what it helped to overcome.

For Universalists, the end of the nineteenth century had brought a measure of maturation as well as decline. Although statistics are unreliable, it was evident by 1890 that membership had shrunk significantly in the previous fifty years.[432] It is often popularly assumed that as more people migrated to cities,

Universalism lost the support that had sustained its growth in rural areas. The decline was probably due to more than a demographic shift. The Universalist message had long opposed traditional Calvinist warnings of hellfire and brimstone. By the twentieth century, many mainline Protestant sects had adopted the more forgiving Universalist theology, attracting people who might formerly have been drawn to Universalism.[433] Meanwhile, according to Charles Howe, Universalism had grown "theologically more orthodox and socially more conservative." In 1870, the denomination had voted to exclude the "Liberty Clause" from its Winchester Profession. This effectively required adherence to a creed for ministerial fellowship. Behind this action was a sense of needing to repudiate the Boston Free Religionists and Emerson's "natural religion."[434] In consequence, exclusion of the "Liberty Clause" firmly tied Universalist belief to Biblical sources of revelation. In the same year, the General Convention moved to create a more centralized organizational structure that resembled Presbyterian administration. A new three-tiered representative arrangement emerged made up of the General Convention, the state convention, and the parish. This new format took power away from individual congregations.

The reorganization was a reactionary move intended to establish theological and organizational unity. It ran up against the desire of most Universalists to maintain congregational autonomy and preserve personal freedom of belief. By century's end, both the Liberty Clause and a decentralized congregation-based organizational structure were reinstated. Furthermore, the greater theological latitude allowed by the Liberty Clause coincided with the impact of the 1893 World Parliament of Religions. The Parliament had hosted a separate Universalist meeting, which claimed the attendance of 55 ministers and hundreds of lay people. The Parliament led to the formation a year later of the American Congress of Liberal Religious Societies, which was supported by a growing liberal wing of Universalist ministers.[435] These were the ministers who wanted closer relations with other religious liberals. In 1905, representatives of the Universalist General Convention and the American Unitarian Association worked together as part of the International Congress of Religious Liberals to host a conference in Boston. Astonishingly, the conference drew an attendance of 7000 from around the globe.[436]

As these events unfolded, Clarence Russell Skinner proved deeply influential in reviving Universalist morale in the first half of the twentieth century. We have seen that his pacifism in World War I led to his being ostracized at Crane Theological School. Skinner was a man who lived at his core a unique vision of the good society and worked his entire life to bring that vision about through his call to Universalist ministry. As a youth he shared his uncle's interest in acting, and while a student at St. Lawrence University, he served as president of the drama society and editor of the school newspaper. After graduating he married a classmate, a fellow Phi Beta Kappa, Clara Louise Ayres. In their marriage of forty-three years, they were seldom apart. Skinner was ordained into Christian Universalist ministry at the Church of the Divine Paternity in 1906, where he had been working as an assistant to the minister.[437]

Skinner soon established his presence with a Social Gospel focus. He had been active in the University Settlement House on the East Side in New York City, but saw its potential as limited. He believed that a more radical approach was necessary to address social problems, as Walter Rauschenbusch advocated in his *Christianity and the Social Crisis* (1907). In 1911 he was a leader in establishing at a denominational level the Commission on Social Service, which was in keeping with the Social Gospel movement prevalent in American Protestant churches.[438] His belief in practical Christianity was more fully articulated in his first book, *The Social Implications of Universalism*, published in 1915. Going beyond the scope of Protestant Christianity, Skinner offered a radical interpretation of the Social Gospel that redirected the mission of the Universalist Church. Its call for a broad theology and global social ethic spelled out a "prophetic and comprehensive theological, ecclesiastical, and social program for the denomination."[439] The ideas in this book were embodied in Skinner's 1917 proposition "A Declaration of Social Principles," which was adopted by the Universalist denomination as the basis for its social witness.[440]

In 1911 Skinner had accepted an invitation to serve as minister to the Grace Universalist Church in Lowell, Massachusetts. Here is where he met Lee S. McCollester, Dean of the Crane Theological School at Tufts College. The theology school was at low ebb, with only thirteen students out of a total of 479 enrolled at the college, and McCollester was looking for someone to build it up. Skinner accepted the appointment of Professor of Applied Christianity at Crane[441] and soon was teaching a number of courses in such topics as Applied Christianity, History of Religions, Church History, and Religious Education. From these beginnings, he organized the Department of Applied Christianity, which offered courses in social psychology, principles and methods of social service, home and foreign missions, and country church problems. The program also required students to perform practical service in settlement houses or other charitable agencies.[442] Skinner's work in college and seminary teaching was a prophetic community ministry that would have a deep impact on Universalism.

After encountering persistent criticism for his pacifist and internationalist views, Skinner established the Community Church of Boston, where he would be free to speak his own mind. For thirty-one years, Skinner led the Community Church while also holding his faculty position at Crane, attracting large numbers of students to his courses and eventually becoming dean. A defining feature of the church was its involvement in social causes, including the Sacco and Vanzetti case (the Skinners attended many sessions of the trial), the Scottsboro case, and Margaret Sanger's right to speak publicly in Boston.[443] Skinner's church, where attendance sometimes ran to over 1200, paralleled in time, theology, and mission the Community Church of New York established by Unitarian minister John Haynes Holmes. Indeed, drawn together by their shared pacifism, theological liberalism, and social-action-oriented humanism, Holmes and Skinner worked together in the founding of the Boston church.[444] Notably, Holmes' church in New York broke from the body of

Unitarians, while Skinner's church remained tied to the Universalist denomination.

Over time, Skinner's theology changed. In a 1924 essay, "In Times of Disillusion," he voiced his bitterness but ended on a triumphant (Howe suggests defiant) note. "The world has grown unutterably old . . . [but] I'll still proclaim the 'Vision Splendid' . . . God's unsurrendered! SO AM I! . . . I light the candle and—I DREAM."[445] Later works followed: *Liberalism Faces the Future* (1937), *Human Nature and the Nature of Evil* (1939), and *A Religion for Greatness* (1945). By the end of World War II, Skinner's religious position had evolved from an earlier conception of liberal Christianity to an all-encompassing, all-compassionate humanism. He called for a "radical religion" in which "man touches infinity; his home is in immensity; he lives, moves, and has his being in eternity."[446]

In this "radical religion," humankind would not need to name in any specific way the powers that exist beyond the self. Our "village stage of existence," Skinner reasoned, required such "partialist" views. But our modern world requires a "cosmic religion" and demands that we "expand our spiritual powers" in order to "increase the range of our understanding and sympathy." To make this happen, Skinner believed, people must embrace "the universals," that is, the absence of all barriers. This was the "essential human task. There is no middle way. It is greatness—universalism—or perish."[447] After the fire of two World Wars and the strain of a Depression, here was Skinner's vision of a united world community.[448] At the age of 64 and in seriously failing health after surgery for colon cancer, he wrote his final book, *Religion and the Well Ordered Life*, published posthumously in 1955. Refusing to go to a hospital, Skinner died at his summer home in Long Ridge, Connecticut, in 1949.

Skinner's bold thinking laid the foundation for a more expansive Universalism that would eventually find sympathy with Unitarianism. His hope of uniting Unitarians and Universalists was still a long way from being realized when he died, but much progress had been made. In 1927, Universalists had rejected a

Unitarian proposal for unification because they feared losing their more Theist-centered identity. Indeed, Universalists at this time considered joining with the Congregationalists, a move which the outgoing AUA president, Samuel Eliot, described as a "step backward into orthodoxy," leaving behind the trails blazed by Unitarians and Universalists. In a brief moment of like-minded Unitarian and Universalist inspiration, a Free Church Fellowship was formed and met from 1934 to 1937. Its dissolution after three years was due to quarrels over the Unitarian acceptance of Humanism, as well as to the absence of a grassroots base.[449]

The emergence of Humanism, and the signing of the Humanist Manifesto in 1933, would profoundly influence—and divide—liberal religious thinkers in the twentieth century."[450] In the face of Darwin's evolutionary hypothesis, historical studies of biblical evidence, and other scientific and technological developments, supernatural belief met with new levels of skepticism, and atheism gained ground. Among Unitarians, the absence of creedal restraints allowed Humanism to open the door to a new faith in humankind.[451] In 1935 Universalists crafted a new statement of faith that made no explicit mention of Jesus as Christ, nor did it specify a doctrine of universal salvation. Rather, it emphasized the social gospel. This may be seen as a step toward acceptance of Humanism in Universalism, but serious debates continued for decades as to whether Humanism was a legitimate religious view for Unitarians or Universalists.

In addition to these questions, the Depression contributed to a kind of malaise among Unitarians and Universalists. Both denominations found that financial strains undermined their sense of spiritual purpose. Unitarian churches were in decline, being either consolidated or closed. In New England alone, 500 Unitarian ministers were unemployed.[452] Fortunately, strong leaders emerged near the end of these difficult years to revive the spirit of the people in both denominations, to put Humanism into an acceptable context of freedom of conscience, and to establish greater financial security. This kind of leadership furthered the conditions that would in time unite both Unitarians and Universalists around a broad theological vision and shared social commitment. For the Unitarians, this leadership came from Frederick May Eliot, president of the AUA from 1937 to 1958; for the Universalists, it came from Robert Cummins, General Superintendent of the Universalist Convention from 1938 to 1953.

In 1934, the AUA called for the Commission on Appraisal[453] to assess the liabilities facing the denomination, as well as the assets, and to determine a course for future action. The world at this time was in the depths of the Depression, and Fascism loomed frighteningly on the horizon. Unitarian membership was at a low point, and morale was lower still. Frederick May Eliot, minister of the Unity Church in St. Paul, Minnesota, and grandson of William Greenleaf Eliot, was appointed to head the Commission. He and Commission members like James Luther Adams advocated important changes, such as a decentralization of decision-making and a greater emphasis on religious education. In regard to the latter, Frederick urged the view that what holds the free church together is a sense of "common memories and common practices." The church, said Eliot, "must remember where it has been."[454] To fulfill this goal, the Commission urged the writing of a new religious education curriculum to replace what had been published by Beacon Press thirty years before. This vital task of ministry fell to Sophia Lyon Fahs, whose religious journey had followed a long path from orthodox Christianity to liberal naturalism and humanism.

Sophia Lyon had been born in 1876 to Presbyterian missionaries in China. When she married in 1902, she joined the Methodist Church so she and her husband would be in the same denomination. In these early years of the century, Sophia had taken courses at the University of Chicago and the City University of New York. These courses led her to appreciate William Rainey's Higher Criticism of the Bible and John Dewey's progressive ideas in education. Further, she would later say, her own five children were unwittingly her "major teachers" as to the ways that children learn. Fahs chose to work in religious education and spent years teaching Sunday school, lecturing at religious education conferences, and writing related articles, all the while integrating her increasingly liberal religious ideas into her work. Edith Fisher Hunter writes that Fahs found herself "drawing less exclusively on the Judeo-Christian tradition and more on the natural sciences, on the religion of primitive people, and on other world religions."[455] What developed out of this was her desire to offer experience-centered religious education whereby children would explore their reactions to primary phenomena like birth and death, sun and stars, wind and rain, dreams and shadows. This seemed more appropriate to her than early childhood study of Bible stories, which should be saved for when children had a better understanding of history. After obtaining a bachelor's degree in religious studies at Union Theological Seminary, Fahs was invited in 1933 to implement some of her ideas in the religious education program of the new Riverside Church in New York City. This church had been built to house the pulpit of the Rev. Harry Emerson Fosdick, a champion of the Modernist school that Fahs had come to embrace.[456]

In 1928, *Religious Education* magazine published an article authored by Fahs, "How Childish Should a Child's Religion Be?" Albert C. Dieffenbach, editor of the Unitarian *Christian Register,* read this article favorably, and Fahs' reputation among Unitarians began to grow. In 1930 Edwin Fairley, a Unitarian minister who was taking a course from Fahs at Union Seminary, invited her to be a leader at a religious education conference at Star Island, a well-known Unitarian conference center. Fahs' acceptance of this invitation began her association with the AUA, which led to her serving as editor and co-author of children's religious education materials for the New Beacon Series. This work incorporated three contemporary themes into its curriculum: the liberal movement in theology, the progressive movement in education, and the critical movement in Biblical studies.[457] In the New Beacon Series, titles by Fahs would include *How Miracles Abound, From Long Ago and Many Lands, Beginnings of Earth and Sky*, and *Men of Prophetic Fire*. One writer asserts that the appointment of Fahs as editor of this series was the crucial event in the modern history of Unitarian religious education.[458]

As for the further work of the Commission on Appraisal, we return to Aurelia Henry Reinhardt, president of Mills College since

1916 and a committed peace activist since the time of World War I. In 1934, Reinhardt was invited by the Commission on Appraisal to write a chapter on Worship. This contribution would be of singular importance to the Unitarian understanding of liturgy and worship. Reinhardt wrote that worship played "a basic part in all mature religions," uniting worshippers in a "common kinship of existence and understanding." Because liberal religionists know that "a final definition of God has always been beyond man's ability to conceive or state," we are more "deeply alone than St. Augustine," who wrote: "Our hearts are restless 'til they find rest in Thee." Reinhardt expressed the idea that worship should be held in a consistent manner at a usual time on the Sabbath, as this would best provide a "stable background for the shifting drama of civilization." She further advocated that the content of worship include traditional sources like the Bible and the Catholic Missal, but that it also bring in "the new science, the visions of integrated humanity, and wider concepts of deity."[459]

Finally, Reinhardt recommended that form and beauty in worship be retained from the past. Tapping into deep human emotion, worship should reflect all customary forms of art: architecture, music, poetry, color, and design. Beyond these, it required the art of an "adventuring spirit" and an awareness of the variety of people's spiritual quests. In her report Reinhardt recognized the "comprehensive human and spiritual needs which find articulate expression only through religion" and recommended that "the liberal fellowship set its hand and mind to the task of reviving adequate public worship."[460] In this period, she also served as Trustee for the Starr King School for the Ministry in Berkeley, predicting that "the future includes more women in the ministry than we have ever known before."[461]

The Commission on Appraisal of 1936 has been said to have caused the renaissance of Unitarianism in the twentieth century. James Luther Adams played an important role in calling for the Commission and influencing its recommendations. Adams believed that the vitality of liberalism depended on a continuous process of reexamination. "Only where there is a sincere recognition of incompleteness and failure, only where there is a recovery of depth, breadth, and length, only there is the authentic spirit of religious liberalism to be found."[462] Robinson writes that the "sense of a return to ultimate foundations in order to find renewed vigor" is very much at the heart of the Commission's report. It was both an analysis and a plan for action—to set about reviving discouraged Unitarians and their disheartened churches. Its recommendations reveal much about the state of Unitarianism in that period, most remarkably in its list of what Unitarians agreed on and what they disagreed on. The foundations of agreement included affirmation of the social implications of religion, the necessity for worship, and the rational nature of the universe; points of disagreement included the wisdom of maintaining the definitely Christian tradition and the adequacy and competency of man to solve his own problems. World War I, the Depression, and Humanism had taken a toll. In the words of James Luther Adams, it was a time for "repentance" and "return." "The report received overwhelming support at the annual meeting," states Carol Morris. "Unitarians were ready to move forward in the direction marked out."[463]

Frederick May Eliot had led the Commission on Appraisal with uncommon wisdom and good sense. When it was time in 1936 to elect a new president of the AUA, he seemed the natural choice. It took a little convincing for him to accept that his serving as president, after directing the Commission, would not be a conflict of interest. Assuming office in hard times, Frederick was drawn to humanitarian endeavors. In 1936, the Unitarian Service Committee, then a part of the AUA, had become involved in assisting Czech Unitarians prior to and during the Nazi occupation of Czechoslovakia. With the full backing of the AUA and Frederick Eliot, aid was extended to any Czechs in need, regardless of their religious affiliation. Eliot regarded the creation of the Unitarian Service Committee as "the most important event in this century."[464] From today's perspective, we might call it one of the most important community ministries in the twentieth century. Unfortunately, the Service Committee was soon separated from the AUA by a vote of the AUA Board of Directors due to political anxieties of the day. On the one hand, the USC was praised for rescuing Spanish liberals from death under Franco; on the other hand, conservative Unitarians feared the USC was giving aid to communists living under Nazi siege in France.[465] Thus political fears distorted perceptions of a world in need.

Frederick Eliot himself came under attack in the late 1940s by a highly conservative Unitarian group known as the Committee of Fourteen. Members of this group believed Frederick was too politically socialist and too theologically humanist. These attacks were not atypical for the time. The Cold War was beginning to heat up, and anyone with socialist ideas was suspect. Moreover, absence of belief in God was seen as a sign of insufficient Americanism. Frederick responded that he had no authority to tell Humanists what to think or preach and no power to expel them. He allowed that he was a Humanist, believing that it "feeds the souls of men" better than any sort of faith. Nonetheless, he regularly referred to God, believed in prayer as a means of cleansing and refreshing the spirit, and deplored disdainful remarks about Christianity. Finally, he shared with others before him the desire to bring people of all liberal faiths together into a united group, including liberal Hindus, Muslims, and Jews. Facing down the tensions of the postwar years, Frederick Eliot's vision continued in the reconciling tradition that had been enunciated by the Congress of Religious Liberals in 1905.

Of necessity, the war years called for new forms of community service. In 1936, the AUA Board members expressed regret for sanctions imposed in 1918 on pacifist ministers in the denomination. By 1942, however, it was understood that every church had "a duty to make the utmost contribution to the defeat of the Axis powers." In response to Nazism, the *Christian Register* published numerous articles on religion and democracy. Titles such as "Democracy as a Modern Religion" and "The Religious Basis for a New World Order" were common. The Unitarian Service Committee, based in Lisbon during the war, directed relief efforts for refugees from 1940 with the fall of France until the time of allied liberation in 1944. At home, the AUA Board voted in 1944 to establish the Unitarian Church of the Larger Fellowship to serve isolated religious liberals with no opportunity to join a local congregation. Run by Dr. Albert Dieffenbach, the Church of the Larger Fellowship maintained contact with its adherents through a monthly pastoral letter and the distribution of denominational publications. In two years, the Church of the Larger Fellowship had a membership of 775, with a constituency of 1500. Every state was represented, as well as several Canadian provinces.[466]

The leadership of the Universalists in these years also proved powerful and influential. Robert Cummins became General Superintendent to the Universalist General Convention in 1938. Having served as a parish minister for twelve years, Cummins spent his first year as Superintendent visiting Universalist churches and analyzing the problems facing the denomination. He found that since 1910, the number of churches had declined from 819 to 544 and the number of family units had dropped from 52,272 to 39,827. In his first address to the General Convention, he called for "a renewed consciousness of worth, dignity, and confidence" to replace "despair and indifference." Organizationally, Cummins worked toward greater centralization with separate departments assigned distinct responsibilities. Critics questioned his centralizing of authority, but were silenced when a majority of delegates voted to continue his program, aptly named "Forward Together." It was time, he urged, to stop looking nostalgically to the past and look instead to the future. He devised a program of revitalization and focus, advocating as well a change in name from the Universalist General Convention to the Universalist Church of America, a change that became official in 1942.[467]

Theologically, Cummins encouraged the broader outlook advocated by Clarence Skinner. Cummins believed that the survival of Universalism depended on its becoming more inclusive. "Ours is a world fellowship," he urged in 1943. All must be welcome: "Theist, Humanist, Unitarian, Trinitarian, colored, and color-less. A circumscribed Universalism is unthinkable." Howe comments that the call for a "colored and colorless" church held particular relevance in this time. Jeffrey Campbell, an African

American, had graduated in 1935 from the Canton Theological School at St. Lawrence University, and had been ordained in spite of opposition from the State Superintendent to both his admission to seminary and his ordination. "It was a waste of money," so it had been argued, "to educate a 'colored' man."[468] Cummins repudiated these old ideas of bigotry and, as a consequence, was enthusiastically accepted by the younger generation of Universalist ministers.

Ironically, it was rejection by the Federal Council of Churches of Christ in America that led Universalists to fully claim the worth of Robert Cummins' open theological vision. The Universalist Church in America had been invited to apply for membership in the Federal Council of Churches of Christ (forerunner of the National Council of Churches). Howe states that Universalists decided to apply for membership in order to "join forces with other denominations in addressing the pressing human needs resulting from the war." Further, the Universalist Washington Avowal (1935) had committed the denomination to "cooperate in establishing the Kingdom for which Jesus lived and died."[469] Twice the application was submitted and twice it was denied, the second time in 1944 by a vote of twelve to six. The reason given for the rejection was that no Universalist statement articulated acceptance of Jesus as Divine Lord and Savior. After this, states Howe, "the Universalist break with institutional Christianity was complete."[470] In bringing more clarity to what Universalism had come to be, this episode provided the necessary point of departure from which a future alliance with the Unitarians could be initiated.

CHAPTER SIXTEEN

Unitarians and Universalists at Mid-Century

With the end of World War II came a sense of relief and a readiness to explore new opportunities for growth. In 1944, the AUA voted to organize the Church of the Larger Fellowship (CLF), by which isolated Unitarians could receive worship and educational materials by mail. Two years later, the Universalist Church of America formed a similar program. Within a year of the CLF being formed, the Fellowship Movement emerged within Unitarianism. The AUA Board of Directors voted on May 14, 1945 to explore forming lay-led "centers" in communities where there were not enough Unitarians to form a church. By May 1948, a Lay Fellowship Plan was developed, based on the realization that there were not enough trained ministers to serve new congregations. Appropriately, a lay leader, Munroe Husbands, was chosen to serve both as Clerk of the Church of the Larger Fellowship and as Director of the Lay Fellowship Plan. Under the fellowship plan, lay-led groups would be permitted to "choose their own leaders" and develop their own "purposes, methods of operation, philosophy, and emphasis."[471]

The first seed among the hundreds of fellowships to follow was planted when a four-year old boy in Boulder, Colorado went knocking on doors in his neighborhood, looking for someone to take him to Sunday school. Not comfortable with sending her son to the local traditional Sunday school, his shocked mother contacted the AUA and was told, "You'll just have to do it yourself." Lenore Stewart wrote away for Unitarian curriculum materials and organized an informal structure of classes and meetings. Her husband, Omer C. Stewart, served as president of the group that emerged. Soon Munroe Husbands visited Boulder and explained the new fellowship program. On July 28, 1948, the Unitarian Fellowship of Boulder was officially recognized by the AUA as the first of its lay-led congregations. There would be many others. In Bismarck, North Dakota, fifteen members formed a fellowship in 1952. At first they met in each other's homes; then they acquired an existing building; and finally, in 1959, they erected a building of their own. Bismarck is more isolated than Boulder but shared with Boulder the experience of having a minister travel from an established Unitarian church to lend whatever assistance was needed. Both congregations succeeded. The Bismarck fellowship is still functioning today, serving a small congregation with its own resources. The Boulder fellowship grew into a large congregation and in 1959 retained a full-time minister. Twenty years later, forty-two of the 375 members followed their preference for a lay-led fellowship and broke off to form a new smaller congregation. Now there are two Unitarian congregations in Boulder, one a church and one a fellowship, with a total membership of 500.[472]

The Fellowship Movement was successful in bringing a large number of lay-led congregations into being. This was in part due to Munroe Husbands, who developed a strategy all his own. "He would come into town, book a public site for a presentation, meet with people interested in forming a new group, provide them with resources, and then keep going."[473] By 1958, there were 249 fellowships, and by 1968, there were 500.

David Robinson maintains that the fellowship movement "affirmed the importance of individualism in the liberal tradition" while also proving "the need for corporate worship."[474] Carol Morris points to the Fellowship Movement as one of the great success stories of the post-war years.[475] The Fellowships led to a 53 percent increase in adult membership in the Unitarian societies: from 69,104 in 1947 to 106,000 in 1957. Church school enrollments gained 169 percent in these same years, many of them utilizing the New Beacon Series developed by Sophia Lyon Fahs. Frederick Eliot, still at the helm of the AUA, optimistically read a deeper significance into this phenomenal growth. The years of Depression, War, and Cold War had been rugged. To Eliot, these numbers were evidence of a new "vitality, a freshness of attitude, a confidence of mood and spirit that show promise of future growth beyond anything we have dared to prophecy."[476]

There were, however, tensions and pitfalls within the Fellowship Movement. As fellowships grew, it became a matter of conflict as to whether they should call a minister and end their "adventure in self-sufficiency." A minister could offer support in times of crisis, deliver pastoral counseling, and raise the visibility of the congregation; on the other hand, lay leadership offered the variety of having members and guests lead services and generated a rich sense of community. This issue of whether or not to call a minister led to the break-up of many fellowships. They also foundered over more mundane matters: what Husbands had described as "creeping apathy, the domination of the group by a few people, and personality problems." Further, many who were drawn to fellowships were "come-outers" who associated any traditional signs of religious practice with past experiences of indoctrination. Even the use of hymns or a collection plate became problematic.[477]

The fellowships were a community ministry in themselves as well as a vehicle for individuals to become lay community ministers. Unitarianism had traditionally been both hierarchical and patriarchal. The new fellowships rejected both of these models, letting both men and women explore their own creative potential for leadership and spiritual expression. They inaugurated more informality in worship with sermon talk-backs, interpretive dance, drama, and non-traditional music.[478] Finally, one Boulder fellowship member described a deeper intangible reward of the fellowship experience: "I wonder if the true meaning of Unitarianism can be known to anyone who has not struggled and bumbled through his own first sermon, and who has not respectfully listened to the spiritual birth pangs of his fellow laymen [and women]."[479] This kind of experience shows the ambivalence felt by many in the fellowships toward calling a minister. In the end, the fellowships facilitated the geographical spread of Unitarianism; though they could be suspicious of spiritual forms and might lack continuity, they generated enthusiasm among younger people and fostered experimentation.[480] As it turned out, the more common pattern for the fellowships that survived was to form a church led by at least a part-time parish minister.

In the midst of this unprecedented period of growth, AUA president Frederick May Eliot died quite unexpectedly, on February 17, 1958. He was only 68. The leadership of the AUA had been his life's work—his larger ministry—for 21 years. Of him it was said: "He transformed a frightened movement into a courageous one. He gave us heart, an intelligent direction, a driving force. The present explosion in the Unitarian population of our country . . . is his living monument."[481] Indeed, his leadership had been central to fostering greater freedom for theological dialogue among Unitarians, enabling them to once again transcend their differences. One of Eliot's greatest contributions was that he gave Humanists an increased sense of belonging in the family. Finally, the closer cooperation that would bring Unitarians and Universalists together into a "wider fellowship" had been his dream. His work opened that door and made possible a foundation for merger with Universalism.[482]

Among Universalists in this same period, a more liberal wing had emerged, looking to move beyond Christianity to a universal religion. In the late 1940s, a group of Universalist ministers formed the Humiliati, espousing a Universalism that "blended functional, naturalistic, theistic, and humanistic views."[483] Significantly influenced by Clarence Skinner, the Humiliati were the chief element within a movement among Universalists embracing a one united world view. As Unitarians had woven into a whole the humanist and theist threads of their movement, the Universalists had integrated non-Christian orientations into what had previously been a predominately Christian theology. Both denominations of liberal religion had come to accept greater diversity within their ranks. Credit for this kind of openness must be attributed in no small part to the leaders of each group: Frederick Eliot for the Unitarians, Clarence Skinner and Robert Cummins for the Universalists.

Then too, perhaps the most radical feature of the movement to bring Unitarians and Universalists under the same tent was that young people led the way. There had been a long history of parallel youth ministries among both Unitarians and Universalists. The Unitarians had established the Young People's Religious Union in 1896 to 1941; this became the American Unitarian Youth between 1941 and 1953. Among Universalists, there was the Young People's Christian Union from 1889 to 1941 and the Universalist Youth Fellowship from 1941 to 1953. It is significant that in 1941, both movements amended their names to reflect the more theologically open orientation they had come to accept. In 1953 American Unitarian Youth joined with the Universalist Youth Fellowship to form a combined Unitarian and Universalist youth organization. Taking the new name of Liberal Religious Youth, they anticipated by eight years the merger that would bring their two movements together.[484] Liberal Religious Youth was a ministry that embodied in tangible form the vision of a combined Unitarian Universalist community.

A similar development took place among college students. Among Unitarians, Channing Clubs had been around since 1855, when one was founded at the University of Wisconsin at Madison. The club took its name from William Ellery Channing, who first claimed the name of Unitarian Christianity in 1819. Channing Clubs convened at major American universities and existed in connection with nearby Unitarian churches. For Universalists, Murray Clubs derived their name from John Murray, the earliest Universalist English minister to migrate to America. In 1908, a combined Channing-Murray Foundation formed a campus ministry at the

University of Champaign-Urbana in Illinois. Then, in 1955, this instance of unified work was replicated generally, when, six years before the merger, the Unitarian Channing Club joined with the Universalist Murray Club. Together they became the Channing-Murray Clubs, known alternatively as Channing Murray Centers. The Channing-Murray Clubs often involved students in lectures and discussions, but they did other things too. At Madison, Wisconsin, the Channing-Murray Club operated a student-cooperative rooming house that offered space to hold their meetings. The money for this house had come from the sale of an earlier house bought in the 1940s to provide racially integrated student housing at a time when none was available.

In the 1960s, Orloff Miller was hired by the UUA on a full-time basis to do campus ministry. Miller had been ordained in a Methodist church in 1954 and served a Congregational-Unitarian church in a New Hampshire village from 1956 to 1959. He then "field tripped" (his words) on North American college campuses as Associate Director of Liberal Religious Youth from 1959 to 1961.[485] Having been accepted in 1961 into UU ministry, he was appointed the first Director of the UUA Office of College Centers and Staff Advisor to the college-age group Student Religious Liberals (SRL). Over the next five years, he made many more campus field trips, led two European Study Trips for SRL, and was the UUA's representative on the board of the Albert Schweitzer College in Switzerland.

By the late 1960s, the UUA was facing financial difficulties and had no funds to sustain a campus ministry focus. Added to this was the concern, shared by mainline Protestant denominations, that campus ministries were giving sanctuary to campus radicalism and the drug scene.[486] Campus ministries faded away at that point. Student Religious Liberals operated informally for about ten years beginning in the late 1960s. Through SRL, students on college campuses organized and led activities with nominal support from the UUA and local UU churches. At the same time as SRL, the College Centers Program established forty chapters with local ministers dedicated to doing campus ministry. Funded on a small scale by the UUA, the College Centers Program organized study and field trips designed to deepen students' connections with liberal religion. Because college-student and young adult programs lost vitality and presence in the 1970s and 1980s, it is easy to forget the combined strength they demonstrated in joint association, as did high school groups, prior to the UU merger. They would gain fuller denominational commitment in the 1990s.

Meeting at Syracuse in 1959, representatives of the Universalist Church of America and the American Unitarian Association hammered out the compromise language that would define the identity and purposes of the consolidated religious movement. This was language that drew on the long traditions of liberal religion "To cherish and spread universal truths taught by the great prophets and teachers of humanity in every age and tradition, immemorially summarized in the Judeo-Christian heritage as love to God and love to man."[487] The congregations voted in favor of adopting the language and consolidating the two liberal denominations: Unitarians, 555 to 54; Universalists, 183 to 49. The long-awaited merger took place in 1961. For community ministry, the consolidation of the new Unitarian Universalist Association was timely. It coincided momentously with the crises of an age that demanded uncharted ministries in justice, compassion, and healing.

CHAPTER SEVENTEEN

New Occasions
Teach New Duties

T he Civil Rights Movement in America called for levels of courage and commitment that exceeded anything customarily experienced among fellow citizens in a time of peace. Here were southern African American men, women, and children claiming their right to sit in any empty seat on a bus, eat at any lunch counter, make normal use of bus terminals in interstate travel, attend their own neighborhood schools, enroll in colleges alongside qualified whites, be hired for appropriate job openings, and vote. For those who joined in their struggle, whether white or black, there was real danger in confronting the defenders of white supremacy. The Civil Rights Act of 1964 pried off the locks that barred African Americans from equal opportunities in education and employment.[488] It did not, however, address the fact that black Americans in southern states were still barred from voting due to the use of poll taxes and unfair literacy tests.

President Lyndon Johnson and the Congress were under pressure to pass a voting rights bill. Then came the shooting death of Jimmy Lee Jackson, a 26-year old African American Civil Rights activist, in Selma, Alabama. At his memorial service, the Southern

Christian Leadership Conference (SCLC) announced there would be a march from Selma, Alabama, to the state capital in Montgomery, to protest for voting rights.[489] Voting rights for blacks posed a fundamental threat to the maintenance of southern white supremacy, attacking it at its core. On what became known as "Bloody Sunday," an initial attempt to stage the march met with armed confrontation on the Edmund Pettis Bridge. Martin Luther King, Jr. sent telegrams to ministers all over the country asking them to join him in Selma for a rescheduled march. Among the 450 or so clergy who rallied to King's call were about 100 Unitarian Universalist ministers, including James Reeb, Orloff Miller, and Clark Olsen. In one of his earliest sermons Reeb had claimed, "American society is today indicted for what it is doing to the Negro. In that struggle we should be prepared to make any sacrifice."[490]

James Reeb had already made critical life decisions guided by a depth of conviction. He had left his associate ministry position at the prestigious All Souls Church in Washington, D.C. to undertake a community-based ministry among the poorest of the poor in Roxbury, one of Boston's most deteriorated neighborhoods. There he worked for the American Friends Service Committee to direct efforts toward improved housing for African Americans in Boston's inner city. In 1961 he had told a congregation, "For as long as I can remember, what I have always thought of as the light within has been of more importance to me than anything else in life. To take the light within and . . . consciously set it before men is keeping faith with the best that is in us."[491] It is an unfortunate irony that Ministerial Fellowship rules at the time required that Reeb's fellowship be revoked because he was no longer serving a UU congregation. J. Ronald Engel describes the sense of absorption he and his friend James Reeb shared with regard to redefining their faith: "We were concerned to reject what we perceived as the prevailing model of religious understanding—a model which assumed God acts through the church to save the world." Whether motivated by Theism or Humanism, stated Engel, "we rejected any notion that the church is the [only] sacred center." He explained further, "The world is filled with sacred centers, and it is the mission of the church to identify, celebrate, and serve the creativity of those places."[492]

In Selma, Reeb met up with Olsen and Miller on the evening before the march. They were standing in a crowd in front of the steps of Brown Chapel. King was waiting for a federal injunction against the march to be lifted. He asked all who had shown up for the second march to return the next morning for a third try. Reeb, Olsen, and Miller had determined to stay for the march. They went to dinner in a black section of town, eating at the crowded integrated Walker's Café. Leaving the restaurant after dinner, they turned left to follow the shortest route back to Brown Chapel. This route took them into a white segregationist neighborhood. As they neared the Silver Moon Café, four white men, one of whom was carrying a club, came towards them from across the street. Reeb and Olsen warned, "Just keep walking." But before anyone could stop it, the club came swinging at Reeb's head. "The sound," Olsen reported later, was "just awful."[493] Reeb fell to the ground on his back; Miller dropped to the sidewalk in a crouch and covered his head; Olsen tried to run but was caught and punched. Then, just as quickly as the attackers appeared, they left. Reeb's head injury was deadly. The first ambulance blew a tire; a second ambulance eventually replaced the first and delivered him to one of the finest hospitals in the South, the University of Alabama Medical Center in Birmingham. There, neurosurgeons soon discovered the irreversible damage done to Reeb. He died two days later, on March 11, 1965.

Reeb's death prompted widespread expressions of horror and grief, with memorial services held across the country. President Lyndon Johnson publicly bemoaned the death of James Reeb and declared the events at Selma "an American tragedy." Privately he arranged for a plane to carry Reeb's wife, Marie, to her husband's side in Birmingham. Four days later, Johnson delivered his televised voting rights proposal to a joint session of Congress, invoking the memory of "that good man" in his address. This proposal was soon followed by legislation that was attributable in large part to "the martyrdom of James Reeb."[494] Within the Voting Rights Act of 1965 was a provision that opened the way for federal oversight of state and local elections. If only a small percentage of eligible African Americans were voting, the law assumed this was due to the prejudicial use of literacy tests. Federal election agents would automatically be placed in such districts to oversee registration and voting. The Act also invited Attorney General Robert Kennedy to challenge the constitutionality of the poll tax, which he did. The Supreme Court soon struck down the poll tax, which passed forever into its own ignominious history.

What is not well known about this story is that King delivered the eulogy at Reeb's funeral in Selma, held the same day as Johnson's televised address. King was clearly moved by the life story and tragic death of James Reeb. His powerful eulogy honored Reeb as a "martyr in the Judeo-Christian faith that all men are brothers."[495] He pointed out that Reeb was not just concerned about justice for blacks away from home. "He and his family," stated King, "live in Roxbury, Massachusetts, a predominantly Negro community, [where they] devote their lives to aiding families in low-income housing areas." King's eulogy lay the blame for Reeb's death not only on the man who wielded the club and the racist sheriffs who allowed it, but more fundamentally on "the indifference of every minister of the gospel who has remained silent behind the safe security of stained glass windows" and on "the irrelevancy of a church that will stand amid social evil and serve as . . . an echo rather than a voice." King also blamed civil officials and "the timidity of a federal government that can spend millions of dollars a day to keep troops in South Vietnam, yet cannot protect the lives of its own citizens seeking constitutional rights." Finally, he blamed "the cowardice of every Negro who tacitly accepts the evil system of segregation." King believed that the "marvelous ecumenical" spirit of Reeb's funeral would come alive in the world only through the commitment of everyone in Alabama, the entire deep South, and ultimately the entire United States to bring it about. Finally, King placed Reeb's death in a context Reeb himself would have owned: "Out of the wombs of a frail world, new systems of justice and equality are being born."[496]

There were many others besides Reeb, of course, who died to bring about justice in the land. One of these was Viola Gregg Liuzzo, a Unitarian Universalist laywoman from Detroit. Liuzzo was shot in her car after driving Selma marchers back to Montgomery and returning to Selma to pick up more. The tragic deaths of Jimmy Lee Jackson, Viola Liuzzo and James Reeb exemplify the immense risks endemic in the fight to achieve human rights. Dr. King's favorite hymn, "Once to Every Man and Nation," speaks of the moment when individuals and nations must decide, "in the strife of truth with falsehood, for the good or evil side."[497] King referred to the words of this hymn in numerous speeches. The hymn reminds its hearers: "new occasions teach new duties, time makes ancient good uncouth; they must upward still and onward who would keep abreast of truth." Racial confrontation in 1960s America was a new occasion demanding new duties. Jackson, Reeb, and Liuzzo, along with far too many others, made costly decisions for the side of truth, forcing a reluctant nation, at long last, to follow their lead.

Jesse Cavileer was a parish minister whose commitment extended to the interracial urban constituency that lived beyond the walls of his church. To all who knew him, he was simply Jesse. His life had always been a ministry of scholarship, faith, and action. He had graduated from Syracuse University as "the senior most accomplished in scholarly pursuits" and obtained his Master of Divinity from Union Theological Seminary in New York City. While a student, Jesse set records in track and qualified to compete in the 1936 Olympics, but was unable to go at the last minute due to a training injury. In these years, he also organized a Student Liberal Club and a campus chapter of the NAACP. His work with young people and migrant workers, and with the League for Industrial Democracy, led to his serving on the faculty of Columbia University as a trainer in outreach to the community. At various times, he was also a steel worker, working open-hearth furnaces in Youngstown, Ohio, Gary, Indiana, and Glasgow, Scotland. Simultaneously, he served as minister to either Unitarian or Universalist churches, whichever was nearest the mills.

From 1966 to 1985, Jesse served the Allegheny Unitarian Universalist Church in Pittsburgh, Pennsylvania. The church was situated on the North Side, where a distinct community mentality stemmed from its early incorporation as Allegheny City. The Allegheny Church, once named the North Side Church, had long felt a responsibility to the North Side neighborhood, which was 55 percent African American in the 1960s.[498] This was the kind of church to which Jesse Cavileer was typically drawn, a small congregation focused on social justice. As minister to the Allegheny Church, Jesse opened himself and the church to the neighborhood.[499] As a case in point, the construction of a highway connector through the neighborhood had deprived local businesses of a base from which to work. Jesse invited representatives of these businesses to use the church building for their meetings. Since he lived next door, it was easy for him to let them into the building as needed.[500]

Perhaps more dramatically, Jesse became involved in an effort to utilize federal anti-poverty funds granted to the North Side. When city officials were unable to decide how to use the funds, Jesse organized the Central Northside Neighborhood Council and determined there was a need for training "untried" people in how to organize and make decisions. "I was named Citizen Chair of the federal program council," he remembered. "I got the University of Pittsburgh to set up an undergraduate course in social work, to enable African Americans to take up leadership positions."[501] Sometimes, Jesse knew, the best strategy was direct intervention. In 1967, he led a prayer meeting with a monsignor, a rabbi, and several priests and ministers in front of the home of a notorious landlord who had so-called "police friends." Jesse later wrote, "We were taken to jail and prayed there. Not long. It is not illegal to pray on a public sidewalk. I wasn't a board member all those years of the ACLU for nothing."[502] On another occasion, when the city attempted to construct a brick wall that would have cut off nearby residents from a 100-acre park, Jesse lay down in the very place where construction workers were about to build the wall. It was enough to cause the city to give up on the wall, and still today the park is open to the neighborhood it serves.[503] Jesse Cavileer died unexpectedly on June 4, 2004. He is remembered by those who knew him for his heartfelt leadership and open ministry to the community.

Neil Shadle's ministry is another example of the urban community ministry that defined this period. In the 1960s, states Shadle, "our awareness of urban issues was enlivened by the War on Poverty in combination with urban studies courses being offered at major colleges and universities."[504] Like Reeb and Cavileer, Shadle felt called by the "new occasions" of the times. He had been serving an internship at a church in St. Paul, Minnesota, when the church burned. Across the street was a settlement house where residents offered the use of the building to the congregation. Prior to this time, the church had had no connection to the settlement house or any other neighborhood entity. The experience of meeting in the settlement house led the congregation to see how isolated they had become from the community around them. Shadle explored with the minister, who was a very conscientious man in Shadle's mind, ways to change the congregation's sense of mission. When Shadle returned to Chicago, he designed his fourth year of study to prepare himself for a very different kind of ministry. The president of Meadville Lombard expressed support for it and asked Shadle and his classmate Ron Engel if they would like to start up an urban ministry in Chicago as a program of the school. Engel had interned at All Souls Church in Washington, D.C. Shadle and Engel welcomed this opportunity. They were given faculty status at Meadville Lombard, which gave them financial support for their ministry. It also provided the UUA institutional affiliation that was necessary for them to be fellowshipped. Shadle states, "Had Ron and I not been hired as faculty at Meadville Lombard, we would not have been fellowshipped."

For Shadle, urban ministry opened up a new way of doing theology. "I operated in a mode of action/reflection—my work in the community led me to reflect on its deeper meaning. And this led me to further action." Shadle and Engel became advocates for community ministry. "But," Shadle recalls, "when we went to the

New Ministers Conference in Boston in 1964, our denominational leadership discouraged what we were doing. Out of twenty-five new ministers, there were about six or seven of us who were doing community ministry. We were told, 'The UUA is interested in congregations and we had better be too.'" Their work in the urban setting led them to develop a new direction in theological education. Shadle taught courses around such professional topics as social ethics, clinical pastoral education, and various kinds of chaplaincies. Shadle became the school's authority on all such programs, which was a natural outgrowth of his work in the community. "I believed that recognition of our ministry should be based on our work in the community."[505] Shadle states simply, "This was not yet encouraged in the 1960s."

In an early first step toward meeting the challenge of social action ministry, the Unitarian Universalist Association revised the rules of the Ministerial Fellowship Committee (MFC) to formalize in 1969 a category of ministry known as "Specialized Minister."[506] The old rules for fellowship required a minister to serve a parish. Specialized Ministers might be fellowshipped even if their ministry lay outside a parish. The new category was not easily implemented, however, as early instances did not fit with conventional parish ministry expectations.

The first to seek official recognition in a "Specialized Ministry" was Howard Matson, who had already been fellowshipped as a parish minister. Matson had served as associate minister for ten years at the First Unitarian Church of San Francisco. During that time, he gave volunteer support to the farm worker movement and became a founding member of the interfaith National Farm Worker Ministry. Through this group, and the Unitarian Universalist Migrant Ministry, which he also founded, Matson organized church support for boycotting and picketing, raised funds for the United Farm Workers union, gave support to Cesar Chavez, and preached for better pay and conditions for migrant farm workers.

Matson and his wife, Rosemary, were at their summer home in Carmel Valley while a lettuce strike was underway in Salinas

Valley. They learned that Cesar Chavez needed a safe place to stay and offered their summer home.[507] Chavez and the farm worker leaders were very happy to accept this offer. Rosemary wrote that one neighbor, a prominent grower, gave them some trouble over the presence of Chicanos living in their summer home. He called the Matsons at their home in San Francisco and warned them, "The good people of Carmel Valley will not let you get away with this." Surprisingly, the neighbor never learned that Chavez himself was staying there. When Matson retired from his San Francisco church in 1972, his part-time ministry with farm workers became full-time ministry.

Matson was present in the dangerous confrontations between Teamsters and the United Farm Workers. "The clergy were present to help cool the violence," he wrote. He was present when farm workers were killed on the picket line and participated in their funerals. Of such times as this, Matson wrote, "In the years I was minister for migrant farm workers it was clear to me that the mere presence of a caring person in a crisis situation is the most important contribution one could make. Migrants are so alone as they wander from field to field in search of work. To live in a labor camp and to work fields close to where people live in real houses is a depressing experience."[508] With the California Agricultural Labor Relations Act of 1975, union organizers were supposed to be free to talk to field workers, but some growers arrested such organizers in spite of the new law.[509] Matson showed up with two other clergy, a nun and a United Church of Christ minister, to stand with those who were arrested. For many hours, the clergy collectively refused all offers to be released. The outcome of their confrontation was that union organizers were allowed on the ranch the next day. Matson reflected, "It is not often ministerial action has such a direct result."

It was after Matson left full-time parish ministry and entered full-time migrant ministry that he sought and was granted recognition as a Specialized Minister. For the denomination, this was a leap into the unknown. For Matson it seemed a superfluous exercise that he be recognized as newly fellowshipped at the next

General Assembly. It was a ritual he chose to enact, however, because to do so gave sanction and visibility to this new category of ministry. It brought Howard Matson as Specialized Minister before the Assembly; it also brought the Assembly into covenant with his migrant farm workers ministry. Matson's migrant ministry was a team effort with his wife Rosemary Matson. He did the speaking and lobbying to gain support for the workers. Rosemary created informational materials, brochures, and mailings. When Chavez died in 1993, Matson wrote movingly of having worked with "this servant of the people" for two decades. "He sought justice for the lowest paid workers in our nation. That the very people who work to put food on our tables would themselves live in poverty is a gross injustice. That today their wages are higher, their working conditions improved, their dignity restored, is a tribute to Chavez." It was not long after this letter was written that Howard Matson died, August 17, 1993. Rosemary writes, "I promised him I would carry on our support of the farm worker movement. That I have."[510]

Soon after Howard Matson was ordained as a specialized minister, Ric Masten requested official recognition as a Troubadour Minister. Masten's early life seemed unpromising. He grew up with severe dyslexia, commonly understood in that time as an intelligence failure rather than a reading disability. He had also suffered from a hearing impairment, and after high school he had proceeded to fail out of one college after another. He made a living working in a print shop and doing construction work, all the while composing poems and singing songs to fulfill an inner call. Having no defined religious affiliation in his youth, he first came to Unitarian Universalism when he and his wife of ten years attended the Unitarian Universalist Church of the Monterey Peninsula. After six months the minister there asked him to do a Sunday service. The service he performed was a moment of discovery, both for him and for his audience; his poems and songs moved people on a spiritual level that neither he nor they had anticipated. Soon he was doing services throughout California, promoted in part by Rosemary Matson, who had heard him at the Monterey church.[511] These engagements led to Masten being hired to perform at the 1968

General Assembly in Cleveland. From there, the UUA assigned him the task of "taking the spirit of liberal religion to college campuses and churches around the country." Before long, he began to connect his work as a *minstrel* with the work of a *minister*. "Poets and pastors are people who help us see things more clearly," he said. "Slowly it dawned on me that what I was doing was ministry."[512] When he first sought recognition from the Ministerial Fellowship Committee in 1971, the committee was ambivalent. How could a folk singer and poet be a Unitarian Universalist minister? Masten told them, "I think I do ministry, an evangelical circuit-riding kind of ministry. [What I do] is the way circuit riders did it. I am doing the same thing for liberal religion."[513] The MFC's eventual decision to recognize Masten opened the door to his thirty-year ministry of performing songs and poems before over 500 Unitarian Univer-salist congregations and other groups across the country. Writer Frances Cerra Whittelsey heard his poetry at an event arranged by her congregation, the Unitarian Universalist Fellowship of Huntington, New York. "I was captivated immediately," she writes. "Sometimes his poems made me laugh out loud. At other times, I could feel tears welling in my eyes. He offered himself as proof that life was worth living despite periods of despair and suicidal impulses. He voiced thoughts about death that most of us are afraid to think, making them less fearful for the airing.... Somehow he managed to be so hopeful, so open, so tender, and so wise, that by the end of the evening I felt as if I had been to a remarkable worship service."[514]

In 1999, Masten was diagnosed with prostate cancer. He says he always liked the idea that death might take him by surprise, but now admits that his life "really began" when his oncologist promised him a "graceful end." It has added a new dimension to his ministry. Unable to travel while under treatment, he began producing a website where he could share his songs and writings. In particular, the site features his "Cancer Pages," which produce some 500 hits a week. "Every week people who have visited the website call from around the country wanting to talk," says Masten. When he has performed for cancer patients, his effect is like "a shaft of sunlight angling through the storm clouds." "Most patients are almost entirely focused on 'have you heard about this drug, or that drug?'" states Harry Pinchot, who runs a prostate cancer helpline. "It's very hard to bring up the psychological issues because no one wants to face their mortality. Ric is able to get them to face that."[515] In the end, they are singing Masten's signature hymn, "Let It Be a Dance," which says in part, "Morning star comes out at night, without the dark there is no light. If nothing's wrong, then nothing's right. Let it be a dance."[516]

In 2001, Masten published a book of poems and line drawings entitled *Let It Be a Dance: Words and One-Liners.* Masten's poems have not been esteemed for their literary merit. It is telling that most college and university invitations have come from departments of psychology and religious studies, not English. Called a people's poet, a priest, a preacher, and a philosopher, Masten writes poems that touch people in the heart and soul of their daily lives. It is in this sense that his poetry is community ministry. He states, "Everything I do has to do with wanting to find ways for me to have the feeling of being part of the larger self, and hopefully presenting something that you can come through to have that same feeling."[517]

The category of Specialized Minister made it possible for Howard Matson and Ric Masten to gain official UUA recognition for their community ministries. The Ministerial Fellowship Committee nonetheless struggled with the category of Specialized Minister, which lacked a template by which to gauge a ministerial path. As MFC members considered criteria for credentialing, a critical factor was whether they had prior familiarity with the nature of the work. This was somewhat counter-intuitive to the innovative nature of the category. Yet, as Dan Hotchkiss put it twenty years later, "If a committee is to certify competence at all, there needs to be a reasonable match between the skills assessed and those of the assessors."[518] As it turned out, most people who were identified as Specialized came into their work after having first been ordained as parish ministers. It seemed to the Ministerial Fellowship Committee (MFC) that the category of Specialized Minister was unworkable, and in 1974, it was ended.[519]

This decision posed a dilemma for people like Scotty (William L.) McLennan, who from 1970 to 1975 pursued both a divinity degree and a law degree. In 1971, his plan for training as a specialized minister was approved. "It was never my intention to be a parish minister," states McLennan.[520] By the time he completed his studies in 1975, however, the category of ministry for which he had been trained no longer existed. He received a letter from the MFC asking what he intended to do about becoming fellowshipped, since his work did not fall into the only category of fellowship available—parish ministry."[521] Fortunately, McLennan had gained some experience working at the First Parish of Framingham, Unitarian Universalist, and he had begun work as an associate minister-at-large for the Dorchester area of the Benevolent Fraternity of Unitarian Universalist Churches in Boston. On that basis, he was able to be fellowshipped, serving the fifty parishes of the Benevolent Fraternity.

In the early 1980s, McLennan played an influential role in urging the MFC to broaden the definition of parish ministry. He felt parish ministry should include work in interfaith ministries and in other UU institutions. This story began when he became co-chair of the Center Cities Advisory Committee, set up by the UUA to report on how churches in the cities were doing. From this advisory group emerged an advocacy group known as the Urban Church Coalition, which McLennan also co-chaired. More is said about the work of the Urban Church Coalition in the next chapter. Comprised of clergy and lay representatives from fifty churches nationwide, the Urban Church Coalition successfully lobbied the MFC to expand the definition of parish ministry. As a result, by 1982, MFC rules allowed that parish ministry included "pastoral counselors, chaplains, and community ministers" working in institutions such as "prisons, universities, and hospitals—as well as counseling clienteles, urban missions, and ecumenical centers."[522]

This broader definition of parish ministry followed McLennan as he moved in 1984 from urban ministry to university chaplaincy at Tufts. According to McLennan, the fact that Tufts was historically a Universalist institution facilitated MFC acceptance of this transition.[523] Both inner city and university communities have been "my parish," states McLennan. As a counselor and campus chaplain, the minister's role is "to aid others in understanding the nature of their own quests, to provide a constant reference in times of tribulation [and] to speak prophetically to issues of the day. . . . I have felt responsible to every person within those communities as pastor, prophet, priest, and preacher-teacher—whether or not they know it."[524]

The Civil Rights Movement woke up the country to a new awareness of it own social wounds. These times began to give ministers and leaders in the denomination a new way to think about ministry—what it might look like, where it might take place, and whom it might serve. Obviously there were new challenges in view. The changed MFC rules marked a significant breakthrough, from which there would be no turning back. Implicitly the new rules demonstrated recognition of the changed tenor of the times. These changes soon found application as increasing numbers of community ministers responded to the new duties of a new day.

CHAPTER EIGHTEEN

Engaging Social Change
in the 1980s

T he decade of the 1980s marks a period of significant growth in community ministry. Building on figures like Reeb, Shadle, and Matson, community ministers in the 1980s recognized the potential for liberal social action ministry to address the interpersonal and community crises brought forward from the previous generation. These ministers perceived a changed landscape where the social inequities, economic and racial disparities, war policies, and patriarchies of modern life had been thrust into the open, calling for a healing force. The following examples show that such community ministry often integrated professional expertise in counseling, psychology, music, sociology, and urban studies into spiritual witness. The emphasis, as Tom Chulak points out, was to deal "not just with issues, but with communities" and to utilize congregations as partners in the process.[525]

Orloff Miller is well known for being with James Reeb when he was attacked in Selma, and for his involvement in UU campus ministry in the 1960s. What is less known about Miller is the full scope of his community-based ministries, incarnations of what he called "religion with its sleeves rolled up." Appointed in 1967 as the first district executive for the UUA's Mountain Desert District, Miller concurrently served a parish in Colorado Springs. During these years, he publicly opposed U.S. involvement in Vietnam, refused to pay taxes in support of that war, aided and abetted candlelight marches to draft board offices, and assisted war resisters in protesting and/or moving to Canada. While in Colorado Springs, he founded the Pikes Peak Center for Human Ecology to deal with issues of problem pregnancy, abortion, and sex education, and convinced the Unitarian Universalist Church of Colorado Springs to provide office and meeting space for an early chapter of the National Organization for Women (NOW).[526]

In 1973, Miller moved to California to serve as half-time minister to the San Luis Obispo County Unitarian Universalist Fellowship. At the same time, he served as coordinator of the local Human Relations Commission and oversaw the city's first Human Needs Assessment. He was also active with Mothers for Peace in its fight against construction of the Diablo Canyon nuclear energy plant, which was to be situated over California's major earthquake fault. In all of these ministries, Miller's work was a response to the crises of the 1960s and 1970s. When a California taxpayers' revolt led to funding cuts for the SLO Human Relations Commission, Miller left San Luis Obispo to work toward a doctorate in human sexuality in San Francisco. In 1979 his focus shifted as he became deeply involved in the earliest stages of the AIDS crisis as a volunteer with Shanti and Hospice.[527]

Here he came face to face with the victims of a little-known but deadly virus. His ministry was to console the dying and their families as they worked through the sickness, grief, and shame of AIDS. There was no support for this work coming from anywhere, nor did it fit with any existing category of UU ministry. "In this period, 1983–1989, AIDS was still considered the 'gay disease,'" states Miller, "and many folks, including UUs, were wildly fearful of bodily fluids and physical contact with PWAs (persons with AIDS)."[528] With no official funding, Miller supported himself by driving a taxi and doing word processing. He traveled across the nation on behalf of the AIDS Interfaith Network, urging Unitarian

Universalists and all Americans to wake up to the threat of HIV and AIDS. He served on the AIDS Action Working Group of the UUA and on the AIDS Task Force of the National Council of Churches.[529] Ultimately a combination of burnout and the loss of many friends with AIDS took its toll on Miller. In the hope that the work he started would be carried on by others, he accepted an invitation to live in Western Europe, where he married a German Humanist leader and served as a volunteer minister-at-large to European Unitarian Universalists. In retirement, he has traveled in Russia and Poland on behalf of the International Council of Unitarians and Universalists (ICUU).

Jeremy Taylor's community ministry gained official recognition under the expanded MFC rules of the early 1980s. Taylor's ministry has been an exploration the world of dreams and how their meanings can lead to wholeness and peace. Taylor was raised in a politically radical family. Growing up on the perimeter of what was considered acceptable mainstream culture, Taylor found friendship among like-minded peers in Liberal Religious Youth. "The LRY saved my life," claims Taylor, adding, "I think it also paved the way for my life in ministry."[530] In 1969, Taylor was called upon by the UU Project East Bay[531] in Emeryville, California, to do some retraining exercises aimed at "overcoming racism." As participants in the exercise told their stories, it seemed they started to "feel better." Beyond the stories, Taylor recognized a deeper unspoken "meta-message" that lay within the (often unconscious) layers of self-deception—yet accessible through an awareness of one's dreams.

Taylor was intrigued by the discovery of the connections between rapid eye movement (REM) and dreaming. This work showed that all human beings dream and are able to recall their dreams with little effort, if they cultivate the habit of doing so. Taylor observed, "When we examine dreams with an eye to their deeper meanings, we find that all dreams come in the service of health and wholeness, and speak a universal language of metaphor and symbol."[532] Identifying these symbols can become the basis for conversations that explore the deeper meanings of dreams and reveal "the deep-shared common humanity out of which our dreams spontaneously spring." Starting in 1971, Taylor began to teach group and individual projective dream work at the Starr King School for Religious Leadership (now School for the Ministry). At the same time, he began practicing and training others to practice projective dream work as a community organizing and counseling ministry, all over the world. In 1982, the Berkeley Fellowship of Unitarian Universalists offered Taylor ordination as a community minister engaged in "performing and promoting 'group projective dream work' in the service of facilitating both personal growth and nonviolent social change."[533] At the same time, the Unitarian Universalist Ministers' Association (UUMA) accepted him into their ranks as a full member, conferring official recognition on his innovative ministry.

Taylor is the founder of the Association for the Study of Dreams, located in San Francisco. He has also published seven books integrating dream symbols, mythology, and archetypal imagery. His latest publication is *Living Labyrinth: Universal Themes in Myths, Dreams, and the Symbolism of Waking Life* (1998). He has a doctorate of ministry from the University of Creation Spirituality and an honorary doctorate of sacred theology from Starr King School for the Ministry. Currently he directs the Marin Institute for Projective Dream Work. He states, "Paying closer attention to the symbolic messages of our own and other people's dreams can release more conscious understanding of confusing emotions, suggest creative solutions to our most pressing problems, and bring us to deeper recognition and acceptance of one another."[534] His now internationally known dream ministry identifies him as a community minister to the world, yet his ministry remains deeply tied to his Unitarian Universalist roots. "Our genius as UUs," says Taylor, "lies in our vanguard status."[535] Recognizing the need for ministries of wholeness to the world at large is vital, in Taylor's mind, to living out the best of what it means to be a Unitarian Universalist.

The 1960s and 1970s witnessed the rise of counseling as community ministry. In Seattle, Washington, Jim Zacharias founded the first Unitarian Universalist counseling services program in 1969.

He made a proposal to the Puget Sound Council of Unitarian Universalist Churches to begin the counseling service. The Council came up with a small amount of financial backing, and he was able to set up counseling groups in church buildings. This was the first instance of this kind of ministry being done among Unitarian Universalists, and the way that Zacharias made himself and his work an integral part of the area Unitarian Universalist churches became a model. Having been fellowshipped in 1964 as a parish minister, he maintained close relationships with his supporting congregations and never lost his fellowship status. A key to his success as a Unitarian Universalist counselor, too, was the fact that he had attained professional credentials and licensing in the field of counseling.[536] This is the additional training qualification, beyond a ministerial credential, that community ministers in counseling, or other professional roles, must achieve. The same is true for David Arksey, who ran a counseling program at the First Unitarian Church of Chicago during most of the 1980s.

David Arksey's pastoral counseling ministry is located in Chicago, where his 1970s training for ministry emphasized what was then a new specialty: marriage and family therapy. Heeding an inner call, Arksey left a work-study program at the World Bank to volunteer for a few months in the UU House of Soul in Trenton, New Jersey. The House of Soul was a "store-front" after-school program funded by the New Jersey Unitarian Universalist Council. Arksey states, "Working in this program was my transition into ministry, a work for which I had no family models." Returning to school, he transferred into a religion and philosophy major at Kalamazoo College and then obtained a Master's Degree in Theological Studies from Meadville Lombard in 1974. Following this, he felt led to pursue a doctorate of ministry in Pastoral Care and Counseling, which he obtained in 1977 from the Chicago Theological Seminary. During these years of schooling, Arksey worked at the Depot, a community ministry program sponsored by the First Unitarian Church of Chicago. Begun in response to an epidemic of runaway children, the Depot was a family-counseling program that primarily served socioeconomically disadvantaged families. A crucial innovation adopted at the Depot involved active outreach to families by meeting with them in their own homes. Rather than requiring them to come to a public place for therapy, therapy was brought to them. Explained Arksey, "In this way, we affirmed the importance of the family's own space and community—and its own resources for healing."[537]

When Arksey completed his program at Chicago Theological Seminary, the First Unitarian Church agreed to ordain him. Much to his surprise, the church also called him to a ministry-at-large in which he would conduct a ministry of pastoral care and counseling to the larger Chicago community. This call was an affirmation of Arksey's work at the Depot—first as a student, then as an intern, and finally as its executive director from 1982 to 1989. In 1986, nine years after being ordained, Arksey was fellowshipped according to the MFC's newly expanded understanding of parish ministry. Arksey explains, "My congregation was always very supportive of me, and I have been very grateful for that. But the MFC was for a long time not sure what to do with me." His ministry came to include programs for emergency psychiatric care, child and family therapy, and homeless and runaway youth. Since 1992, Arksey has served on the staff of Counseling Ministries Incorporated, which continues his ministry-at-large, now in an affiliated status with the First Unitarian Church. It is important to see how Zacharias' and Arksey's pastoral counseling ministries developed in tandem with the rise in professional psychological counseling. Their work has been understood in this context as a compassionate liberal religious response to the individual and family stresses of the late twentieth century. Like the counseling ministries in Puget Sound, Arksey's ministry has also served as an important model to other community ministers and to the Unitarian Universalist movement of how a congregation-based community ministry can work.

The First Unitarian Church of Chicago is well recognized for its historic commitments to community ministry, begun with the Ministry-at-Large held by Robert Collyer in the mid-nineteenth century. More recently, in addition to running the Depot, the First Unitarian Society became the home of the famed Chicago

Children's Choir, organized in 1956 by Christopher Moore. Having grown up in Michigan, Moore did his undergraduate studies at Harvard, where he became entranced with G. Wallace Woodworth, director of the Harvard Glee Club. As a member of the Glee Club, Moore developed a "strong sense of music as a community-building, rebuilding, community-celebrating operation, not just great art to be placed on a pedestal."[538] After Harvard, Moore pursued theological studies at Meadville Lombard, and after a brief period as a parish minister in St. Louis, Missouri, he accepted an invitation from Chicago's First Unitarian Church to organize "a really good children's choir." This "delightful side-slipping into music" (his words) became his call to a full-time ministry of music as the choir he organized became a three-decade-long experiment, exploring what the Choir could become to a community as well as to individual children.

There were soon approximately 450 children involved in the Choir at any given time. They came from all religious, racial, and ethnic backgrounds, and were representative of all social and economic levels, including the ghettoes of Chicago. Moore emphasized the ability of all youngsters to perform "serious" music. Under his direction, they performed music that included sixteenth-century motets, Hebrew liturgical pieces, Mozart masses, Purcell anthems, Negro spirituals, and folksongs in a half dozen languages. In the beginning, funding was hard to come by, and at times, the Choir even drew on the church's endowment. But with faith and perseverance, the Choir soon gained financial backing from church members, choir parents, Urban Gateways, foundations, businesses, the Illinois Arts Council, the National Endowment for the Arts, the University of Chicago, and earnings from concerts and recordings. They performed concerts all over the country; they appeared with the Chicago Symphony Orchestra and the Joffrey Ballet in its Chicago performances. The Choir even toured Europe in 1970, with funding raised through an appeal made by the *Chicago Tribune*.

Moore was a leader in the First Unitarian Church in other ways, acting the part of an associate minister for three decades as senior ministers came and went. The Choir, however, was the jewel of Moore's ministry, described by a church historian as the "large nonsectarian community agency of our Society."[539] Moore's own words eloquently testify to the religious purposes behind his choir ministry: "I have been deeply concerned about this country and the world in which we live. My way of attempting to help change it has been working with children and youth in and through music to assist them to a deeper understanding of the whole process of building and maintaining a culture that nourishes and ministers to its people."[540]

The rise of community ministry in recent decades, claims Tom Chulak, cannot be separated from the social revolutions brought about by the anti-war, civil rights, and women's rights movements. Chulak spent time in the 1970s as a labor organizer in Flint, Michigan. Feeling called to ministry, he entered Chicago Theological Seminary and began ministry in 1979. He served a Universalist church in Yarmouth, Maine initially, and then took a position in the early 1980s as director of the New Congregations Program at the UUA. In 1988, he became the senior minister of the First Church of Chicago. Chulak believes that congregations need to be participants in community ministry. While serving at the First Church of Chicago, he made a conscious effort to build a positive relationship between the church and Meadville Lombard Theological School. This was facilitated in large part by his continuing friendship with Spencer Lavan, who was then president of the school. Chulak taught at Meadville Lombard; Lavan became a member of the First Church. This was a relational form of ministry, rather than programmatic; both institutions benefited in the form of greater connection and growth.

Chulak moved on from Chicago to serve the Unitarian Universalist Congregation at Shelter Rock; after four years he accepted the position of district executive for the St. Lawrence District. Today, Chulak works with congregations to assist them in responding to societal challenges around them. He believes recent history has presented our generation with "new duties." Moreover, he contends, recent community ministries have not only responded to the press of these needs, they have openly engaged them when the churches seemed paralyzed. The effect ultimately was that community ministries helped rejuvenate a denomination that by the 1970s was becoming moribund.[541]

One mark of the decline in congregations lay in the passions arising over the anti-war movement. Many congregations became divided over the question of whether to support the war in Vietnam and/or give sanctuary to draft resisters. U.S. involvement in Vietnam had begun in the 1950s with aid to the French and deepened after the French surrendered their Indochina claims. Increasingly Americans became alarmed over the neo-colonial nature of their government's intervention, and beginning in 1964, Unitarian Universalists at the annual General Assemblies (GAs) passed yearly resolutions to condemn this policy. With continued troop escalation and bombing after 1965, death tolls in Vietnam mounted among both U.S. and Southeast Asian people. The conviction that young men who resisted the draft were obeying a higher law put pressure on Unitarian Universalists and others to consider their just response. Should Unitarian Universalist congregations speak out against the war? Should UU churches give sanctuary to draft resisters? Serious debates over these questions led to acrimony and disillusionment, as ministers and congregations often found themselves at odds with each other over what to do.

The memory of this struggle was still fresh when the General Assembly went on record opposing the nuclear arms race and calling for a plan of disarmament. In 1984, the Rev. Eugene Pickett, president of the UUA, brought together a coalition of Unitarian Universalist organizations—the UUA, the Unitarian Universalist Service Committee, the IARF, the Women's Federation, the United Nations Office, and the Unitarian Universalist Peace Fellowship— to create the Unitarian Universalist Peace Network (UUPN). The UUPN became the national Unitarian Universalist voice for peace and nuclear disarmament.[542] In 1985, General Assembly delegates passed a resolution to protest U.S. military intervention in Central America, particularly in Nicaragua and El Salvador, to establish a clearing house for the dissemination of information regarding any such intervention, and to work toward joint cooperation with such peace groups as the Unitarian Universalist Service Committee, the

American Friends Service Committee, *Pax Christi*, and Mobilization for Survival.

Stephen Shick was involved in movements for peace in Philadelphia from the time he graduated in 1969 from Crozer Theological Seminary.[543] Crozer was important to Shick because of its emphasis on uniting social ethics and religion. "There was a School of Nonviolent Social Change that deeply influenced me," recalls Schick. He worked on organizing national and local peace demonstrations and appeared frequently on local radio and television. "I worked tirelessly in those years to end the Vietnam War and establish new national spending priorities." Linking up with Citizens for a Sane Nuclear Policy (SANE), an organization begun in 1954, Shick founded the SANE Education Fund of Pennsylvania in 1974 and served as its director. Through SANE, he began a radio program, "Consider the Alternatives," that focused on nuclear disarmament. It would in time achieve national syndication on over 400 commercial and non-commercial stations.[544] With generous support from the National Endowment for the Humanities, Shick's radio program produced in 1979 a special thirteen-part series, entitled "Shadows of the Nuclear Age: A Series on the Social, Religious, Cultural, and Artistic Impact of the Bomb."[545] Shick also aired a number of pre-recorded interviews with well-known peace advocates, including Sen. George McGovern and activist actress Jane Fonda.

In 1978, personal circumstances led Shick to attend the Unitarian Society of Germantown, Pennsylvania, where he experienced a profound sense of rebirth. There he met up with many of his radio supporters—and found the religious community he had been looking for. "I discovered a place where my Humanism was seen as religious and where I could publicly embrace my Christian heritage defined as I experienced it. Here I found prophetic practice, intellectual honesty, and exploration of the mystery of the spirit." This led to Shick's becoming a Unitarian Universalist and being ordained into UU ministry at the Germantown church in 1986. Here was another instance in which parish ministry achieved more fluid definition—in this case to accommodate Shick's radio peace ministry. He had anticipated that being a credentialed minister would give him greater access to pulpits and foundations. It also enabled him to bring his religious identity together with his peace work.[546] He was producing radio shows and working with SANE when UUA President Pickett and other UU ministers asked him to direct the new Unitarian Universalist Peace Network (UUPN). "They came to me because of my long record of peace activism," Shick states.[547]

Shick remained director of the UUPN until 1989. A look at what he did in that position is a window into the larger community ministry of the Peace Network. "One of the things we did," states Shick, "was the ad campaign, 'Say Your Peace.' We used radio, TV, and billboards to advertise this phrase, to raise consciousness against the policy of nuclear weapons build up. We also provided resources to congregations to declare their properties Nuclear Free Zones."[548] About 150 UU churches across the country participated in this campaign. As with "Say Your Peace," this was an instance of the UUPN providing resources on an issue of national importance to local congregations. Indeed, to promote the work of the UUPN, Shick preached, lectured, and conducted worship before hundreds of congregations, at summer camps and conferences, district meetings, and the UUA General Assembly. Finally, for an event called "Desert Witness," the UUPN got about 150 Unitarian Universalists to show up at the desert testing site in Nevada to protest the U.S. government's refusal to enter into a nuclear test ban treaty. Shick states, "This grew out of an interfaith effort, but we were the only denomination whose leadership got arrested."[549]

The UUPN was the principal organization through which Unitarian Universalists participated in the Great Peace March for Global Nuclear Disarmament in 1986. This march across the country had been the brainchild of David Mixner, who, though not a Unitarian Universalist himself, had come to the 1985 General Assembly in Atlanta to get affirmation for the Peace March. The GA delegates warmly endorsed Mixner's idea, and the UUA supported it with several resolutions. When the march was launched, UUs made up the largest contingent of the initial 1400 marchers. Though organizational problems played a role in leading 1100 marchers to turn back, a core group of 350 people carried on across

3700 miles for nine months, marching from the West Coast to Washington, D.C. "We were a traveling city, with food trucks and tents for sleeping," recalls David Pettee.[550] Pettee was one of four seminary students from the Starr King School for the Ministry who completed the march. He integrated the experience of the march into his degree program, preparing reflections of his experience to share with his academic mentor and earning credits toward his degree in the process. Along with Pettee were SKSM students Stephanie Nichols, Carol Powers, and Phil Schulman, all of whom went on to become community ministers. Shick hired Carol Powers to be the UUPN liaison with the march. Later she became a UUPN staff member. Stephanie Nichols later became the Director of UUPN. Sue Guist, a UU laywoman, also completed the march and wrote a book about her experience, *Peace Like a River: A Personal Journey across America*. She recalled tents blowing down and problems with bathing; she also described the support offered by UU congregations and families who opened their churches and homes to the traveling marchers.[551] The Great Peace March for Global Nuclear Disarmament was an event that spoke to the deepest concerns of Unitarian Universalists, and others, for the well-being of the planet and of all humankind.

Tom Chulak points out that a second source of division in the churches was the movement for black empowerment. Unitarian Universalists and community ministers in particular had supported civil rights for African Americans and believed in the "One World" goal of racial integration. When riots began erupting in northern cities after 1965, UUs were among the first to respond. In 1967 the UUA's Commission on Race and Religion convened a gathering in New York City: the Emergency Conference on Unitarian Universalist Response to the Black Rebellion. The conference did not go as planned.[552] Thirty-seven of the 140 attendees were African American. Once the conference began, thirty of the African American delegates removed themselves from the main body of the conference to hold their own meeting. Mark Morrison-Reed explains that his mother was present at that meeting: "This black caucus tapped into the raw emotion hidden behind middle class reasonableness. They were searching for an identity that was more authentic than the futile attempt to be 'carbon copies of white people.'" It could not be just about integration. "Civil rights had proved ineffectual at remedying black poverty, and liberal religion had failed to address the experience of blackness."[553]

By the time they emerged, these thirty delegates had formed the Black Unitarian Universalist Caucus (BUUC), which created the Black Affairs Council (BAC). From 1967 to 1970, the Black Affairs Council resisted collaboration with white UUs; moreover the BAC existed in conflict with Black and White Action (BAWA), a group coming out of the Community Church of New York, which had long been committed to integration and integrationist strategies. UUA intentions were good, and generous funding for the BAC was pledged. But the UU budgetary crisis of those years ultimately forced the UUA to reduce this support. In the end, the BAC disaffiliated itself from the UUA to do its own fundraising, and the UUA dropped the BAC from its budget.[554]

Leslie Westbrook remembers this time well. She had first been inspired to pursue ministry in the 1960s as a member of Liberal Religious Youth at All Souls Church in Washington, D.C. There she had felt affirmed by James Reeb's belief in the worth of all persons. When the Black Empowerment Movement "blew on the scene in the UUA," as she recalls, "I was the assistant minister at the Arlington Street Church in Boston. There was so much conflict between the church's senior minister, who was a member of BAC, some of the members of the church, and the UUA. There was a surprising amount of tension over issues of equal rights and human dignity."[555] This controversy divided the entire denomination for a number of years.

Morrison-Reed writes, "The black empowerment controversy was a denominational tragedy.... The pain was so great that we as a denomination recoiled from the 'Empowerment Controversy' and a legacy of distrust lingers still."[556] Betty Reid anticipated with sadness the strain that would come from these developments. While she welcomed the "new birth of blackness," she knew that whites who had helped it to occur in its "first stages" would not understand this new stage of "release."[557] The resulting disorientation among whites and alienation among blacks, together with the flight of many churches to the suburbs, led many African Americans, as well as whites, to leave their UU churches. The parishioners that remained, Chulak reflects, "turned inward," even as "the larger society was pressing on all these other issues."[558]

Chulak believes the Civil Rights and Black Empowerment struggles generated developments that helped inspire new interest in community ministry.[559] The first development was the founding in 1979 of the Urban Church Coalition, a grassroots advocacy group, co-chaired, as we have seen, by Scotty McLennan and evolving out of the Center Cities Advisory Committee to the UUA. What drew members of both urban and suburban congregations to the Urban Church Coalition was the recognition that everyone has a stake in what happens in the cities that form the core of their locale. Attendees to the 1982 pre-GA conference "The Urban Church— Growing Diversity" at Ferry Beach, a UU conference center in Saco, Maine, established the Whitney Young Fund for Urban Ministry. This fund was to be used to aid struggling UU urban congregations, train UU leaders for urban ministries, provide seed money for UU congregations of diverse racial and ethnic make-up, and create channels for urban-suburban connections.[560] In 1983, Ministerial Fellowship Committee rules were changed to allow for "inclusive" or dual fellowship, a move that was endorsed by the Urban Concerns and Ministry Committee, because of its potential impact on ministers of color and urban ministries.[561] The Urban Concerns people had been working to bring African American ministers of other denominations into dual UU fellowship.[562] In that same year, the Urban Church Coalition began an annual Jenkin Lloyd Jones Lecture at General Assembly to highlight urban concerns. Then in 1984, the Commission on Appraisal issued a report entitled *Empowerment: One Denomination's Quest for Racial Justice, 1967–1982*. This was an important effort to take stock of what had happened and why. Finally, a revised UUA Statement of Principles and Purposes was issued in 1985, which, to Mark Morrison-Reed, "reflected a new consciousness" that had developed out of the challenges of the 1960s and 1970s.[563] Mark Morrison-Reed believes the new Statement was

important in this time. The lack of a creed had made it more difficult to transcend the struggles of the 1970s. The new Principles were
"formative in providing grounding and a transcendent narrative"
that could help bridge differences in the future.[564]

Chulak recalls that the Urban Church Coalition and its supporters drew on two main models. The first was the ecumenical
Institute for the Church in Urban and Industrial Society, begun by
the Presbyterian Church (USA) in the 1930s and joined by the
UUA in 1985. The second was the Industrial Areas Foundation,
begun by Saul David Alinsky. Coming out of 1930s Depression-era
Chicago, Alinsky was known as a leading organizer of neighborhood citizen reform groups. His book *Reveille for Radicals* had
provided philosophical direction for organizing the poor, in the
belief that widespread poverty left America open to the influence
of demagogues. Alinsky had organized the black communities
in Chicago's South Side to challenge then-mayor Richard Daly's
political machine with a radical political registration project.[565]
"Everyone was reading about this kind of urban activism, and all
the justice-related ministers were working in this area," Chulak
states. "You cannot separate the growth of community ministry in
this period from the Urban Church Coalition."[566]

In this context, Steve Shick moved with his family to Boston
in 1989 to accept a senior position with the Unitarian Universalist
Service Committee, as founding director of a new Citizen Action
Department. Shick's prior connections and visibility in peace work
facilitated his putting in place a new U.S. Programs Department,
emphasizing opportunities to work for peace and justice in the
United States. He became widely known for his successful efforts in
the Promise the Children and Just Works programs. Promise the
Children was an idea initiated by the UUSC board and carried forward by many people, with Shick providing the leadership. Aimed
at addressing issues of child poverty in the United States, the program made educational materials available to UUs on a national
scale. In six state-wide networks, people decided at the local level
how they would focus their efforts. There were trainings in Boston
to work with 50 representative local activists on choosing issues

and using resources. When Shick left the UUSC in 1996, Marian Wright Edelman wrote to praise his work. "Under your leadership, the Promise the Children Campaign grew to become an effective network for service and advocacy on behalf of children." In Just Works, Shick initiated a program based on the work camp training strategy once employed by Universalists. Young people received training in work camps for leadership. "I felt this would help create the next generation of people to be involved in UUSC."[567] One of the efforts to come out of Just Works was the rebuilding of burned-out churches in the South.

Steve Shick left the UUSC in late 1996, having "discovered a deep longing to work locally" in parish ministry. As minister to the Unitarian Universalist Church of Haverhill, he involved the congregation in providing bi-monthly meals to homeless people served out of a section of the church building specifically renovated for that purpose prior to his arrival. The church also established the Cornucopia Project, which grows an acre of sweet corn for area pantries each summer. As a result of his work at Haverhill, Steve Shick was named an Urban Fellow by Harvard Divinity School for 2000–2003.

Beyond urban concerns, community ministry was sensitive to the gender revolutions of the last thirty years—putting women in leadership roles, and supporting the rights of gay, lesbian, bisexual, and transgender people. "UU support on these issues has flourished in the context of UU community ministries, and has benefited our movement as a whole."[568] In 1977, General Assembly delegates passed the Women and Religion Resolution, encouraging all Unitarian Universalists to examine the religious roots of sexism in the denomination. A UU laywoman, Lucille Shuck Longview, spearheaded movement toward this resolution. There had been previous resolutions on issues of importance to women, but Longview believed that sexism within the denomination was itself "the great untouched area" needing action.[569]

About 100 people attended meetings on the resolution during GA week. When the Women and Religion Resolution passed unanimously, its proponents wondered if the delegates really understood the implications of what they had agreed to.[570] UUA President

Paul Carnes created a new staff position for Leslie Westbrook as UUA Minister for Women and Religion and appointed a Women and Religion Committee to work with her on implementing the resolution. Westbrook had accepted a position with the UUA the previous year as director of the Social Action Clearing House. Prior to that, she had served the Arlington Street Church, which had been in the forefront of peace and justice activity.

The newly appointed Women and Religion Committee recognized the need to gather together representatives from the various districts of the UUA to determine how to move forward on the resolution. Meeting at Grailville Conference Center in Loveland, Ohio, in May 1979, they named the conference "Beyond this Time: A Continental Conference on Women and Religion." First the conference addressed the problem of sexist language in hymns and in the UUA Principles and Purposes. A list of hymns was drawn up for rewriting, and the long process was begun that would eventually lead to the new set of Principles and Purposes adopted in 1985.[571] Then, following a model often used in denominational programming, conference participants were to return to their districts to organize similar district-based conferences.

To further implement the Women and Religion Resolution, UUA President Carnes appointed a second committee: the Affirmative Action for Women Ministers Committee. This committee followed a model in use among women in the Presbyterian Church, training consultants from the districts to go upon invitation to the churches to talk with church search committees about women in ministerial and professional leadership roles. Westbrook reflects that these initiatives had a consciousness-raising effect that was both internal and external. "When I was ordained in 1973, there were only about thirty women ministers in the denomination. Within ten years, that changed dramatically and today we are about half of all UU ministers."[572]

Soon the UUA Women and Religion Committee planned a Women and Religion Convocation on Feminist Theology, which was held in November 1980 in East Lansing, Michigan. From this convocation "grew the urgency for a UU curriculum that would explore approaches to feminist theology."[573] As Minister for Women and Religion and also the Adult Programs Curriculum Editor, Westbrook approached Shirley Ranck to write such a curriculum. What Ranck produced was the popular *Cakes for the Queen of Heaven*. The title was taken from the biblical story in which Jeremiah warned the Hebrew people of the Lord's wrath over the "women who knead dough to make cakes for the Queen of Heaven."[574] Rejecting this warning, the people reasoned, "Since we ceased burning incense to the Queen of Heaven, we have wanted everything and have been consumed by sword and famine."[575] The curriculum was not released for five years, in part because of the need to obtain permissions for the many art images it contained. These images depicted women in roles of power and influence in goddess mythology and were regarded as vital to the purposes of the curriculum.[576] After it came out, however, it became the most widely used adult curriculum the UUA has ever published. It was followed in 1994 by Liz Fisher's multicultural *Rise Up and Call Her Name*.[577]

Deborah Pope-Lance recognized these trends. Ordained into parish ministry in 1978, Pope-Lance was the only UU woman parish minister in the UUA's Metropolitan New York District at that time. She was also one of the first consultants trained by the UUA Affirmative Action for Women Ministers Committee and was frequently called upon to lecture or teach on the role of women in religion. Pope-Lance served two parishes, the Unitarian Universalist Church of Washington Crossing in Titusville, New Jersey from 1978 to 1983, and the First Parish of Sudbury, Massachusetts from 1986 to 1996. In between, from 1983 to 1987, she did community ministry as a therapist to battered women with the Unitarian Universalist Counseling and Education Service in Belle Meade, New Jersey.[578] "This was community ministry before there was language to name it as such," she states.[579] For Deborah Pope-Lance, the rise of community ministry and the use of community ministry language cannot be separated from the flood of women into the ministry in the 1980s. "Women had a broader view of ministry," reflects Pope-Lance, "and could not always see themselves as pulpit ministers." Westbrook agrees. In her mind, "Women understood ministry differently. They seemed to see it more as walking with you."[580] Pope-Lance suggests that some in the denomination perceived that there would "not be enough pulpit jobs available" to place all those coming out of the theological schools and, regrettably, may have discouraged women from looking at parish positions. It was in fact true that "many women ministers were unable to get settled in a congregation after completing their internships."[581] These practical realities, in combination with the societal urgencies they witnessed, led women ministers in greater numbers to embrace community ministry.

In her ministry to battered women, Pope-Lance believed that the church needed to be supportive, compassionate, and justice-seeking toward victims of domestic violence. However, she found that religious institutions seemed generally ill equipped to address victims in those terms. Making harmful use of patriarchal scripture, their framing of domestic abuse tended to find fault with the woman. In response, Pope-Lance wrote a training manual for clergy and conducted a related training program in pastoral counseling. From this evolved a long-term community ministry in which she has served as a consultant on sexual ethics, counseling religious leaders in parish or extra-parish settings on the ethics of ministerial practice and advocating for clearer standards for ministers on this issue. Her ministry has addressed an issue made more visible—and more approachable—because of women's increased presence and consciousness in ministry.

For Pope-Lance, an imperative of her ministry has been to recognize a theological grounding for her social, practical, and clinical work. "My work, as well as the innovative ministries being done by others, is challenging traditional expectations for ministry. It is ministry as activity and witness, where word becomes action and action becomes word." Reflecting aloud, she adds, "Community ministry may well be 'a thorn in the side of our imagination,' compelling us to think more broadly. You know, this was how Margaret Fuller was described in her day."[582] The thorn would not go away. This was the context, in her mind, for the formation in 1987 of the Society for the Larger Ministry.

PART V

Community Ministry
Gains Formal Standing

These chapters show the innovative spirit that continued to enliven community ministry in all its forms.
They also provide an inside look at how those ministries led to institutional change, beginning with the formation
of the Society for the Larger Ministry and the formal recognition
of community ministry in 1991. Meanwhile campus ministries
were founded, as congregation-based community ministries sought
to "mind the gap" with college-age and young adult UUs. The
Community Ministry Summit in 2003 established a framework
for organizational leadership with which community ministry
could move forward into the future.[583]

CHAPTER NINETEEN

Founding the Society for the Larger Ministry

Among community ministers there was a sense of needing to find a place of shared experience and affirmation. They felt isolated and unrecognized in a religious institution historically structured to recognize primarily parish-based ministers. As their numbers grew, they looked for ways to connect with each other and assess the meaning of what they were doing. With their locations so widely dispersed, two organizations formed independently of each other. Each group sought its own goals, which were not dissimilar, though initial memberships and strategies bore a slightly different look.

In June 1981, thirty chaplains, pastoral counselors, and other ministers who worked outside of congregations came together while attending General Assembly in Philadelphia. They were responding to an informal invitation posted by Robert Rafford. Rafford's past experiences told him that such a meeting might be welcome. He had been ordained in 1971 as a pastoral counselor in the United Church of Christ (UCC) and was fellowshipped in 1979 as a UU minister. In 1980, Rafford started his own UU congregation in Woodbury, Connecticut, which was very successful. Meanwhile he continued his full-time chaplaincy in Waterbury. What troubled Rafford was that he and others like him were not being recognized for their ministries outside the parish setting. Compared to the more fluid UCC definition of ministry, the single category of parish ministry in the UUA seemed to him closed and archaic, out of sync with the liberal UU theology he had come to embrace. Even at the 1979 GA, he was disappointed when the first vote to establish a second track of ministry for religious education did not receive a stronger show of support.[584]

The ministers who met with Rafford in 1981 were mostly chaplains and counselors, along with a few college professors. They continued to meet yearly at subsequent General Assemblies. As Rafford expected, they found a kind of support in this group that they were not getting from their parish-based colleagues or from the UUA. At the Columbus, Ohio meeting in 1984, they made a decision to identify themselves officially as the Extra-Parochial Clergy (EPC). By now, they comprised about 40–50 members. In the fall of 1986, they secured a grant to hold a pre-GA conference at Little Rock, Arkansas in 1987. This conference would have important implications for the future of community ministry. To plan for this conference, they met in January in Boston.

In Berkeley, California, another group of ministers, seminary students, and lay ministers—all active in a wide variety of ministries—became conscious of themselves and each other as community ministers. They worked in community service, peace groups, shelters for battered women or homeless persons, and a variety of social advocacy organizations. They found a mentor in Jody Shipley, who had been drawn to community ministry when she took an administrative position with the Pacific Central District office housed at the Starr King School for the Ministry. Here Shipley met students with dreams of creating new ministries, like "retreat places or women's monasteries, or centers that would merge religion with social service."[585] Shipley decided to enter seminary herself; upon completing her studies and becoming ordained in 1979, she began a decade-long career of parish ministries combined with various community ministries. She attended the 1986 meeting of the Extra-Parochial Clergy in Rochester as an interested observer. That same week, she also attended the meeting of the Commission on Appraisal, where she suggested that the Commission should be looking at community ministry. The Commission invited her to submit her concerns in writing, which she did the following August.[586] At the conclusion of this meeting, Jane Boyajian, a member of the Commission and a community minister in Seattle, invited Shipley to attend a Convocation on Community Focused Ministries to be held the following November in Boston.[587]

Organized by the Benevolent Fraternity and the UUA Department of Extension, and funded by a UUA grant, the November 1986 Convocation on Community Focused Ministries aimed to begin the process of networking among those who were ministering in non-church settings.[588] Thirty justice-oriented ministers met for four days and engaged in a visioning process to determine a course of action to promote community ministry. The Convocation offered a welcome tone of affirmation. David Pohl, then Director of Ministry at the UUA, assured them that the Department of Ministry was "supportive of efforts to broaden our understanding of what constitutes ministry."[589] Ministerial Fellowship Committee rules had expanded the definition of parish ministry in the early 1980s, due in large part to the persuasive urging of Scotty McLennan and the Urban Church Coalition. "These changes have broadened our definition of 'parish'" said Pohl, "rather than establishing and validating 'specialized' ministries as such."[590] Here Pohl intimated that the expanded 1980s definition of "parish" established firmer institutional grounding for community ministry than did the short-lived 1970s experiment with the category of "specialized minister."

Pohl's address to the Convocation provided a context for the rising number of community ministers. Out of a total of 1150 UU ministers, 640 were settled in parish ministries and 100 were serving in ministries outside of congregations. (The others were retired or inactive.) He spoke warmly of the theological and ethical imperative "that calls us together in our search for a better world," and concluded by lifting up a shared vision of mission and direction. "Together we need to explore and support ways to reach beyond the local congregation, particularly to minister to the alone, the disinherited, the powerless, the battered, the shunned, the disillusioned, the overwhelmed, the alienated, the homeless, and the dying. We commend what you are doing, and what you hope to do, and what you would like the Association to do, to shape what James Luther Adams called 'the community of justice and love.'"[591] Those who were there agree that feelings of high energy and expectation prevailed at the meeting. Stephen Shick remembers how good it felt to be among so many like-minded peers. "It was exhilarating," he said, "to connect with so many who were living out their call to community ministry.[592]

The community ministers at the Convocation established a new group, the Community Focused Ministers (CFM), which formed a steering committee and initiated a newsletter. In the newsletter's first issue, editor Jody Shipley announced the group's birth: "Just as the religious knows no boundaries or limitations, so the expressions of ministry in our liberal religious movement are not limited."[593] The newsletter featured Thom Payne's description of the gathering at Boston, noting how it brought together for the first time "fellowshipped, ordained and lay ministers actively engaged in community ministry."[594] The inclusion of lay ministers was one of the characteristics that made the Community Focused Ministers distinct from the Extra-Parochial Clergy and would be a point of tension when the proposal was raised to merge the two groups into one.

The Steering Committee of the Community Focused Ministers held its first meeting in January 1987 in Boston.[595] Chaired by David Cole, then interim director of the Benevolent Fraternity, the Steering Committee pursued steps to institutionalize CFM by applying for affiliate status with the UUA. These justice-oriented ministers, often working in tandem with outside institutions in their work, understood the need for this kind of institutional connection.[596] Coincidentally, it seems, the steering committee of the Extra-Parochial Clergy was meeting at this same place and time, which led to conversations between their members about whether the two groups should join forces. In the following months, Rafford's inquiries among EPC members revealed that many were ambivalent about such a move. The tension they felt rested on the CFM acceptance of lay ministers. "We were trying to get a conservative institution to recognize our status outside the parish," states Rafford. "The idea that we would include lay ministers seemed too radical and might jeopardize our standing in the UUA even more."[597] In retrospect, Rafford praised Shipley for "casting the net a little wider."[598] As for the Community Focused Ministers, they worried that the EPC was too conservative and lacking in innovative spirit. The Rev. Roberta King Mitchell, a member of both groups, properly characterized their differences in a letter to the grants panel, describing the EPC as "client-centered" and the CFM as "socio-political."[599]

From January until June 1987, these discussions among the Extra-Parochial Clergy and Community Focused Ministers evolved toward a shared sense of alignment. In spite of their differences, there were already instances of overlapping membership. Moreover, they had a mutual purpose in their "concern for the further involvement of community ministry in the life of our UU movement."[600] When they came together at GA in Little Rock, Arkansas in 1987, leaders from both groups worked into the wee hours of the morning to draft by-laws for a combined group. They agreed to a name, the Society for the Larger Ministry (SLM), which would neither exclude nor privilege either constituent group or any potential members, whether they were ordained or lay ministers. When the proposed merger was subsequently brought before the CFM Board, it was approved. The formation of SLM marked a significant moment of shared vision and common ministry, from which further planning and organizing would take place.

Indeed, a conference was already being planned by community ministers at Berkeley for November 1987.[601] This conference became the first official meeting of the Society for the Larger Ministry. Because conference planners hoped to increase the visibility of community ministers in the district where they were meeting, they invited other area UUs to attend a dinner during the conference. Thirty-five UU leaders joined the fifty-four conference participants on Friday evening. In her conference report Shipley stated: "The most moving moment for me . . . occurred [when] the community ministers stood and introduced themselves and received a warm welcome and recognition. For the many UUs who envision a wider ministry in our movement, it was a very special moment."[602] At the next General Assembly, in June 1988, the UUA's Department of Social Justice presented the Holmes-Weatherly Award to the Society for the Larger Ministry. This is the most important social justice award given out at GA. Shipley took it as an opportunity to remind SLM members that this remarkable show of support recognized the value of their individual ministries.[603] Many community ministers appreciated this type of mentoring from Jody Shipley. She was vital to their sense of empowerment in ministry; her community ministry was centered in nurturing their ministries.

Neil Shadle was asked if he would make arrangements to hold the next SLM conference at Meadville Lombard Theological School, where he was on the faculty. This conference met in November 1988 and took as its theme "Continue the Conversation." It was an appropriate title because everyone felt, with much optimism, that they were picking up the conversation where they had left off the year before. Spencer Lavan, president of Meadville Lombard Theological School from 1988 to 1996, recalls that there was a lot of questioning going on as people earnestly sought to assess the importance and relevance of their work in the context of their UU faith and its institutions.[604]

One of the key issues to be decided was the nature of membership in SLM. In the past, ministers' groups had been open only to ordained clergy and students preparing for ordained ministry. The early members of SLM, however, felt that membership should also be open to lay ministers, who were among the most active in their work in the wider community. Among them, for instance, was Carolyn McDade, a laywoman from Massachusetts, whose years of work with women in Central America motivated her to speak about their poverty before groups all over the United States. Carol Graywing described her as an extraordinarily inspiring person: "Carolyn articulates the depth of prophecy wrapped in spirit."[605] McDade believed that community ministry was happening at the boundaries of Unitarian Universalism as an institution. "Boundaries are where one finds vitality," she stated. "What concerns me is what happens to that vitality when it flows from the boundary into the institution."[606] After significant debate, carried over from the Berkeley meeting in 1987, the decision within SLM overwhelmingly came down on the side of inclusiveness. The Society for the Larger Ministry would be open to laypersons as well as clergy "who are in harmony with the purposes of the Society."[607] As Jody Shipley wrote, "The simple measure of good practice is in the question, 'Is what I do empowering to those I serve?' It is a question that tests all action . . . that separates out ministry that is self-serving from real ministry."[608]

Attendees at the Chicago conference worked with a consultant and met in ministry working groups focused on pastoral counseling, chaplaincy, peace and justice ministries, community/ urban ministries, academic ministries, and healing ministries. Each of these groups formulated a theological position paper, which was then carried to a central working group huddled together in Neil Shadle's office. There the language in the position papers was carefully integrated into what became known as the Society for the Larger Ministry Proclamation. The importance of the Proclamation was that it united the widely varying community ministers behind a common identity and mission, defined in broadly inclusive terms. The Rev. Neil Gerdes, librarian at Meadville Lombard, became involved in the organizational aspects of community ministry at this meeting. The meeting "evoked one of the better group processes," according to Gerdes, in that "the synthesis it produced resulted from ideas collected over the previous year. People were elated when it was over," he recalls. "There was a great feeling of euphoria and solidarity."[609]

That evening, SLM members came forward one by one, as they were inwardly moved, to sign the Proclamation. Judy Morris remembers, "We signed that statement finally in candle light, and I sang harmony with Carolyn McDade on 'Spirit of Life,' the hymn Carolyn had written.[610] She was standing next to me, and Doug Morgan Strong stood across from her, and he signed it for her [in American Sign Language]. I was in tears because I was singing with Carolyn McDade, and Carolyn was in tears because Doug was signing her song." McDade reported later how much this moment affected her because she had never before seen anyone sign her song.[611] The Proclamation described SLM as "a Unitarian Universalist movement of lay ministers and ordained clergy committed to promoting a broad spectrum of healing and social justice ministries." It declared, "We believe that only through many diverse forms of ministry can we heal the broken, create justice, and live in harmony with the spirit of life. We hold a vision of a larger ministry that sees the world as its parish."[612]

The next morning, November 13, 1988, SLM conference participants held a worship service across the street at the First Unitarian Church of Chicago, where senior minister Tom Chulak issued the welcome. David Arksey, Jody Shipley, and Carolyn McDade jointly delivered the sermon, "Community Ministry in Our Midst: A Voice for Justice." Arksey, the minister-at-large at the First Church, spoke of the numerous community ministries historically supported by the Chicago church. These ministries, he stated, "have continued to actively make manifest this church's belief in a ministry of justice and hope for those who are most in need."[613] Shipley's message added further urgency to the meaning of the weekend's events. "During this weekend we talked about ministry. We shared visions of ministry that reach with our imaginations into the world we are all called to serve. There is a spirit moving through us. By 'us' I mean Unitarian Universalists. It is deep and it is hungry. [The spirit] is calling us to declare our mission ... and without reservation to carry that mission out."[614]

Shipley believed that part of SLM's mission was to call upon the UUA to incorporate the vision of community ministry into its institutional structure. In preparation for the 1989 SLM conference at Brookline, Massachusetts, she stated, "The ... identification of the work of community ministry . . . is changing our denomination's view of the breadth and possibilities of our mission. . . . Because community ministry reaches deep into the meaning of our work as a movement, it calls us to examine . . . the nature of ministry today."[615] In this same year, SLM formed a Task Force on Ministerial Fellowship, chaired by Steve Shick, to promote a positive relationship between SLM and the Unitarian Universalist Ministers' Association, and to begin a dialogue with the Ministerial Fellowship Committee and the UUA Department of Ministry. As representatives of SLM, Jody Shipley and Steve Shick were invited to attend the UUA-sponsored Convocation on the Future of UU Ministry. Roberta King Mitchell made a presentation about community ministry at the UUA Convocation. Neil Shadle remembers: "Our effort was to show that ministry was a broader category than was acceptable for fellowship at the time."[616]

There is little question that consciousness of community ministry increased in this period and assumed greater priority within the denomination. In 1989, the Commission on Appraisal began a study of ministry. Flo Gelo, who was present at the signing of the Proclamation, was a new member of the Commission. Gelo urged the COA to seriously address the concerns of community ministers. Moreover, as a representative of the COA, Charles Howe attended the UUA Board Meeting in October 1990 and urged the Board to pay more attention to community ministry. "There is a tidal wave fast approaching, made up of many people eager to do community ministry," he warned, "and the UUA needs to get ready for it before it hits."[617] The Commission on Appraisal released its report in 1992. Titled "Our Professional Ministry," it gave significant attention to community ministry.

After many months of dialogue and careful consideration, the Ministerial Fellowship Committee recommended adding community ministry as a recognized option for UU ministry.[618] In 1990 the General Assembly held the first of two annual votes required to make the change, proposing to reword the bylaws to add "community ministry" as one of three tracks of ministry that already included tracks for parish and religious education ministries. The final vote for a third track of ministry was planned for GA in 1991. SLM made considerable preparations to assure its passage, as cluster groups met in New England and in the San Francisco Bay Area.[619] The SLM steering committee wrote a position paper on the third ministerial track, emphasizing their interest in pursuing professional development with the Department of Ministry.

The UUA's Committee on Committees appointed John Weston and Neil Shadle to represent SLM's position on the UUA's Task Force on Community Ministry. As the vote neared, SLM turned its attention to what would come next. In particular, they wanted to see an article in *UU World* illuminating the work of community ministers.[620] In May, one month before the 1991 vote at GA, the UUA's Task Force on Community Ministry was quoted as saying, "we urge settled Parish Ministers and Ministers of Religious Education to make themselves aware of community ministries in their areas and to encourage them and to embrace them to the fullest extent possible."[621]

The much-anticipated vote took place at the 1991 General Assembly in Hollywood, Florida. Prior to the vote, David Pohl, Director of the Department of Ministry, spoke directly about the proposed by-law amendment: "An affirmative vote ... will enable us to formally validate this ministry, adopt appropriate academic and professional requirements for its various forms, and broaden our understanding of how and where we may place our particular gifts at the service of our free faith." The bylaw change establishing community ministry as a third track of UU ministry was passed unanimously by the General Assembly with no delegates speaking against it.[622] SLM members were elated. Pohl articulated warm support for the change, eloquently capturing the co-equal status all shared in regard to ministerial work. "Your choice [of community ministry] makes you neither nobler nor less than your colleagues in the parish. To paraphrase Paul: 'There are varieties of gifts, but the same ministry. There are varieties of service, but the same ministry.'"[623] Here was expressed the hoped-for spirit of acceptance and collaboration. Implementation faced further hurdles, however, and the road ahead was anything but smooth.

CHAPTER TWENTY

Community Ministry
Since 1991

In the years following the 1991 vote, numerous questions surfaced as to how community ministries might be carried out. How would innovative and untried community ministries be identified as worthy professional representatives of Unitarian Universalism in the world? Would ministers who were already engaged in community work but fellowshipped as parish ministers need to go through the accreditation process again? How would community ministers be connected to the congregational life that was historically central to the movement? How would community ministers be sustained spiritually? How would they be held accountable? How might relationships between congregations and community ministers be developed? One of the central issues was funding, critical both for community ministers and for congregations if they chose to engage a community minister to work with them. Although some community ministers worked for outside agencies that provided their compensation, many times such agencies did not exist, and community ministers needed to develop resources on their own.

To settle some of these questions, Steve Shick and Cheng Imm Tan were appointed by the Society for the Larger Ministry to the Liaison Committee working with the UUA and the Ministerial Fellowship Committee. At the November 1991 SLM conference, Shick reported that a subcommittee of the MFC had been formed to work on appropriate academic requirements for community ministry candidates, internship sites, and renewal terms for community ministers in preliminary fellowship.[624] Carl Seaburg spoke at this same conference on "Ministries Beyond the Local Parish: An Historical Overview," a speech recognized for years to come as a community ministry landmark. In January 1992, Cheng Imm Tan and Steve Shick reported on their monthly meetings with David Pohl at the Department of Ministry. The SLM Steering Committee drafted a proposal to the MFC for the "grandparenting" in of existing community ministers: those who were currently in final fellowship as parish ministers and seeking re-classification, those who had been ministering for years but had never approached the MFC to be fellowshipped, and those who had achieved preliminary fellowship long before but had not sought final fellowship. Plans were also drawn up to confer with established community ministers and identify possible mentors for new community ministers in preliminary fellowship. Lastly, SLM felt the need for a community minister on the Ministerial Fellowship Committee. This was made possible with an amendment to the UUA bylaws in 1993, and Ralph Mero became the first community minister on the MFC.[625]

Many became fellowshipped for community ministry they were already doing. Neil Gerdes had previously been fellowshipped as a parish minister because of his position as director of the library and professor on a joint appointment at Meadville Lombard Theological School and the Chicago Theological Seminary. After the 1991 bylaw change, Gerdes applied for community ministry credentials as minister librarian and educator. "I saw this as an important designation for myself; I also wanted to give it more credence, some legitimacy."[626] He had been a member of the First Unitarian Church of Chicago since 1973; after the bylaw change he acquired affiliate status there. David Arksey, who had been fellowshipped in parish ministry as a minister-at-large with the First Unitarian Church of Chicago, was also grandparented in as a community minister. Now he was fellowshipped as both a parish minister and a community minister. Steve Shick, who had held credentials as a parish minister since 1986, was grandparented into community ministry. Later, in 1997, Shick left full-time community ministry to become a parish minister to a church from which he engaged in community ministry. Ralph Mero saw the third track of ministry as an opportunity to restore the official ministerial status he had lost when he left parish ministry. He sent a letter to the Department of Ministry detailing his work as Director of Planned Parenthood of Seattle and was soon grandparented in as a community minister.

Mero had served as parish minister for a UU congregation in Kirkland, Washington, after graduating from Meadville Lombard in 1965. Then, in 1971, after an economic reversal at Boeing brought financial hard times to the Kirkland church and others in the Pacific Northwest, Mero accepted a position as Director of Planned Parenthood in Seattle. Mero's intended three-year leave of absence, granted him by the Department of Ministry, turned into a twenty-year leave, and he lost his fellowship status.[627] Now he was able to be fellowshipped as a community minister, recognized for his work with Planned Parenthood and with Compassion in Dying, which he had founded as one of the nation's first "right-to-die" organizations. Mero's ministry to these external communities gained sanction because of his affiliation with the University Unitarian Church of Seattle, where he had for many years performed ministerial services on a voluntary basis. In addition, Compassion in Dying operated out of the church. When Mero left Seattle in August 1996 to become Director of Church Staff Finance with the UUA, he was the first fellowshipped community minister to serve on the staff of the Department of Ministry.

Scott Giles was ordained to ministry in 1978 and served as a parish minister from 1978 to 1991. In those years, he also became a Board Certified Chaplain specializing in hypnosis for patients dealing with pain control, appetite issues, mood maintenance, and other problems related to physical and mental health. Giles joined a counseling practice in 1990, and when the UU community ministry track was added, he was grandparented in without having to go through preliminary fellowship. "The community ministry designation was liberating for me," he states. It secured continued ministerial recognition for "the area [of work] where I would achieve my greatest success—I found the call that God set for me."[628] In his counseling ministry, Giles operates four Chicago-area free clinics run on the philosophy that physical healing is not the only goal in treatment. Patients are encouraged to use treatment to heal their spirit, their relationships, and their heart.[629] Giles left full-time parish ministry in 1992 and, like Gerdes, maintains an affiliate status with his congregation, the Countryside Church of Palatine, Illinois.

Michelle Bentley was grandparented into fellowship as a community minister in 1996. As an African American woman, she had been involved in community work long before being ordained into parish ministry in 1986. Bentley experienced a call to ministry in the late 1970s, while serving as the principal of a special school in downtown Chicago for serious male juvenile offenders. In a painful case involving the arrest of a sixteen-year-old male student, she realized that many boys turned to criminal activity for reasons that needed to be addressed on a religious level.[630]

Through a series of connections and decisions, she found that her broad theology, her social activism, her womanism,[631] and her African American cultural heritage would be at home in the liberal religious atmosphere of Meadville Lombard Theological School. She worked under the mentorship of Gene Reeves and Neil Shadle; Shadle's work in urban ministry fit with her own commitment to inner city needs. She wrote a proposal to La Rabida, a hospital for chronically and terminally ill children where her daughter was being treated, to be a chaplain to the children, their families, and the staff. The hospital loved the idea, and Bentley served in this chaplaincy for ten years. Having also started two churches, she became involved in an organization known as BRASS, Inc., an acronym for Behavior Research and Action in the Social Sciences Foundation. She wrote a proposal to BRASS that they add a spiritual therapeutic component to their substance abuse treatment and prevention program, which they accepted. She served in this capacity from 1990 to 1991. This was the beginning of what would be a dual path of ministry for Bentley—serving, alternately and together, ministries in both parish and community settings.

From 1991 to 1992, Bentley served as a half-time associate minister with the First Unitarian Church in Chicago, the first woman of African descent to be called as an associate UU minister. From this parish position, she initiated a variety of community ministries: organizing marches to protest U.S. military action in Kuwait, heading up an anti-racism committee, and arranging meetings of interfaith clergy in Chicago. When the senior minister, Tom Chulak, left in 1992, Bentley became the full-time interim senior minister for the church, a position she held for a year and a half. After this, she accepted a faculty appointment at Meadville Lombard, serving as lecturer and Dean of Students for most of the next five years. This is when she became fellowshipped as a community minister. As a lecturer, she focused on cultural diversity, contextual learning, and social analysis; as dean, she called together the African American seminary professors in the Chicago area. "This was good for us and good for our students of color."[632] Then, under a three-year grant, she brought in African American speakers and sponsored special cultural dinners for the faculty, the students, and their families.

In 1998, Bentley became the first African American woman called as senior minister to a historic UU church, the Third Unitarian Church of Chicago. Along with congregants and neighborhood residential and business leaders, she organized and coordinated the 3-M Community Organization. With some support from the church's endowment funds, they undertook to shut down neighborhood drug houses and restore the Harriet Tubman Center, a residential alcohol rehabilitation facility for women and children. With additional grant money, church members and neighbors organized CAPS (Community Alternative Policing Strategy) meetings, established a Gardening Project for community children to grow their own produce in a community garden, and created the not-for-profit Rosa Parks Center to run programs for children.

"I feel I have to work inside and outside the church. How can I come into the church and forget that there are people hungry outside?"[633]

Bentley left parish ministry in 2002 to work with the UUA as the Chicago-based Director of Professional Development in the Department of Ministry and Professional Leadership. She has at the same time maintained her ministries in the community. As an Expert Pastoral Consultant for the law offices of the Cook County Public Defender's Office of Alternative Sentencing Program for Capital Criminal Cases, she has "anytime access" to men and women charged with murder. She finds this work worthwhile, but bemoans the size and workings of the prison-industrial complex. Finally, she also works with the Society of Sankofa, so named for the West African Ashanti word that means "looking back in order to go forward." The African American Unitarian Universalist women of Sankofa use their varieties of expertise to work with and mentor women and young girls in crisis. These ministries are continuing evidence of Bentley's theology of community, which she describes using the words of James Luther Adams: "Every personal problem is a social problem and every social problem is a personal problem."[634] Racial injustice toward an individual derives from racial injustice in the community and is the responsibility of the community.

Bentley's ministry is important for those whom she serves and also for what she brings to the Unitarian Universalist movement. The consciousness evident in her work is an effective reminder of the work being carried forward into the 1990s by the Urban Church Coalition (established in the 1980s). At General Assembly in 1992, the Urban Church Coalition, along with virtually every other UU social justice advocacy group, proposed and passed the Racial/Cultural Diversity Resolution of Immediate Witness, affirming and supporting a "vision of a racially diverse and multicultural Unitarian Universalism." The following year, twenty-eight ministers attended (by invitation) the Urban Ministers consultation "Restoring Our Theology of Hope," to discuss issues important to urban ministry, among them being "community identity."

The 1994 Urban Church Profile, created by the Urban Concerns and Ministry Committee, made all too clear the bleak circumstances that characterize urban neighborhoods, describing "high population density, economic distress, middle-class flight, crime, unemployment, low education levels, and family and cultural breakdown."[635]

Efforts to raise awareness of racial justice needs were complemented in 1995 by the creation of the Latino/a Unitarian Universalist Networking Association (LUUNA), to implement ministries of justice with and for Latinos/as. At the 1997 General Assembly, the Racial and Cultural Diversity Task Force, created by the 1992 resolution, urged UUs "to examine carefully their own conscious and unconscious racism as participants in a racist society, and the effect that racism has on all our lives, regardless of color." Here is where attention toward the racial disparities in our cities expanded to address the racist assumptions and structures that permeate all of our lives and our institutions. The Task Force recommended the creation of a committee to monitor and assess the UUA's transformation into an anti-racist, anti-oppressive, multicultural institution. The result was the 1997 resolution, "Toward an Anti-Racist UUA," which urged "the Unitarian Universalist Association, its congregations, and community organizations to develop an ongoing process for the comprehensive institutionalization of anti-racism and multiculturalism, understanding that whether or not a group becomes multi-racial, there is always the opportunity to become anti-racist."[636] Based on this initiative, the Board of Trustees appointed in October 1997 the Journey Toward Wholeness Transformation Committee (JTWTC) with the charge "to strategically plan, coordinate, monitor, assess and guide the transformation of the UUA into an authentically anti-oppressive institution."[637]

The 2001 report of the JTWTC to the 2001 General Assembly, "Continuing the Journey," describes the work up to that time. The vision has been "to build an institution that is open to a transformation of mind, heart, and spirit. We seek an association that is anti-oppressive in all its guiding practices, policies, structures, and actions."[638] Premised on the idea that "we cannot love, wish, or educate racism away," the JTWTC builds upon the work of the Black Concerns Working Group formed in 1985 (now the Jubilee Working Group) and its Jubilee Workshops that had earlier helped many UUs better understand the realities of racism.[639] The Jubilee workshops are week-end long events in which members of congregations hear each other's stories, specially trained leaders facilitate lessons about the presence of racism in society, and participants reflect on what actions they might take as a result of their raised awareness of their participation in the racist structures of society. The JTWTC suggested broadening the analysis to include Native Americans, Asians, and Latino/as; to see linkages between the oppressions of race and class; and to help European Americans understand themselves as beneficiaries and perpetrators (however unwitting) of institutional racism, which is different from personal bigotry.

Kurt Kuhwald, a community minister working with the Faithful Fools Street Ministry in San Francisco, was a member of the JTWTC and worked as a Jubilee Workshop trainer for many years. Since its founding in 1998, the Faithful Fools has offered a "ministry of service and witness" in the Tenderloin District, convening Street Retreats, hosting an after-school day care, and staging dramatic performances such as *The Witness* to involve audiences in the mission of the Fools.[640] Racism, says Kuhwald, is different from simple prejudice. We all carry prejudice. Racism points to the institutional structures that give power to one race over another and inherently privilege one race over another, whether the members of that race know it or not.[641] The goal of the Journey Toward Wholeness program is to raise awareness of those structures within the UUA and in society and to eradicate them.

Tom Chulak, now district executive for the St. Lawrence District of the UUA, writes of his early interest in helping to make Unitarian Universalism become more multi-racial. "I believed that the sociology of a group is important in determining its way of being in community. I knew that my whiteness and that of Unitarian Universalism caused life to be skewed because it emerged from power and privilege and therefore was partial." Serving as a parish minister in two racially diverse UU congregations helped him begin to take a less skewed view of life. He writes that he read and talked with those who were not white to learn of their history, stories and customs. "Ignorance was not an acceptable response to not knowing. Being white and being in the dominant position means that one has to seek the truth of the other; it will not be delivered to your doorstep."[642] Here is a sense of the intention that inspires the ongoing Journey Toward Wholeness.

Paula Cole Jones is an African American consultant and member of All Souls Church in Washington, D.C., where she grew up. She sees that there are deep sensitivities involved when one brings racial concerns to the table. From her experience of working with the All Souls congregation since 1998, she acknowledges that the kind of transformation sought in anti-racism work takes a long time. "It should not be treated as a project, but rather become infused into the ongoing life of the church."[643] She feels this work is about individual transformation that operates from a larger framework of power and accountability. "We have to ask, 'What does it mean to be members of a group that has historically been marginalized?'"[644]

For Frances Barnes, an African American laywoman at the First Unitarian Church of Pittsburgh, anti-racism means seeing into the "eye" of racism and changing one's behavior out of that new consciousness.[645] Michelle Bentley offers such a challenge to Unitarian Universalists. "We need to have a world view that includes the 'other' as sister and brother." She echoes Shadle in calling for a model of liberation theology in which study and spiritual reflection generate social action, and social action produces spiritual reflection and further study. This theology offers a critical challenge to each person in the UU denomination, states Bentley, "to look more carefully at what we think we know and how fully we walk our walk."

Dorothy May Emerson came to community ministry in the mid-1980s while in seminary at Harvard. From 1985 to 1986, she held the first MFC-approved community ministry internship, working jointly at Tufts as a chaplain intern and at the UU Legal Ministry, a program of the Benevolent Fraternity in Boston.[646] A formative experience for Emerson was attending the first gathering of community-focused ministers in Boston in 1986 and hearing Tom Chulak's keynote address.[647] Chulak spoke of the kind of community that UU churches sought to create, where reconciliation and communal well-being were made possible. It was important to extend this vision and capacity to the larger community. "As people committed to the wholeness of the community, may we be under-girded and overarched by a common vision of the public good," Chulak urged.[648]

Through ten years of parish ministry, Emerson believed that her call to ministry was a call to community and sought ways to incorporate a community ministry vision into her parish work. She was called to a small congregation in Medford, Massachusetts, where the congregation had expressed a desire for a minister to help them be a presence in the community. Emerson worked with the congregation to start a campus ministry and initiate a Food Bank that is today widely supported by the Medford community. She was invited to join the UUA's Task Force on Anti-Racist Multi-Cultural Congregations and helped facilitate a gathering of fifteen of these congregations in Atlanta in 1996. From that gathering came a decision to propose a General Assembly business resolution challenging the UUA to make anti-racism a core principle.[649] With backing from the church, Emerson launched Friends of the Mystic River, a community group that "adopted" the river and still holds regular river clean-ups and educational programs. "Though some were drawn to the church through my community work," she reflects, "others saw my work in the community as a distraction from my work with the congregation."[650] Leaving parish ministry in 1998 opened the way for Emerson to pursue significant work in the wider world.

Emerson is probably most widely known for her work in women's history. Beginning in her student years, she founded and directed the Unitarian Universalist Women's Heritage Society "to promote appreciation of the important roles Unitarian and

Universalist women have played in the growth of our movement and in the establishment of justice in the wider community." Through the Women's Heritage Society, with financial support from the Unitarian Universalist Funding Program and the contributions of many authors, she assembled and edited an invaluable collection of biographical sketches and corresponding documents into the volume *Standing Before Us: Unitarian Universalist Women and Social Reform, 1776–1936* (Skinner House, 2000). More recently, she wrote a successful grant proposal to the Ministerial Sisterhood UU (MSUU) to fund the publication of her anthology *Glorious Women: Award-Winning Sermons about Women.* Emerson was also a recipient of the Margaret Fuller Award, from the Unitarian Universalist Women's Federation, for her programs about Unitarian Universalist women and peacemaking. "The message of my ministry" reflects Emerson, "is to empower people to take action for justice," and she believes the study of women's history is a force for empowerment.[651]

After leaving full-time parish ministry in 1998, Emerson's focus shifted to economic justice, and she became a consultant to several UU and interfaith justice organizations writing curriculum and grants and providing program and organizational development services. With her life partner (now spouse) Donna Clifford, she founded Rainbow Solutions, a business entity whose purpose is to help people and institutions live, work and invest their money in environmentally and socially responsible ways. "One of my goals is to help people and organizations heal their relationships with money so they can translate their dreams into action," states Emerson. "At Rainbow Solutions we help individuals and congregations use their financial assets to further their commitment to their values and principles."[652]

One example of this financial ministry is Emerson's work to promote investment in microcredit banks, which make small loans primarily to women in developing countries, enabling them to develop businesses and lift themselves out of poverty. There are amazing success stories behind such investing, where "small loans to people in poverty are empowering women and transforming local economies around the world."[653] Congregations have been drawn to this work because they see that "when you provide women with access to money, they put food on the table and educate their children." Emerson concludes, "By supporting the microfinance movement, Unitarian Universalists and others are putting their resources to work in the revolution against poverty."[654]

Cheng Imm Tan has put Asian-American women at the center of her ministry. Tan was ordained as a community minister in 1992. An unusual feature of Tan's ordination was that she was not ordained by any one church, but rather by twenty-eight of the congregations that were members of the UU Urban Ministry (formerly the Benevolent Fraternity). The fact that several congregations in the UUUM raised objections to her "renegade" ordination was evidence of the concern some people felt regarding congregational connection and accountability in community ministry.[655]

Tan grew up in her native Malaysia in a Confucian/Buddhist family but was educated for thirteen years in a Catholic school. It was not until her years as a student of feminist theology at Harvard that she fully realized the negative impact of having been taught that girls were a "doorway to the devil." In 1982 she began work as an intern at Renewal House, an emergency shelter for battered women, founded in 1978 by the Rev. Elizabeth Ellis-Hagler as a program of the Benevolent Fraternity.[656] Here is where Tan became familiar with Unitarian Universalism and learned to appreciate its inclusiveness and commitment to social justice. With clergy and laypersons serving at the Benevolent Fraternity, she attended the 1986 Convocation on Community Focused Ministries and became convinced that the UU community could be a home for her.

At Renewal House, Tan created a space for Chinese, Vietnamese, and Cambodian women. She put out brochures in a variety of Asian languages, encouraging battered women to seek shelter from abusive husbands. She hired bilingual, bicultural staff that enabled women to better negotiate shelter services and the legal system. The lack of multicultural services and understanding, Tan would later say, meant that "Asian women were forced to face their batterers over and over again."[657] She saw that the problems of poverty and domestic abuse were compounded by the difficulties of racial discrimination. On the one hand, Asian immigrant women were "viewed as competitors in a world where there are too few resources," and on the other hand, they were seen as "commodities to be used at will."[658] In response, she created a catering business that employed Asian women in recovery from abuse, and by 1994, she had raised $900,000 to build and operate New England's first battered women's shelter exclusively for Asian women.[659] In 1997, she initiated Ricesticks and Tea, the only food pantry in Boston supplying Asian-appropriate food to low-income Asian immigrants.[660] Tan believes that "anger over injustice must be met with love and compassion—toward ourselves as well as toward those who cause us to feel oppressed." This spiritual discovery in ministry is where "transformation begins to take place."[661]

Working independently of the UU Urban Ministry, Tan led the Asian Women's Task Force Against Domestic Violence in sponsoring an annual fund-raising cultural event, the Silk Road Gala. This led to her being asked in 1998 to direct the New Bostonians, a program created to assist the economic, social, cultural, and civic life of Boston's immigrant community. Tan accepted the directorship of this program, realizing it would enable her to "make a difference" to a larger constituency of Boston's immigrants. In leaving the Benevolent Fraternity, she regarded the New Bostonians as her community ministry.[662] In that same year, Tan founded Gund Kwok, an Asian women's lion and dragon dance troupe—a martial-arts based performance group in which women perform traditional dances dressed as lions and dragons. Historically and culturally, such dancers would only be men, so it is personally empowering and culturally revolutionary for Asian women to perform this dance. In this way, Gund Kwok offers a symbolic message that speaks fully to the heart of Tan's twenty-year life in community ministry.

In the 1980s, Maddie Sifantus was working as a professional singer and also serving as the youth director at the First Parish in Wayland, Massachusetts. In 1988, she established a chorus for senior singers, the Golden Tones, viewing her work with this group as an extension of her Unitarian Universalist faith. While working with the singers and their families through the Golden Tones, she became involved in organizations dealing with death and dying and end-of-life issues. She was an outreach worker for the Bill Moyers PBS series "On Our Own Terms," which included a cyber-ministry with the UU Church of the Larger Fellowship. She became chair of the Massachusetts Compassion Sabbath Working Group, helping to educate clergy who work with people who are seriously ill or dying. Sifantus was sitting in the plenary at General Assembly in 1991 when the motion to create a third track of ministry was passed. She realized on that day that the option of community ministry "made sense" for what she was already doing.[663] It would also give her "the accountability and colleagues" she had been looking for without success in the other paths she had been pursuing. Her seminary years at Andover Newton Theological School improved her skills and helped her gain a deeper theological understanding of her work.

Sifantus struggled with many questions in the beginning, chief among them being the need for ordination and the question of financial support. Drawing encouragement from Jody Shipley and other pioneers in community ministry, she completed her master's degree in Divinity and was ordained by the First Parish in Wayland, Massachusetts, where she first recognized her call. She has continued to lead the Golden Tones for nearly two decades. Having achieved non-profit status in 1996, the Golden Tones has been financially supported by a large grant from the State Street Global Philanthropy Program, additional smaller grants, modest performance fees and member dues. More recently the interfaith mission of the group has attracted support from the local faith community.

There are approximately fifty-five singers in the Golden Tones. Members need not audition; they need only be at least sixty years old and have a love of singing. The oldest member is ninety-nine and has been singing solos and duets since the group began. They perform about sixty concerts a year—at faith communities of all kinds, schools, prisons, nursing homes, and in intergenerational settings. They sang for the women inmates at the Massachusetts Correctional Institution's Framingham prison in September 2005. Each year, they sing at an Earth Day celebration at the local land-fill. One of the most meaningful things they do is sing at members' funerals. Sifantus describes the singing as more than the act of per-formance. States Sifantus, "This is an arts ministry—which is one of the best ways to get the community together." It is also about addressing issues like "depression at the end of life, family systems, death and dying, and the physical limitations of old age." It is a ministry that "brings my musical gifts and my Unitarian Universalist faith together with the gifts of the Golden Tones and their needs, as well as those of the greater community, to co-create what we do."[664]

Jose Ballester became a Unitarian Universalist in 1979, attracted to the movement by the Universalist message of hope. He notes that the congregations he has served have Universalist roots, such as his current congregation in Houston, founded by Quillen Hamilton Shinn. In seminary at Andover Newton, Ballester took five courses in religious education and others with a community focus, but he became a parish minister since that was the recom-mended path at the time. His first ministries were interims, where he gained a reputation for his skill in dealing with congregations in crisis.

In 1992 Steve Shick hired Ballester to work with the Just Works program at the Unitarian Universalist Service Committee. Ballester drew on the model of Universalist work camps to design innovative programs bringing young people and adults into direct relationship with people in severe poverty. Their goal was to work together to build something specific that the community needed. He comments, "My work at UUSC was my dream job. It did more for my ministry than anything else."[665] In that capacity, he was able to combine his commitment to religious education with his com-mitment to community ministry, and bring both commitments to people in congregations. Now he serves as co-minister at the First UU Church in Houston, where his role is to preach and be involved in the larger community. He is thus able to carry out a community ministry in the context of a parish ministry. Jose Ballester, who jokes that his Spanish first name was initially misspelled as Hosea by the UUA Department of Ministry, insists that any ministry among people of color requires community ministry. "The Latino church lives in the plaza. Only twenty percent of the people actually go to church, so if you want to reach the community you need to be involved in public works. You need to take a stand for justice."[666]

Jade Angelica found that her experience at Harvard Divinity School from 1988 to 1992 was intellectually stimulating but spiritually empty. "The most connecting piece for me was the weekly Friday night worship service held among UU ministerial students."[667] Angelica expected to pursue community ministry but felt very alone in her path. When she met Steve Shick at an SLM meeting in Brookline in 1989, she found in him a supportive mentor and colleague. In the early 1990s, they would work together in the Massachusetts Bay District to plan conferences and promote the interests of community ministers.

When Angelica determined that she belonged in community ministry, she arranged an internship with the local district attorney's office to serve as a community minister on a child abuse project. Ordained as a community minister in 1993, she developed a child abuse ministry and published two books: *The Moral Emergency: Breaking the Cycle of Child Sexual Abuse* (1993) and *We are Not Alone: A Guidebook for Helping Professionals and Parents Supporting Adolescent Victims of Sexual Abuse* (2002). She admits this ministry aided in her own healing from abuse. But this was not to be the only chapter in her ministry.

During a period of living in Maine, she gained spiritual healing in consultation with a spiritual director and felt called to a similar ministry. In September 2005, she began a doctoral program in faith, health, and spirituality at Andover Newton Theological School. "My goal," states Angelica, "is to be a spiritual director at a seminary. It is so hard for people to hold on to their call—that is why I want to do this." This work will bring her back to where she began, searching for deeper spiritual direction as an integral part of the divinity school experience. What Angelica envisions as her own work is yet another form of community ministry arising in response to an evident need. A network of spiritual directors is currently being established across the country.

David Pettee entered Starr King School for the Ministry in 1985. From the beginning, he was certain that his call to ministry was not toward the parish but toward a larger service. Within months of arriving at Starr King, he helped organize an early community ministry meeting, held in January 1986 at the Berkeley Unitarian Universalist Fellowship. Two months later, he was one of four Starr King students who took a leave of absence to walk with the Great Peace March for Global Nuclear Disarmament, the transcontinental peace walk that gained the support of delegates at the 1985 General Assembly in Atlanta.[668] Pettee claims, "The experience of living in community in a walking city for nine months secured in me the promise of Unitarian Universalist witness and leadership in the community."[669] When he graduated from Starr King in 1988, he went to work as a consultant with a public nonprofit agency, serving people with developmental disabilities. When SLM was born, he supported its efforts to bring about formal recognition of community ministry.

The passage of the 1991 bylaw change prompted Pettee to leave his work as a consultant and begin his preparation for ministerial fellowship. He completed a yearlong hospital chaplaincy, successfully interviewed with the Ministerial Fellowship Committee in 1993, and soon after that took a full-time hospice position with the Visiting Nurses Association (VNA). His UU faith was essential to his hospice work. He explains, "Many of my clients were still learning to love themselves and others and to decipher the meaning of their lives. It was my theological grounding that put me in a position to help them."[670] In 1994, he was ordained to community ministry—the first in the Pacific Central District—by the First Unitarian Universalist Church of San Francisco, which endorsed his hospice ministry.[671]

During his nearly ten-year stay at the VNA, the Rev. Pettee was invited to be a minister-in-residence at Starr King, where he taught a course in the history of community ministry.[672] In 2002,

Pettee accepted a position with the UUA as Ministerial Credentialing Director. His interest in credentialing had grown as he counseled many students who came to him for advice about pursuing community ministry. He had also served for three years during this time on the West Regional Sub-Committee on Candidacy. He brought all this experience to the credentialing position in Boston. He also brought the presence and perspective of a community minister. Pettee reflects, "I have been in conversation on community ministry for twenty years; others have been in it longer than I. The earlier challenges deeply imprinted feelings of marginality and estrangement for many, but I believe there have been dramatic changes since 1991."[673]

In fact, the 1991 decision to grant official recognition to community ministers inaugurated a long process of assessment and accommodation. The community ministers that were recognized after the 1991 bylaw change welcomed the official change that granted them fellowship on the basis of their community ministry, whether or not they already held fellowship in parish ministry. Community ministers wanted their ministries to be granted equal and official standing by the Ministerial Fellowship Committee; they also wanted acceptance among their peers in the UUMA. At the heart of their vision was the potential for good to the world made possible with a more open definition of ministry.

The chief difficulty in implementing the vision of community ministry lay in the fact that the Unitarian tradition, more so than the Universalist tradition, had most often tied ministry to a particular congregation, which served to confer ordination and provide compensation.[674] These concerns have not gone unnoticed. Ralph Mero allows, "We are not like the Episcopalians, who have a tradition of NEEPS (Non-Ecclesiastically Employed Priests)." Pointing out a financial reality, he adds, "We have been focused on congregations because congregations support the UUA."[675] Similarly, Scotty McLennan observes, "We do not have an Episcopalian model where ordination by a bishop grants you a new status of being. Perhaps we have to ask what it means to be ordained."[676] Neil Gerdes offers yet another denominational comparison: "Who has authority to oversee the work? We are not like the Catholics who have their orphanages and their schools."[677]

Then too, some in the UUA spoke to the question of compensation, warning, "We cannot pay you." But as Director of Church Staff Finance since August 1996, Mero understood that there were many more people coming out of the seminaries than there were churches to place them.[678] Ironically, acknowledgment of this practical reality helped create a more encouraging environment for aspiring community ministers.

Skeptics did not question community ministry as work worth doing; rather they wondered how this work could be recognized in the same congregational tradition as ordained parish ministry. Among the critics was Daniel Hotchkiss, whose 1995 statement to the UUA Department of Ministry raised what Neil Shadle called "some sharp intelligent questions."[679] Hotchkiss was at the time a staff member of the Department of Ministry. Having listened to the discussions about community ministry, he took some time to formulate in writing his view of the issue. Framing his ideas in essentially positive terms, he began with an acknowledgment that the 1991 bylaw change was motivated by a sense of fairness to UU ministers working in community settings and by a vision of increased social outreach through ministry. He then listed what he thought the UUA would need to do to successfully implement the change: (1) raise money to help fund community ministries; (2) more fully recognize the ministries of laypersons; and (3) develop a common theory by which to structure community ministry within the existing framework of ministry. How would the idea of ministry as a mutual covenant between a leader and followers be adapted to community ministry, where the "followers are more diffuse and unlikely to engage in a covenant?"[680]

Having raised these questions, Hotchkiss reasoned out ways to enlarge the current view of concepts like "the church" and "ordination." "If a congregation is ordaining a community minister," he stated, "it is the congregation's social mission that the minister is charged to help fulfill." He promoted the idea that community ministers might fulfill the historical congregational relationship by maintaining "an institutional tie to a congregation, District, UUA affiliate, or to the UUA itself."[681] This plan had been lifted up by community ministers as well. Indeed, in January 1992, a change in MFC rules required that every candidate for fellowship, including candidates for community ministry, be sponsored by a UU congregation. The following February, the SLM newsletter, *Crossroads*, reported this change in positive terms, stressing the fact that sponsorship "is intended to be a relationship that provides denominational connection, encouragement toward ministry, and in some cases financial assistance."[682]

From 1996 to 2003, Leslie Westbrook served on the Ministerial Fellowship Committee.[683] Westbrook recognized there was a dual task. "The MFC wanted to recognize people working in the community, but it also wanted to support the congregations."[684] It was a difficult duality to negotiate, however, because, as Jody Shipley explained in 1994, "most UU congregants see a church as a place to belong, not as a launching pad for social action or other community work."[685] Moreover, as Ralph Mero offers, "Part of the problem is—how does one lift up new ideas without posing a threat."[686] Finally, reflecting on her own experience, Shipley had concluded: "I knew that somewhere the work that we were calling 'non-parish ministry' was hollow [if] it did not touch the life of a congregation."[687]

As community ministry gained more visibility and focus, Shipley urged community ministers to tie their work to congregations and to see how their ministry could be inherited by succeeding generations.[688] Over time, states Westbrook, what came about was a model whereby "community ministers needed to show how what they do serves a congregation's ministry." In Westbrook's mind, this model led to a more sympathetic relationship between community ministers and congregations.[689] Here is evidence for what David Pettee sees as a change in institutional vision.[690] It is an indication of the possibility Hotchkiss articulated in 1995: "Healthy institutions need clarity but not rigidity. The UUA can choose its own institutional commitments . . . to harmonize with our abilities, our history, and our purposes."[691]

CHAPTER TWENTY-ONE

The Revival of
Campus Ministry

At the same time that community ministry was growing, campus ministry was revived. Campus and young adult ministries had lost support in the late 1960s, due in part to the dire financial straits of the UUA and UU churches at that time. In addition, campus ministry meeting spaces were targeted as suspected havens for drugs and campus radicals.[692] Finally, the migration of urban churches to the suburbs made them less accessible to campuses in cities.[693] In sum, a number of factors contributed to the decline of campus ministry by the early 1970s. In 1985, UUA president Gene Pickett argued that it was time to get out on the campuses again.

College students and young adults (officially aged 18 to 35) were recognized as a special population bearing the unique burden of a generation making tough choices in a time of accelerating change. They were a generation that ought not be lost from the church, yet the UU churches were not meeting the needs of college students and young adults. In response to Pickett's challenge, the UUA Board prepared a report examining the history and status of campus ministry. On the basis of this report, Pickett asked Tom

Chulak, serving then as New Congregations Program Director and Urban Extension Consultant for the UUA, if he would lead the first phase of this new effort. Chulak agreed to fold this work into his existing duties, and from 1986 to 1988, he did what he could to "get things going."[694] Packets were developed on how to start a group; for leaders, training sessions were offered on the needs of young adults. Local programs were begun, recognizing the importance of establishing connections between campuses and nearby UU congregations. When Chulak left the UUA in 1988, Teresa Cooley was hired part-time to disperse funds from a UUA Funding Panel grant to young adult and campus ministry groups. She was succeeded by Beverly Olson.

Of great significance to the revival of campus ministry was Donna DiSciullo. DiSciullo arrived in Princeton, New Jersey in 1989, having served as parish minister at a UU church in Olympia, Washington since being ordained in 1986. She had come to Princeton with her husband, who accepted a position as Dean of Religious Life at Princeton University. At Princeton, DiSciullo combined a consulting position with a church in Hunterdon County, New Jersey, with a one-year position on the staff at All Souls Church in New York City. At All Souls, she was initiated into the experience of working with young adults.[695] It came to her attention through the prompting of a student that there was no UU campus ministry at Princeton. She invited the student to help her start one, and on a voluntary basis, she led the UU campus ministry at Princeton for the next ten years. In the process, she discovered her passion for young adult and campus ministry.

In 1994, DiSciullo accepted a half-time position with the UUA as the Princeton-based Coordinator of Young Adult and Campus Ministry. The following year, the UUA asked her to prepare a program on young adult and campus ministry for the 1995 General Assembly. She welcomed this opportunity, but requested that she now be hired full-time. Her Young Adult and Campus Ministry position was given full-time status in September 1995, the first such position created since the time of Orloff Miller in the 1960s. It marked the re-institutionalization of UU campus ministry at the UUA. By the time DiSciullo left, there were two full-time and two half-time UUA staff people working in Young Adult and Campus Ministry.

DiSciullo focused her efforts on providing resources, training, and materials for students to lead campus groups. She also sought to educate congregations to the importance of their involvement in young adult and campus ministry. The difficulty she recognized was that students don't typically bring big numbers into the pews, nor can they be counted on for much financial support. Even so, DiSciullo argued, students need to be supported and have a place to go with their concerns. They need a UU worship experience, which she insisted should be at the heart of any campus ministry program. They also need to be reminded of social justice principles and learn ways to implement them.[696] In this period, Mary Ann Macklin, Young Adult and Campus Ministry Coordinator at the Unitarian Universalist Church of Bloomington, Indiana, created *A Unitarian Universalist Campus Ministry Manual*. This manual brought together a collection of essays and pieces of wisdom from campus ministry leaders in numerous faiths. They eloquently bear witness to the importance of DiSciullo's vision. Published by the Young Adult Ministries Office of the UUA, this manual became a vital resource for campus ministry leaders of all faith traditions.

A significant program developed in these years was the "Bridging Ceremony," in which graduating high school seniors are invited at GA to cross into young adulthood with the support of other young adults. This moving ceremony is now held at UU churches across the country. Finally, DiSciullo made an important contribution in overcoming the distrust of the Continental UU Young Adult Network (CUUYAN) toward UUA-sponsored campus ministry programs. CUUYAN was, and remains, a broad grassroots organization comprised of young adults, ages 18 to 35. It includes, but is not limited to, college students. The Young Adult Network had retained a remnant of suspicion toward the UUA as a result of past experiences when promised program support had not materialized. DiSciullo was largely successful in building positive relationships with CUUYAN. In 1996 DiSciullo asked Joseph Santos-Lyons to advise and consult on young adult and campus ministry, and in 1998, Santos-Lyons was offered a position in the UUA to develop campus ministry on a more comprehensive basis.

Joseph Santos-Lyons brought to young adult and campus ministry an extensive prior history of working with high school-age youth and young adults. He had worked as a youth leader at the West Hills Unitarian Universalist Fellowship in Portland, Oregon in the 1980s and had served since 1983 as the representative to the UUA's Continental Youth Council for the Pacific Northwest District. From this work, Santos-Lyons went to the University of Oregon, where he organized a campus group and developed a young adult ministry. This is what he was doing when he was first approached by DiSciullo. After taking the position with the UUA in 1998, Santos-Lyons implemented a plan to build networks that would connect campus ministry programs. "This is happening," he says. "We have networked over 300 groups and run numerous workshops for leaders. Right now, there are forty-five paid professionals working in campus ministry."[697]

Leadership in campus ministry has been sustained by an infusion of money from the UUA Campaign for Unitarian Universalism and from "Mind the Gap" Youth, Campus, and Young Adult Sunday fundraising. "Mind the Gap" is a phrase that aptly characterizes the importance of young adult and campus ministry. Santos-Lyons sees that young adults are in a time of "asking profound questions about career, family, relationships, and identity— who they are."[698] Our congregations cannot attend to this, he argues. At the same time, the old idea that young adults are not interested in church or are too busy doesn't apply. "We need to take a lifespan approach so that these people have access to a community to explore their identity and faith as UUs."[699] Important to the revitalization of campus ministry, observes Santos-Lyons, has been an expanded sense of ownership. The Campus Ministry Advisory Council now includes representatives from the Unitarian Universalist Ministers' Association, the Liberal Religious Educators Association, the Youth Network and the Young Adult Network.

This kind of involvement helps assure a fuller denominational commitment. It also helps insure that campus ministry offers more than just social activity, providing an avenue for spiritual growth.

The Young Adult and Campus Ministry program at the First Unitarian Church of Pittsburgh illustrates the current prospect for campus ministry programming. Michael Tino, director of the UUA office of Young Adult and Campus Ministry, came to the Pittsburgh church in April 2002, to meet with the parish minister, David Herndon, and interested college students. Herndon and the Board of Trustees had earlier recognized that the church's location within walking distance of two major universities offered an opportunity for significant outreach in campus ministry. As a follow-up to that meeting, Herndon spent a year working with the Association of Chaplains at the University of Pittsburgh and the Interfaith Council at Carnegie Mellon University to get the First Unitarian Church recognized as an officially welcomed religious presence on their respective campuses.[700] Herndon applied for and obtained a grant from the UUA Office for Young Adult and Campus Ministry. This provided the seed money for the church to hire lay minister Devon Wood as a part-time staff person to begin a campus ministry program. Wood came to this position with an academic background in human development and family studies, as well as religious studies, and a working background in public mental health. "When I came on," reports Wood, "we had an office at Carnegie Mellon, and a CMU staff person began attending our meetings. David's prior work made this happen."[701] Of further consequence to the success of the Young Adult and Campus Ministry Program at Pittsburgh was a grant of $1000 from the Ohio Meadville District, which was used to purchase hymnbooks, and a bequest from a family in the church establishing a $50,000 endowment to help cover expenses of the Young Adult and Campus Ministry Program.[702]

Devon Wood began by meeting with a few students from Pitt and Carnegie Mellon and asking them what they would like to see. When she first set up a table for UU Campus Ministry at student activity fairs, she was astonished at the "massive initial response" she got from students. "I saw students cry when they found our table and saw that we were there," she states. "In a sea of other faiths," one student exclaimed, "I can't believe you are here."[703] From the two campuses, Wood soon developed a combined e-mail list of 130 students, about one-third of whom are UUs. The students from the two campuses voted to hold their weekly meetings jointly, at alternating campus sites. Shortly thereafter, they decided to hold their meetings at the church. Each meeting includes a chalice lighting and brief worship service on a theme that the students choose. Wood reports that this is a collaborative effort, in which UU students have also led the services. Additional time might be given to a special speaker, a social justice or educational project, and sharing some kind of refreshment. Once a month, students go out for dinner together, and currently an effort is underway to involve faculty in hosting dinners for the students. Many campus ministry students also attend Sunday services at the church.

The campus ministry program at the First Unitarian Church of Pittsburgh was featured as one of the most successful new programs in a November 2003 issue of *UU World* magazine.[704] Indeed, coming in on the ground floor of the movement, the campus ministry program at Pittsburgh has become a model for budding campus ministry programs. Devon Wood serves on the national UUA Campus Ministry Advisory Council as an at-large member. She also advises the UUA office on matters of focus, such as formulating a code of ethics for young adults and leaders, and developing resources for campus ministry groups. "When I started," recalls Wood, "I got a Campus Ministry Start-Up Kit, which was very helpful, but the whole movement was new and there was not much to plug into."[705]

Today, with the help of the UUA Campus Ministry Advisory Committee and Strategic Plan established in 2002, "a lot more is being developed, like a web source where you can find campus ministry groups in your state."[706] Wood also works with campus students to connect with OPUS, a spiritual retreat offered annually by the Continental UU Young Adult Network, and Concentric, a program of grassroots planning and leadership development, also sponsored by CUUYAN. Finally, she states, "I encourage our students to attend one of the six to eight UUA-funded regional campus ministry conferences held each year.[707] Among other things, these conferences deal with social justice issues and strategies for raising money for campus ministry groups and projects.

Wood believes campus ministry is having an important impact. "It has kept folks who were already UUs connected to the faith, and it has opened the door to people who are new to the faith. Almost all of our students who have graduated are still involved with a UU congregation." She adds, "One campus ministry student, a life-long UU, has a minor in religion and has decided to go on to seminary; another one, a Florida UU, was the first to obtain a Clara Barton Internship funded by the UU Women's Federation. This funding made it possible for her to work on women's issues for two years with the UUA Office of Advocacy and Witness for in Washington, D.C."[708] Numerous stories of this kind are told in other campus ministry programs across the country.

Mary Ann Macklin has stressed the need for students and young adults to explore their religious and spiritual needs. They need a faith that encourages them to develop their own theology and spiritual path, to openly worship regardless of race, creed, gender, or sexual orientation. They want a place where reason and wisdom affirm a liberal religious view.[709] At Pittsburgh, Devon Wood shares this sense of purpose. "Campus Ministry provides a spiritual home for students. This is the primary thing that has made our program what it is."[710] The 2002 UUA Statement on Campus Ministry further expresses the hope that campus ministry experiences will help students learn to "act for social justice change in their communities and the world."[711]

CHAPTER TWENTY-TWO

The Community Ministry Summit
A Framework for the Future

O nce the intensity of start-up activity was past and the community ministry track was established, the Society for the Larger Ministry appeared to be losing momentum. In fact, however, a lot of institutional connections were being made behind the scenes, and serious work was accomplished through 1996. Jody Shipley left the SLM Steering Committee in 1990, when her term expired. The new leadership, which included Barbara Jo Sorenson, Steve Shick, and David Gilmartin, among others, continued to meet annually. They focused their energy on building the institutional base for community ministry, working with the UUA, the Ministerial Fellowship Committee, and the UUMA to adopt policies that would include community ministers. They continued to hold annual conferences, meeting simultaneously in the Boston, Berkeley, and Chicago areas in 1994 and 1995.[712] At the 1994 General Assembly in Fort Worth, Neil Shadle gave the James Reeb Memorial Lecture[713] on "Community Ministry and the True Church of Democracy." This watershed talk outlined the need for a democratic vision of religion in a pluralistic society. Shadle eloquently advocated a shift from seeing the church as a private enclave to the church as a steward of public life. We must be interfaith to do this, he said, even as we are interracial and intercultural. Later that year, the MFC accepted SLM's invitation to send a representative to its Berkeley conference in November 1994 to learn more about issues of concern to community ministers.[714]

Steve Shick, who had served as chair of the SLM Task Force on Fellowshipping since 1988 and as a Steering Committee member from 1992 through 1996, established a connection between the Unitarian Universalist Service Committee and SLM. This resulted in the UUSC agreeing to provide office and meeting space for SLM at UUSC headquarters in Cambridge, Massachusetts. The UUSC also agreed to recognize Shick's community ministry. His role as liaison among the various UU institutional structures was a significant factor in the progress made in the first half of the 1990s. Indeed, in 1995, SLM received a grant to promote community ministry by hiring an advocate to work out of the office at the UUSC.[715]

A critical point of institutional cooperation took place with the convening of the Consultation on Community Ministry, held in Boston, March 1–3, 1996.[716] Planned by the SLM Steering Committee and the UUA Board Ministry Working Group, representatives from twelve different constituencies participated in the Consultation.[717] Steve Shick came to the Consultation thinking it would be good to get all these interests around the table to promote community ministry. "I wanted to see a strong affirmation of community ministry," he recalls. "I also wanted to see some clarity, because already there was talk of doing away with the three separate tracks of ministry." Shick hoped that the Consultation would put an end to the idea of discontinuing the separate tracks. The recommendations of the Consultation were hopeful and far-reaching. Among them was a proposal to establish a UUA Commission on Community Ministry that would "create a long-term plan for community ministries to include a wider vision of ministry for the denomination" and "establish a staff structure" to meet the needs of community ministries.[718] The recommendations of the Consultation were placed before the UUA Board in April 1996.

Meanwhile, the question that worried Steve Shick had in fact been re-opened. In 1995, the UUMA Executive Committee had conducted an informal survey of its members and found support for instituting a single category of ministry.[719] In 1997, the Commission on Appraisal reported, "Ministers should be received into Ministerial Fellowship with the potential for adding areas of specialization." After the UUMA passed a resolution in 1999 proposing a new structure for categories, a Task Force on Categories was convened in January 2000 including members of the Ministerial Fellowship Committee, the UUMA, and the UUA Board of Trustees. By September of that year, the MFC voted for the second time on the motion "that preliminary fellowship will be granted in ministry without regard to category."

By 1997, the Society for the Larger Ministry fell into a period of inactivity, and its newsletter *Crossroads* ceased publication from 1996 to 1999. The causes were many. Skinner House declined to publish the book *Community Ministry: An Opportunity for Renewal and Change,* edited by Barbara Jo Sorenson and Joan Engel.[720] The proposals of the 1996 Boston Consultation on Community Ministry received little tangible result at the time. There was also a leadership vacuum after Barbara Jo Sorenson left, with no one feeling prepared to take her place.[721] On a personal level, many community ministers were reportedly experiencing burnout or inadequate financial support in their respective areas of work.[722] Finally, there was an emerging sense of confusion over proposals at the UUA and MFC to fold the three tracks of ministry into one.

Where support was missing, many community ministers found an ally in Jody Shipley. "Jody held the banner high, even when nothing was happening," states Maddie Sifantus. Shipley was among several persons who urged the Pacific Central District board to form a district Community Ministry Council in 1996. To address the concerns of community ministers and the UUA, Shipley worked with this Council in formulating guidelines for the affiliation of community ministers with congregations. Shipley liked to think of affiliation as a covenantal relationship. In 1997, she wrote a successful proposal to fund her role as Council staff person. In that capacity, she continued to work on the guidelines, eventually producing a spiral-bound book, *Guidelines for the Affiliation of Community Clergy with Unitarian Universalist Congregations.* This resource helped many community ministers and congregations to develop written agreements defining their relationships with each other. It brought a lot of ideas together and "got a lot of people thinking."[723]

Though she maintained a sometimes-interrupted parish ministry for twenty-six years, Shipley continued her ministry to community ministers. To facilitate communication, she started a community ministry email list that initially served the Pacific Central District but eventually expanded into a national and international network. In 1998, she founded the Unitarian Universalist Community Ministry Center in Berkeley. The Center was set up as a non-profit organization, with a small, mostly local board of directors that could focus on programs in the San Francisco Bay Area. The Center has been described by many as Shipley's personal ministry. It was essentially an organization through which she could combine all of her community ministries—writing grant proposals, holding conferences, running retreats, and offering educational workshops.

At General Assembly in 1998, a group of community ministers began to meet again to determine what might be done to address their concerns and revive the Society for the Larger Ministry.[724] In November 1999 *Crossroads* resumed publication with a grant from the Unitarian Universalist Ministers' Association. In the first issue, Shipley announced that after several years of silence, "we [again] crank up this organization . . . everything is cold . . . a little misplaced . . . but we're underway."[725] SLM resumed offering yearly community ministry workshops at General Assembly, and the membership of SLM climbed to eighty. Shipley had stepped in as the driving force, but she knew that others needed to assume longer-term leadership. She also wanted to focus more of her time and energy on the UU Community Ministry Center she had founded in Berkeley. She recommended in 2001 that Jeanne Lloyd and Maddie Sifantus become the co-chairs of SLM. They agreed to do so only if Shipley would stay on as treasurer for one more year, which she did.

Community ministers still felt the need for parity with parish ministers, and the MFC proposal for one ministry track appeared as a setback in the struggle to achieve that parity. Thus, when the proposal to merge the separate tracks of ministry came up, the ensuing discussion led to a heated debate at the March 2002 Ministers Convocation in Birmingham, Alabama. The debate led ordained and fellowshipped community ministers to establish a Community Ministry Focus Group (CMFG) to advocate for community ministers within the UUMA.[726] At General Assembly in Boston, the CMFG held a reception for community ministers to raise awareness of its existence and to encourage community ministers to participate in a meeting with the UUMA Committee on Categories. Community ministers who attended that meeting expressed their concerns about the lack of inclusive process by which decisions were being made regarding their status and about continuing inequities among different categories of ministers. The UUMA Committee on Categories listened and subsequently recommended to the Ministerial Fellowship Committee and the UUMA Executive Committee that the process of changing the tracks be slowed down. More input and greater consensus was needed before proceeding.

With the formation of the UUMA Community Ministry Focus Group, there were now three community ministry organizations, the other two being the Society for the Larger Ministry and the UU Community Ministry Center. Considered weak in organizational skills, Jody Shipley had nonetheless been central to the development of all three groups. Her strengths, as many have attested, lay in her pastoral care of community ministers and in her ability to serve as a catalyst for community ministry organizing and advocacy. Jody Shipley was awarded the SLM "Community Minister of the Year Award" at the 2002 GA; sadly, she was unable to attend GA to receive the award because she had become ill with lymphoma. Her unexpected death in October 2002 was a shock to everyone and left the separate community ministry organizations with a need to take stock. How would they now be run, by whom, and for what purpose?

The need for clarity led representatives from the three organizations to apply for a special grant for a Community Ministry Summit, to be held the day after General Assembly 2003 in Boston.[727] Each of the three community ministry organizations was asked to prepare in advance a "concept paper" describing: (1) their group's mission; (2) the attributes that made their group unique; (3) their key accomplishments; and (4) their points of confusion about identity, funding, and accountability. Among the thirty people who attended, there were many who came with allegiances to more than one group. All came with the idea of advancing community ministry through cooperative efforts. In addition to representatives of the three community ministry groups, representatives from the UUMA, UUA Board of Trustees, and UUA staff also participated. Facilitating as director of the UUA Ministerial and Professional Leadership Staff Group (formerly the Department of Ministry), David Hubner recalls that there was a lot to work through. "There was grief work to be done over the loss of Jody Shipley. There were also struggles over competing visions and strategies of leadership. It was hard to sort out who to listen to and easy to lose heart in the process."[728]

A report on the Summit was prepared by community minister Nancy Bowen, who also facilitated the Summit planning and proceedings, as well as subsequent meetings of the Community Ministry Coalition formed out of the Summit. Bowen summarized the process by which the three groups had sought to identify how their individual identities and purposes could come together in a shared vision for UU community ministry. With frank honesty, they looked at the current reality of community ministry, with its strengths and weaknesses as well as its benefits and dangers. Strengths included a sense of call, passion, diverse skills, good will, and an entrepreneurial spirit; weaknesses included over-commitment, murky vision, competitiveness, a lone-ranger stereotype, and whining. Acknowledging this last weakness brought laughter and the recognition that it was time to stop whining and move forward with a common vision.

Key decisions made at the summit were to establish a committee to facilitate communication among the organizations, research and prepare a book on community ministry,[729] develop an educational program for parish ministers to learn about community ministry, and develop a manual of community ministry guidelines. At the end of the day, David Hubner "took the bold step . . . to volunteer his office to serve as an ex-officio member of what would later become the Community Ministry Coalition."[730] The creation of the Community Ministry Coalition was perhaps the most significant outcome of the Summit. The 2003 Summit signified a coming of age for UU community ministry. More than anything, it marked an opening up of dialogue between the separate and overlapping community ministry entities, with the UUA as a full partner in that conversation.[731] The summit helped to clarify and generate the kind of changes that needed to take place to strengthen community ministry.

Already underway was a proposal to incorporate SLM as a non-profit organization, in the hope that this status would promote greater legitimacy, stability, and accountability. After a year of meetings with the Coalition, the San Francisco-based UU Community Ministry Center proposed to fold its vision and mission into that of SLM. In December 2004, the membership of the Society for the Larger Ministry voted to change its name to the Society for Community Ministries (SCM). The name change affirmed the group's focus on community ministry and at the same time eliminated the recurring name confusion between SLM and the Church of the Larger Fellowship. In January 2005, Kurt Kuhwald, formerly a board member for the Center, joined the board of SCM and was named Director of Education to carry on the continuing mission of the Center within SCM.[732]

To create a stronger organizational structure and foster the development of new leadership, Jeanne Lloyd and Maddie Sifantus, who had served first as co-chairs and then as co-presidents of SLM, altered their leadership roles. In 2005 Lloyd became president and Sifantus became vice president of the renamed Society for Community Ministries. The nonprofit status of SCM was finalized in June 2005. Now donors could claim a tax deduction, making it easier for SCM to attract funding. SCM is currently focused on reaching out to its membership through better communication, using the SCM website which Lloyd designed. The site provides information about SCM, its goals, organizational developments, the issues and events it is working on, and the work of individual community ministers.[733] Community ministers are invited to post descriptions of their work and a photograph. The SCM website is a channel of communication between the membership, other entities in the UUA, and anyone else in the larger world who wants to know more about UU community ministry. Lloyd and David Pettee have continued with the redesigning and updating of the SCM website.

An important document on the SCM website is the Community Ministry Code of Professional Practice, developed over a two-year period under the leadership of community minister Nadine Swahnberg[734] and approved by the SCM membership in December 2004. The Code is a valuable tool that sets out for both lay and ordained community ministers a standard of ethical commitment for their ministries and their lives. By this code, community ministers agree to "fulfill their responsibilities to their employers" and also "to know and understand their own strengths, weaknesses, and limitations." There are also agreements that pertain to relationships with congregations and colleagues, primarily aimed at respecting traditions, keeping confidences, establishing written agreements, and fulfilling them. Finally, there are agreements whereby community ministers recognize their relationship to the Unitarian Universalist Association and the spread of its traditions. This last item is very important. Ministerial Credentialing Director David Pettee states, "There are frequently those who come to my office seeking ecclesiastical endorsement, who want nothing to do with the UU denomination or a UU congregation. On that basis, we have to turn them away."[735]

Meanwhile, the Community Ministry Focus Group has been establishing its role within the UUMA. One of its challenges has been to develop a complete listing of all ordained and fellowshipped community ministers. This task is more complicated than it might appear, since many of those engaged in community ministry hold fellowship as parish ministers or ministers of religious education. Even the UUA has not had a complete list. The CMFG meets monthly via conference call and hosts an annual meeting and reception at Ministry Days before General Assembly. Its mission is to represent the needs and gifts of community ministers within the UUMA. To help accomplish this mission, the CMFG designed a survey for the UUMA website to collect information about members' ministries, with a focus on how all ministers see their work as serving the wider community.

Since the Summit of 2003, community ministry has come into a place of greater visibility and acceptance within the institutional structures of the UUA. It is encouraging that several ordained and fellowshipped community ministers serve in leadership positions at the UUA, including Bill Sinkford, President of the UUA; David Pettee, Director of Ministerial Credentialing; Ralph Mero, Director of Church Staff Finances; and Michelle Bentley, Professional Development Director. In addition, John Weston, Settlement Director, was one of the original signers of the SLM Proclamation and served on the SLM Steering Committee in the early 1990s. Other UUA senior staff members are ordained ministers, fulfilling roles as community ministers.

Bill Sinkford, it should be said, was elected the first African American president of the UUA in June 2001.[736] A lifelong Unitarian, he was president of LRY at the First Unitarian Church of Cincinnati in his youth. He graduated from Harvard College in 1968 and spent ten years in business management, during which time he also served as a volunteer in community action groups and not-for-profit housing. Sinkford felt called to ministry after returning to his congregation in Cincinnati and becoming involved in the UU Urban Concerns and Ministry Committee. After completing seminary at Starr King School for the Ministry in 1995, he was ordained as a community minister and was hired as Director of Congregational, District, and Extension Services with the UUA. In his work as president of the UUA, he has aimed to extend the voice of Unitarian Universalism into the wider world and has been fully supportive of community ministry.

Jeanne Lloyd rightly credits David Hubner, Director of the Ministerial and Professional Leadership Staff Group, for being "instrumental in raising up community ministry in the UUA and helping it find parity in fellowship, practice, and process."[737] Hubner believes that "community ministry offers a kind of creativity and entrepreneurial spirit that is visionary. It is also of enormous value to congregations because it helps shift the sense of ministry to engage with the world."[738] And finally, there is a movement underway to recognize and credential at some level the gifts and commitments of lay community ministers.

In 2005 the newly formed UU Professional Leadership Coordinating Council invited SCM to participate as one of its member organizations. This Coordinating Council came together in 2004 representing the interests of the Liberal Religious Educators Association (LREDA), the UU Musicians Network (UUMN), the Association of UU Administrators (AUUA), and the UU Ministers' Association (UUMA). The idea was to bring these professional organizations into contact with each other to heal hidden injuries and to recognize the necessary contributions of each group to the health of Unitarian Universalism. The Community Ministry Focus Group has become a regular part of the UUMA organizational structure, with leadership appointed by the UUMA Executive Committee. All of these structural changes are indications that community ministry is becoming an integral part of the Unitarian Universalist movement.

In regard to the issue of separate tracks for ministry, as of its September 2005 meeting, the Ministerial Fellowship Committee agreed it would no longer be asking candidates to indicate which category of ministry they planned to pursue. The MFC began granting preliminary fellowship to UU ministers on the premise that all candidates should be prepared to serve in any ministerial capacity.[739] The General Assembly was not involved in this decision, because it did not involve a bylaw change and the UUA Board had empowered the MFC to resolve the question.[740] Feelings on this issue have differed. For many, it makes official a flexibility that is desirable and already being practiced. For others, it threatens to fragment study that might better be focused on the type of ministry one wishes to pursue.

Meanwhile, though funding for community ministry remains a challenge for some, the flow of people answering the call to community ministry continues unabated. David Pettee estimates that around forty percent of incoming ministerial students are interested in community ministry, and that perhaps sixteen percent will choose community ministry as their specialty. Likewise, Hubner states, "I visit seminaries and my experience tells me that the students want to have community ministry as part of their ministry to the world."[741] Each of these ministers brings new vision and possibility for serving the wider community. The organizational healing and focus that came about with the Community Ministry Summit clarified that sense of possibility for the next generation and beyond.

Conclusion

*We must have a sense of mission to the world.
"We" can't be the "end" of Unitarian Universalism.
To serve is ultimately liberating — to serve people
at their deepest needs. That needs to be primary.*

—Tom Chulak[742]

In a world as imperfect as our own, we are sometimes struck by the magnitude of our mutual human need. To minister to that world is to be open to that need and to connect with it at its deepest, most authentic level. It is here, in this place of recognized shared vulnerability, that ministry takes place. In congregations, ordained parish ministers have for generations opened themselves in thoughtfully conscious ways to the needs made apparent among those who congregate with them. Ministers of religious education have opened themselves in carefully studied ways to the need for lifespan lessons to grow our faith and commitments. In the larger society, community ministers have, since the beginnings of the Unitarian Universalist movement, opened themselves in consciously intentional ways to the needs made apparent among those who inhabit the civic spaces of life. This history is about them.

Their stories of community ministry reflect an evolving apprehension of larger religious purposes in response to a changing world. Such purposes have been informed by a liberal religious imperative, emerging with the earliest Unitarians and Universalists, who conceived of a benevolent God and saw Jesus as the model of perfection God intended in human creation. Out of this theology evolved over time a non-creedal consciousness of human beings as the worthy bearers of life, called on behalf of each other to work for goodness on earth. In this light, freedom of belief did not absolve us from the need to serve.

Community ministers have served the Benevolent Fraternity of Unitarian Churches in Boston, begun with Joseph Tuckerman and William Ellery Channing. Today it is known as the Unitarian Universalist Urban Ministry, supported by sixty area UU churches. In addition to Renewal House, a ministry to women in crisis and their children, the UU Urban Ministry sponsors United Souls, offering assistance to individuals recently released from prison. Ricesticks and Tea distributes food to 130 indigent Asian families each month. Weekend and summer youth programs complement the weekday after-school programs in which students from elementary school through college participate in academic and social support activities.

Community ministers have through time confronted the American tragedy of racial oppression in its many forms. They worked toward the abolition of slavery prior to the Civil War and resisted the Fugitive Slave Law. During the war, they worked for the U.S. Sanitary Commission to supply medical needs, and after the war, they established schools to educate those deprived of education under slavery. At the turn of the century, they mounted legal challenges to black disfranchisement and segregation through the NAACP. In the 1960s, lay and ordained community ministers consciously exposed themselves to bodily harm, demanding the right of full participation in the nation's economic and political life for African Americans.

Community ministers have recently worked within and outside of congregations to make real the mission of the Journey Toward Wholeness Transformation Committee to recognize and eliminate racism within ourselves, within the Unitarian Universalist movement, and in society. Efforts to end racism continue today in the UUA's JUUST Change Consultancy program, which engages congregations in understanding the multi-layered nature of oppression and seeking ways to eradicate it. A success story is the A. Powell Davies Memorial Unitarian Universalist Church in Southern Prince George's County, Maryland. The congregation instituted A Dialogue on Race and Ethnicity (ADORE), adapted from a program at the All Souls Church in Washington, D.C. African American minister John T. Crestwell, Jr. has been instrumental, working with a committed congregation, in building a church in which thirty-seven percent of the members are people of color.[743] Here is where community ministry has influenced parish ministry and parish ministry influences the community in return.

Community ministers in the nineteenth century worked toward humanitarian improvements like prison reform and abolition. Ordained women established the Everyday Church and built communities in places in the Midwest where there was little denominational presence. Ordained women joined lay women to gain woman suffrage, enduring society's scorn in the process. In the 1970s and 1980s, women entered ordained ministry in unprecedented numbers, bringing with them new layers of gender-sensitive community consciousness. A critical factor in the formation of their ministries lay in what they noticed that others had misunderstood or ignored.

Finally, community ministers have been writers, educators and denominational leaders. In the nineteenth century they articulated, challenged, and ultimately found room to affirm competing claims of faith. In the twentieth century, they gave attention and direction to the organizational and educational needs of an emerging generation of religious liberals, schooled in higher biblical criticism and a one-world view of earth's people. Essential to the work of Unitarian Universalism in these modern times has been their peace activism and their larger institutional vision. Among them was Spencer Lavan, who, from the time of his ordination in 1962, served as campus chaplain and professor of the religions of Islam and India at Tufts, brought a blend of ethics and humanities to the New England College of Osteopathic Medicine, and served as Dean and President of Meadville Lombard Theological School. For his community ministry in higher education, Lavan was the recipient of a Lifetime Achievement Award for Service to Unitarian Universalism at General Assembly in Boston in 2003.

In 1961, after earlier attempts had failed, Unitarian and Universalist leaders brought their two denominations together. Lay-led fellowships and youth ministries brought democratic empowerment to an expanding grassroots membership. In recent years, community ministers became prophets of our age, condemning war and nuclear weapons, standing with agricultural laborers, caring for persons with AIDS, and chronicling the deeds of our good models. At this writing, an archival ministry has begun at Meadville Lombard to collect and make available the papers and biographies of ministers of color within Unitarian Universalism.[744] Taken together, our community ministers show how connected our Unitarian Universalist movement has been to the impetus for American social justice reform. Yet sometimes our community ministers have had to stand at the edge of acceptable custom or leave our institutions altogether in order to forge a new path.

Community ministry is grounded in the liberal religious principles of the Unitarian, Universalist, and Unitarian Universalist traditions, fulfilling the promise of a benevolent and life-affirming concept of faith. Community ministers have brought compassion, hope, and energy to the wider world, where empowerment, prophecy, reform, reconciliation, and healing have forever been in short supply. From this history, the inescapable conclusion is that community ministers in this liberal faith have been among the first to push the boundaries of spirituality and culture. In this regard, their vision has been animated by an acute perceptiveness and vigilance, imagining in distinct ways a more just and humane world.

Their history is our history; their story is our own. They have brought sacred service to civic space and have thereby enlarged our understanding of where the sacred may be found. They have connected us to that wider world of need and have thereby expanded our sense of who we are. They have shown us that the community is ourselves and have thereby broadened our view of the human family that we serve.

Notes

Introduction

1. Frederick Eliot was president of the American Unitarian Association (AUA) from 1937 to 1958. He is quoted in James Luther Adams, "Radical Laicism," in *The Prophethood of All Believers* (Boston: Beacon Press, 1986), pp. 93–95.

2. Adams, *Prophethood of all Believers*, p. 95.

Historical Theological Perspectives Toward Community Ministry

3. George Marshall, *The Challenge of a Liberal Faith* (Boston: Skinner House Books, 1966, 1991), p. 42.

4. James Luther Adams, *On Being Human Religiously: Selected Essays in Religion and Society,* ed. Max Stackhouse (1976), p. 10.

5. Adams, *On Being Human Religiously*, p. 10.

6. Roger Betsworth, *Social Ethics: An Examination of American Moral Traditions* (Louisville, KY: Westminster/John Knox Press, 1990), p. 82.

7. Betsworth, *Social Ethics*, 82.

8. James Luther Adams, *On Being Human*, pp. 12–21.

9. Adams, *Prophethood of all Believers,* pp. 100–02.

10. Arthur Simon, *Christian Faith and Public Policy* (Grand Rapids, MI: Eerdmans Publishing Company, 1987), p. 16.

11. George Marshall, *The Challenge of a Liberal Faith*, pp. 44–45.

12. Rev. Kyoki Roberts, a Buddhist priest, describes the "non-self" as a central transformative element in Buddhist practice. Meeting with Kyoki Roberts, July 2006. Zen Center, Sewickley, Pennsylvania.

13. Reza Aslan, *No god but God: The Origins, Evolution, and Future of Islam* (New York: Random House, 2005), 28–29.

14. William F. Shulz, "Our Humanist Legacy: Seventy Years of Religious Humanism," *UU World*, November/December, 2003.

15. Forrest Church, *A Chosen Faith: An Introduction to Unitarian Universalism* (Boston: Beacon Press, 1989, 1998), pp. 81–96.

16. Richard S. Gilbert, *The Prophetic Imperative: Social Gospel in Theory and Practice* (Boston: Skinner House Books, 2000).

17. Gilbert, *Prophetic Imperative*, p. 7. David Robinson also speaks of the labor violence of the 1890s as what sparked liberal ministers out of their complacency in the late nineteenth century and helped create the Social Gospel Movement that followed. See David Robinson, *The Unitarians and the Universalists* (Westport, Connecticut: Greenwood Press, 1985), pp. 133–35.

18. Neil Shadle, "Community Ministry and the True Church of Democracy," James Reeb Memorial Lecture, UUA General Assembly, Fort Worth, TX, 1994.

PART I
The Pressing Rise of Liberal Religion

CHAPTER ONE:
Community Ministry in Early New England

19. David Pettee, "This Grand and Holy Revolution," paper produced for course RSFT 4013, Starr King School for the Ministry, Berkeley, CA, Spring 2001; Carl Seaburg, "Ministries Beyond the Local Parish: An Historical Overview," in *The Challenge of Right Relationship* (unpublished manuscript), 1996.

20. Cambridge Platform of 1648, Andover-Harvard Library, Special Collections.

21. Pettee, "Grand and Holy Revolution," p. 3.

22. Seaburg "Ministries beyond the Local Parish," p. 40.

23. Shadle, "True Church of Democracy," p. 5.

24. David Robinson, *The Unitarians and the Universalists* (Westport, Connecticut: Greenwood Press, 1985), p. 12.

25. Seaburg, "Ministries," p. 41.

26. John Eliot of Roxbury was the first in a long line of Eliots, whose later generations became Unitarians serving the American Unitarian Association well into the twentieth century.

27. Pettee, "Grand and Holy Revolution," p. 2.

28. In "King Philip's War", 52 of 90 Puritan towns were destroyed along with 8000 cattle. The Puritan death toll was somewhere around 2000, the Indian death toll about twice that number. In relative terms, historians see it as one of the most disastrous wars in American history. See James Henretta and Gregory Nobles, *Evolution and Revolution: American Society, 1600–1820* (D.C. Heath, 1987), p. 39. On Eliot's role of protest, see T. H. Breen and Timothy Hall, *Colonial America in an Atlantic World* (New York: Pearson Longman, 2004), p. 183.

29. See *Connecticut's Heritage Gateway*, at www.ctheritage.org, and Jere Daniell, *Encyclopedia of North American Indians*, at http://college.hm co.com/history/readscomp/naind/html/na_010702_dartmouth-col.htm.

30. Brant later took the side of the British in the American Revolution.

31. Robinson, *Unitarians and Universalists*, p. 15.

32. Robinson, *Unitarians and Universalists*, p. 16.

33. Robinson, *Unitarians and Universalists*, p. 19.

34. Robinson, *Unitarians and Universalists*, p. 19.

35. Robinson, *Unitarians and Universalists*, p. 47.

36. Robinson, *Unitarians and Universalists*, pp. 12–14.

37. Cited in Robinson, *Unitarians and Universalists*, p. 13.

38. Gary Nash, *The Urban Crucible: The Northern Seaports and the Origins of the American Revolution* (Cambridge, MA, Harvard University Press, 1986), pp. 118–19.

39. Nash, *Urban Crucible*, p. 116.

40. Robinson, *Unitarians and Universalists*, pp. 20, 50.

41. Robinson, *Unitarians and Universalists*, p. 50.

42. Robinson, *Unitarians and Universalists*, p. 313.

43. Robinson, *Unitarians and Universalists*, pp. 47–50.

44. Russell E. Miller, *The Larger Hope: The First Century of the Universalist Church in America, 1770–1870* (Boston: Unitarian Universalist Association, 1979), pp. 3–10.

45. Miller, *Larger Hope: First Century*, pp. 14–15.

46. Miller, *Larger Hope: First Century*, p. 18.

47. Miller, *Larger Hope*, pp. 18–19.

48. The work of Benjamin Rush on alcoholism is discussed by Pettee in "Holy Revolution," pp. 12–13.

49. Charles Howe, "Benjamin Rush," *Dictionary of Unitarian Universalist Biography* (UUHS), 1999–2004.

50. The Westminster Confession is a Reformed confession of faith, formulated according to Calvinist theology. Though it was drawn up in 1646 by the Westminster Assembly of the Church of England, it became the theological standard for many Protestant sects.

51. George Huntston Williams, "Three Recurrent Conflicts," and Conrad Wright, "The Early Period (1811–1840)" in *The Harvard Divinity School: Its Place in Harvard University and in American Culture*, ed. George Huntston Williams (Boston: Beacon Press, 1954), pp. 3–6, 21–24.

52. Conrad Wright, "American Unitarianism in 1805," *The Journal of Unitarian Universalist History*, Vol. XXX (2005), pp. 1–35.

53. Wright, "Unitarianism in 1805," pp. 8–12.

54. Wright, "Unitarianism in 1805," p. 11.

55. Wright, "Unitarianism in 1805," p. 11.

56. Wright, "Unitarianism in 1805," pp. 17–18.

57. Cited in Wright, "Unitarianism in 1805," p. 22.

58. With Thomas Jefferson as governor, Virginia enacted the Virginia Statute of Religious Freedom, releasing anyone from paying a tax in support of the Anglican, or state church.

59. Shadle, "True Church of Democracy," p. 8.

CHAPTER TWO:
The Early Liberal Moralists

60. Conrad Wright, *The Unitarian Controversy: Essays on American Unitarian History* (Boston: Skinner House Books, 1994), pp. 13–16. See the chapter "The Election of Henry Ware" for a more detailed account.

61. Wright, in Williams, ed., *Harvard Divinity School*, pp. 39–41.

62. Wright, in Williams, ed., *Harvard Divinity School,* pp. 36–37.

63. Robinson, *Unitarians and Universalists*, pp. 225–26.

64. Wright, "Unitarianism in 1805," pp. 18–19.

65. Robinson, *Unitarians and Universalists*, p. 27.

66. Robinson, *Unitarians and Universalists*, pp. 26, 226.

67. Frank Carpenter, "William Ellery Channing," *Dictionary of Unitarian Universalist Biography*, 2004.

68. Carpenter, "William Ellery Channing," *Dictionary of Unitarian Universalist Biography*, 2004.

69. Conrad Wright, *The Unitarian Controversy*, p. 162.

70. Wright, in Williams, ed., *Harvard Divinity School*, pp. 21–27.

71. William Ellery Channing, "Unitarian Christianity," in *Three Prophets of Religious Liberalism: Channing, Emerson, Parker,* ed. Conrad Wright (Boston: Beacon Press, 1961), pp. 47–89.

72. Robinson, *Unitarians and Universalists*, p. 29. David Robinson notes an irony in the fact that the liberal movement was more clearly defined by their stress on moral culture and the corresponding rejection of innate depravity than by their anti-Trinitarianism. In the same vein, Conrad Wright states, "Anti-Trinitarian they were, to be sure . . . [but] their basic disagreement with orthodoxy was over the nature of man and the doctrines of grace. See Wright, Introduction to *Three Prophets of Religious Liberalism*, p. 7.

73. Edward H. Madden, "William Ellery Channing: Philosopher, Critic of Orthodoxy, and Cautious Reformer," *Transactions of the Charles S. Pierce Society*, Vol. XXXIII:3 (1997), p. 577.

74. Madden (and others) note that the ascetic practices Channing undertook as a youth had permanently damaged his health. See Madden, p. 578.

75. David Robinson, Introduction, *William Ellery Channing: Selected Writings*, ed. David Robinson (New York: Paulist Press, 1985), p. 26.

76. Madden, "William Ellery Channing," p. 580.

77. Robinson, ed., *William Ellery Channing*, p. 27.

78. Madden, "Channing," pp. 580–83.

79. Madden, "Channing," p. 583.

80. Madden, "Channing," p. 584.

81. Michelle Walsh, "Joseph Tuckerman's Theology of Community Ministry and Contemporary Unitarian Universalist Theological Struggles," unpublished paper, Andover Newton Theological School, 2003.

82. See Jedidiah Mannis, "Joseph Tuckerman," *Dictionary of Unitarian Universalist Biography*, 2004.

83. Michelle Walsh, "The Dual Missionary: Revisiting the Depth and Intent of Joseph Tuckerman's Theological Vision and Work," unpublished paper, Andover-Newton Theological Seminary, 2003.

84. Frank Carpenter, "William Ellery Channing," *Dictionary of Unitarian Universalist Biography*.

85. Tuckerman looked to the ideas of Scottish social scientist and moral theologian, Thomas Chalmers, who advocated rational relief through friendly visitation. See Joseph Tuckerman, *Joseph Tuckerman on the Elevation of the Poor, With an Introduction by E. E. Hale* (Boston: Roberts Brothers, 1874).

86. Charles H. Lyttle, *Freedom Moves West: A History of the Western Unitarian Conference, 1852–1952* (Boston: Beacon Press, 1952), p. 108.

87. The main proponent of asylum reform was Unitarian Dorothea Dix, whose story appears later in this book. Horace Mann, better known as an advocate for public schools, was also involved in this work.

88. Mannis, "Tuckerman," p. 2.

89. Joseph Tuckerman, "Second Semiannual Report of the Second Year of His Service as Minister-At-Large" (Boston, Massachusetts, 1828).

90. Tuckerman, "Second Semiannual Report," 1828.

91. David Pettee, interview with Kathleen Parker, March, 2005.

92. William Ellery Channing, "Charge to the Ministers, Ordination of Charles F. Barnard and Frederick T. Gray" (1835), in *The Works of William E. Channing, D.D.* (Boston: American Unitarian Association, 1891).

93. Channing, "A Discourse on the Life and Character of The Rev. Joseph Tuckerman," Warren Street Chapel, January 31, 1841, in *The Works of William E. Channing*, pp. 578–99.

94. Robinson, *Unitarians and Universalists*, p. 322; Wright, in Williams, *Harvard Divinity School*, p. 55.

95. Wright, in Williams, ed., *Harvard Divinity School*, pp. 56–57.

96. Cited by Wright, in Williams, ed., *Harvard Divinity School*, p. 57.

97. Wright, in Williams, ed., *Harvard Divinity School*, p. 57.

98. Daniel Walker Howe, *The Unitarian Conscience: Harvard Moral Philosophy, 1805–1861* (Cambridge, MA: Harvard University Press, 1970), p. 15.

99. Cited in Robinson, *Unitarians and Universalists*, p. 322.

100. Robinson, *Unitarians and Universalists*, p. 56.

101. Robinson, *Unitarians and Universalists*, p. 64.

102. Robinson, *Unitarians and Universalists*, p. 65.

103. This story is told in much greater detail in James Sherblom, "The Reverend Thomas Whittemore: Engaging Life Fully in the Early Nineteenth Century," unpublished paper, 2003.

104. John Greenleaf Adams, *Memoir of Thomas Whittemore* (Boston: Universalist Publishing House, 1878), p. 86.

105. John Greenleaf Adams, *Fifty Notable Years: Views of the Ministry of Christian Universalism during the Last Half-Century* (Boston: Universalist Publishing House, 1883), p. 112.

106. Robinson, *Unitarians and Universalists*, p. 68.

107. See Cassara, "Thomas Whittemore," in *Dictionary of Unitarian Universalist Biography*, and Sherblom, "Engaging Life Fully," p. 19.

108. Cassara, "Whittemore," in *Dictionary of Unitarian Universalist Biography*.

109. Sherblom, "Engaging Life Fully."

CHAPTER THREE:
The "New Religion"

110. Frank Schulman, "Ralph Waldo Emerson," in *Dictionary of Unitarian Universalist Biography*.

111. Schulman, "Emerson," in *Dictionary of Unitarian Universalist Biography*.

112. Sydney Ahlstrom, "The Middle Period, 1840–1889" in Williams, ed., *Harvard Divinity School*, pp. 79–80.

113. This essay is cited in Scott Russell Sanders, "Road into Chaos and Old Night: Emerson as Essayist" in *Journal of UU History*, Vol. XXIX, 2003, p. 23.

114. Wright, in Williams, ed., *Harvard Divinity School*, p. 71.

115. Ralph Waldo Emerson, "Divinity School Address," in *Three Prophets of Liberalism: Channing, Emerson, Parker*, pp. 95–98.

116. Emerson, "Divinity School Address," in Wright, ed., *Three Prophets*, p. 100.

117. Wright argues that Emerson was indirectly reflecting on the limitations of the Rev. Barzillai Frost, the minister at the church he attended in Concord.

118. Emerson, *Three Prophets*. pp. 100–11.

119. Sanders, "Road into Chaos," p. 26.

120. Ralph Waldo Emerson, "Self-Reliance," in *American Ground: Vistas, Visions and Revisions,* ed. Robert H. Fossum and John K. Roth (New York: Paragon Publishers, 1988), pp. 164–67.

121. David Robinson, ed., *The Political Emerson: Essential Writings on Politics and Social Reform* (Boston: Beacon Press, 2004), p. 4.

122. Emerson quoted in "Introduction," in Robinson, *The Political Emerson*, p. 7.

123. Robinson, *Political Emerson*, p.30–31.

124. Lawrence Buell, "Emerson's Significance for the Twenty-First Century" in *Journal of UU History*, Vol XXIX, 2003, p. 42.

125. Robinson, *Political Emerson*, p. 56.

126. Emerson, "American Slavery," in Robinson, *Political Emerson*, pp. 122–27.

127. Emerson, "John Brown," in Robinson, *Political Emerson*, p. 157.

128. Robinson, *Unitarians and Universalists*, p. 80-81.

129. Cited in Joan Goodwin, "Margaret Fuller," in *Dictionary of Unitarian Universalist Biography*. The quotation is from *A History of Woman Suffrage*, by Stanton and Anthony (1881).

130. Bell Gale Chevigny, "Margaret Fuller," in *Portraits of American Women: From Settlement to the Present*, ed. G.J. Barker-Benfield and Catherine Clinton (New York: St. Martin's Press, 1991), p. 194.

131. Joan Goodwin, "Margaret Fuller," *Dictionary of Unitarian Universalist Biography*.

132. Chevigny, "Fuller," in *Portraits*, p. 195.

133. Chevigny, "Fuller," in *Portraits*, p. 200.

134. Chevigny, "Fuller," in *Portraits*, p. 199.

135. Paula Blanchard, "Biographical Sketch of Margaret Fuller," in *Standing Before Us: Unitarian Universalist Women and Social Reform, 1776–1936*, ed. Dorothy May Emerson (Boston: Skinner House Books, 2000), pp. 27–28

136. See "Conversations," in Emerson, ed., *Standing Before Us*, p. 184.

137. Laurie James suggests that the relationship between Fuller and Emerson experienced a rift after she pressed the subject of marriage and he "put an end to her suppositions." See Laurie James, "Margaret Fuller," in *Journal of UU History*, Vol. XXIX, 2003, p. 89

138. Northern opponents viewed the annexation of Texas as a southern strategy to expand slavery.

139. See Chevigny, "Fuller," in *Portraits*, pp. 200–01.

140. See Goodwin, "Fuller," in *Dictionary of Unitarian Universalist Biography*.

141. Chevigny, "Fuller," in *Portraits*, p. 204–205.

142. James, "Margaret Fuller," *Journal of UU History*, Vol. XXIX, p. 90.

143. David Robinson, *Unitarians and Universalists*, p. 235.

144. This story is told in Robinson, *Unitarians and Universalists*, pp. 93–95

145. Gregory McGonigle, "James Freeman Clarke," *Dictionary of Unitarian Universalist Biography*, 2007.

146. McGonigle, "Clarke," in *Dictionary of Unitarian Universalist Biography.*

147. Alan D. Hodder, "James Freeman Clarke," in *Dictionary of Literary Biography 235: The American Renaissance in New England*, ed. Wesley T. Mott (Detroit: Gale Group, 2001), pp. 63–76.

148. Robinson, in *Unitarians and Universalists*, pp. 104–05.

149. McGonigle, "James Freeman Clarke," in *Dictionary of Unitarian Universalist Biography,* 2007.

150. Ahlstrom, in Williams, ed., *Harvard Divinity School*, p. 113.

151. This appeared in Clarke's "Vexed Questions in Theology," 1886; cited in McGonigle, "James Freeman Clarke," in *Dictionary of Unitarian Universalist Biography,* 2007.

CHAPTER FOUR:
Community Ministers-at-Large in the West

152. David Robinson writes that liberal ministers in the west faced "a kind of cultural isolation that was debilitating." See *Unitarians and the Universalists*, pp. 93–94.

153. Cahokia was a powerful confederation of Mississippian Indian towns clustered around a large raised area identified later as Monk's Mound. It reached its height of power in the period from 900 to 1300 C.E. and broke up for reasons that are not entirely clear. By the early modern period, when the Spanish, French, and English colonizers first arrived in North America, Cahokia was gone, but the region remained a vital center of development to later generations of Indians, traders, and settlers.

154. Lyttle, *Freedom Moves West*, p. 36.

155. Earl Holt, *William Greenleaf Eliot: Conservative Radical* (St Louis: First Unitarian Church, 1985), p. 24.

156. Holt, *WG Eliot*, p. 49.

157. Holt, *WG Eliot*, p. 32. Eliot made this remark to James Freeman Clarke in a letter penned from Pittsburgh on Oct. 16, 1834.

158. Lyttle, *Freedom Moves West*, pp. 73–74. This story is told in more detail in Kathleen Parker, *"Comrades in a Common Cause": The Arrival and Development of Unitarian Universalism in Western Pennsylvania, 1820–2000*, forthcoming in 2008.

159. Frederic was unable to complete the ministerial curriculum at Harvard because of his bad eyesight. He pursued further studies in Germany after leaving Harvard.

160. Lyttle, *Freedom Moves West*, p. 72.

161. Quoted in Ahlstrom, in Williams, ed., *Harvard Divinity School*, p. 91.

162. Francis A. Christie, *The Makers of the Meadville Theological School* (Boston: Beacon Press, 1927), p. 181.

163. A measure of the affection Peabody felt for the Huidekoper family may be seen in his naming one of his daughters after Harm's daughter: Anna Huidekoper Peabody.

164. Frank Carpenter, "Ephraim Peabody," in *Dictionary of Unitarian Universalist Biography*.

165. Ronald Walters, *American Reformers: 1815–1860* (New York: Hill and Wang, 1981, 1997), p. 215.

166. This story is recounted in David Pettee, unpublished manuscript, and in Charles Lyttle, *Freedom Moves West*, pp. 104–05.

167. Collyer turned to the anti-slavery movement after hearing a speech given by Lucretia Mott, who was with the American delegation to the first International Anti-Slavery Convention in London in 1840.

168. Lyttle, *Freedom Moves West*, p. 104.

169. In this instance, the Ministry-at-Large was created as a special office, referred to by name in upper case letters.

170. Lyttle, *Freedom Moves West*, pp. 51, 105.

171. See Celeste DeRoche and Peter Hughes, "Thomas Starr King," in *Dictionary of Unitarian Universalist Biography*.

172. DeRoche and Hughes, "Thomas Starr King," in *Dictionary of Unitarian Universalist Biography*.

173. DeRoche and Hughes, "Barton," in *Dictionary of Unitarian Universalist Biography*.

174. Russell E. Miller, *The Larger Hope: The Second Century of the Universalist Church in America, 1870–1970* (Boston: UUA, 1985), pp. 341–60.

175. The other Universalist school was Crane Theological School at Tufts College, located in Medford, Massachusetts.

176. Miller, *The Second Century*, p. 343.

177. As General Missionary for the Universalist Church of American, Shinn visited Duluth, MN, Dubuque and Des Moines, IA, Kansas City, MO, Spokane, Seattle, and Tacoma, WA, San Francisco and Los Angeles, CA, Birmingham, AL, Atlanta and Americus, GA, Little Rock, AK, and many other cities. See Miller, as well as David A. Johnson, "A Burr under the Buckle of the Bible Belt," a sermon delivered at the Southwest Unitarian Universalist Summer Institute, available at www.swuuc.org/resources/sermons/swuusi4.htm.

178. Robinson, *Unitarians and Universalists*, pp. 72–73.

179. Robinson, *Unitarians and Universalists*, p. 320.

180. Miller, *The Second Century*, p. 358. After Shinn's death, states created superintendents to carry on the work he had done.

PART II
Liberal Religion and Antebellum Reform

CHAPTER FIVE:
Utopian Societies as Community Ministry

181. Walters, *American Reformers*, p. 40.

182. Miller, *The Larger Hope: the Second Century*, p. 352.

183. We have seen in particular how Channing's early stand against slavery led to his being rebuked by the congregation he had served for three decades.

184. Peter Hughes, "Adin Ballou," in *Dictionary of Unitarian Universalist Biography*.

185. Pettee, "Grand and Holy Revolution," p. 16; Walters, *American Reformers*, pp. 50–51.

186. See http://www.AdinBallou.org , where is found excerpts from Andrew Dickson's *Autobiography* and *The Kingdom of God is Within You*, by Leo Tolstoy.

187. Walters, *American Reformers*, pp. 50, 54, 60; Hughes, "Adin Ballou," in *Dictionary of Unitarian Universalist Biography*.

188. George Tindall and David Shi, *America: A Narrative History*, Fourth Edition, Vol. I (New York: W. W. Norton & Company, 1996), pp. 525. Emerson considered Bronson Alcott the heart and soul of the club.

189. David Robinson, "Transcendentalism and the Utopian Mentality," lecture, Oregon State University, 1997, available at http://oregonstate.edu/ Dept/philosophy/club/utopia/utopian-visions/rob.

190. See David Robinson, "George Ripley," in *Dictionary of Unitarian Universalist Biography*.

191. Robinson, "Ripley," in *Dictionary of Unitarian Universalist Biography*.

192. Robinson, "Ripley," in *Dictionary of Unitarian Universalist Biography*.

193. Nathaniel Hawthorne's *The Blithedale Romance* is the most well known for its darkly fictional depiction of life in the community.

194. Miller, *The Second Century*, pp. 469–70.

195. *Harbinger* quotes are found in Miller, *The Second Century*, p. 470.

196. According to Pettee, a core group from Brook Farm continued to meet every summer for sixty years in the foothills of the Adirondack Mountains, to live again the Brook Farm life.

CHAPTER SIX:
Ordained Ministers as Reformers

197. The term "self-culture" was not used exclusively by Unitarians. It referred to the cultivation of personal awareness and spiritual depth in ways that inspired one to improve one's self and to better society. Often this meant practicing and promoting temperance.

198. See Dennis Landis, "Samuel Joseph May," in *Dictionary of Unitarian Universalist Biography*, 2003.

199. Landis, "Samuel Joseph May," in *Dictionary of Unitarian Universalist Biography*.

200. This was the famous case of Prudence Crandall, against whom the townsfolk passed a "black law," stipulating that no black persons from other states could be educated in Connecticut. Further, neighbors poisoned her well with horse manure, local establishments refused to sell to her, and church doors previously open to her were closed. This was when she turned to Samuel May. See Leonard L. Richards, *Gentlemen of Property and Standing: Anti-Abolition Mobs in Jacksonian America* (New York: Oxford University Press, 1970), pp. 38–40.

201. Landis, "Samuel Joseph May," in *Dictionary of Unitarian Universalist Biography.*

202. Landis, "Samuel Joseph May," in *Dictionary of Unitarian Universalist Biography.*

203. The Berry Street Lecture is the oldest continuing annual Unitarian Universalist lecture, still given yearly at General Assembly.

204. Edward Bellamy, for instance, wrote a socialist utopian novel, *Looking Backward*, in which the protagonist wakes up in the year 2000, after falling asleep in 1887, to find a socialist utopia of shared work and shared material benefit. Bellamy's book sold a phenomenal 160,000 copies in its first two years of publication and was translated into five languages.

205. John Buescher, "Charles Spear" and "John Murray Spear," in *Dictionary of Unitarian Universalist Biography.*

206. Walters, *American Reformers*, p. 101. In his condemnation of slavery, William Lloyd Garrison refused to vote for thirty years, until he voted for Lincoln in 1864, due to Lincoln's Emancipation Proclamation.

207. Buescher, "Charles Spear," in *Dictionary of Unitarian Universalist Biography.*

208. Buescher, "John Murray Spear," in *Dictionary of Unitarian Universalist Biography.*

209. Walters, *American Reformers*, pp. 131–146.

210. Walters, *American Reformers*, p. 12.

211. Later in his life, Higginson acknowledged his excesses in temperance work and attributed them to youthful lack of moderation. See "Thomas Wentworth Higginson: A Representative Life of the 1850s," at www.assumption.edu/ahc/HigginsonDefault.html.

212. Walters describes the "missionary impulse" of evangelical reformers and their drive toward "perfectionism" in themselves and in society: "They wanted to make things right." What became clear over time was that evangelicals were not alone in their reform-minded work. "Some were Unitarians and Universalists," who by the measure of their actions, "came out better than any number of revivalist preachers." See Walters, *American Reformers*, pp. 28, 36.

213. Tindall and Shi, *America: A Narrative History*, p. 474. Tindall writes that "Burns would be the last fugitive slave to be returned from Boston and was himself soon freed through purchase by Boston's black community."

214. The members who burned their documents or issued disclaimers were Samuel Gridley Howe, Franklin Sanborn, and millionaire Gerrit Smith.

215. The Missouri Compromise limited slavery to Missouri and territories south of its southern border; the Compromise of 1850 opened up Utah and New Mexico territories to the possibility of slavery via popular sovereignty.

216. Dean Grodzins, "Theodore Parker," in *American Renaissance in New England*, p. 319.

217. Dean Grodzins, "Theodore Parker," in *Dictionary of Unitarian Universalist Biography*.

218. The violence in Kansas was the result of a compromise bill (Kansas-Nebraska Act of 1854) allowing Kansas citizens popular sovereignty on the question of slavery. Popular sovereignty backfired, as pro-slavery and anti-slavery proponents flooded into Kansas from outside the territory and engaged in armed warfare against each other. Referred to then as "Bleeding Kansas," these events were a telling prelude of what was to come in the Civil War.

219. David Bumbaugh, *Unitarian Universalism: A Narrative History* (Chicago: Meadville Lombard Press, 2000), p. 125; Robinson, *Unitarians and Universalists*, pp. 84–85.

220. Bumbaugh, *A Narrative History*, p. 126.

221. Grodzins, "Theodore Parker," in *American Renaissance in New England*, p. 311.

222. Grodzins, "Theodore Parker," in *American Renaissance in New England*, p. 322.

CHAPTER SEVEN:
Reform Work as Lay Community Ministry

223. Walters, *American Reformers*, pp. 35–37.

224. Joan Goodwin, "Biographical Sketch of Lydia Maria Child," in Emerson, ed., *Standing Before Us*, pp. 295–97.

225. Linda Brent, *Incidents in the Life of a Slave Girl: An Authentic Historical Narrative Describing the Horrors of Slavery as Experienced by Black Women*, with an introduction by Lydia Maria Child (1861), (New York: Harcourt Brace Jovanovich, Publishers, 1973), pp. xi–xii.

226. The text of these letters is found at http://womenshistory.about.com/ library/etext/bl_lmc_as1_03.htm.

227. Joan Goodwin, "Lydia Maria Child," in *Dictionary of Unitarian Universalist Biography.*

228. Janeen Grohsmeyer, "Frances Harper," in *Dictionary of Unitarian Universalist Biography.*

229. Qiyamah Rahman, "Biographical Sketch of Frances Ellen Watkins Harper," in Emerson, ed., *Standing Before Us,* p. 104.

230. An excerpt is in Grohsmeyer, "Frances Harper," in *Dictionary of Unitarian Universalist Biography.* The full text of the letter is in Emerson, ed., *Standing Before Us,* pp. 358–59.

231. James K. Hosmer, son of the Rev. Dr. George Hosmer, minister of the First Unitarian Church of Buffalo, where President Fillmore was a member, wrote that his father had spoken of Fillmore at the former president's death, saying, "I dissented utterly from the Fugitive Slave Bill which was put forward to save the country from civil war." Dr. Hosmer added that Fillmore had said to him, "It is better to do that than that half the nation should be butchered." Dr. Hosmer argued that Fillmore had dreaded war and would by any means prevent such a calamity from happening. He then allowed, "Now all can see, and some saw it then, it was only postponing the horror." See James K. Hosmer, "Testimony, Tribute and Reminiscences from Friends unable to be Present on 'Fillmore Evening,'" Minneapolis, MN, December 7, 1898. Found at http://library5.library.cornell.edu/Hunter/hunter.pl?handle=cornell.library.nys/nys279&id=1.

232. Margaret Harrelson, "Biographical Sketch on Sallie Holley," in Emerson, ed., *Standing Before Us,* p. 340.

233. Among those who were at least uncomfortable with slavery, most believed it would be gradually abolition and eventually extinguished in the southern states. Garrison, on the other hand, insisted on immediate abolition and universal extinction everywhere, even in the South.

234. The New England Institute for the Blind was later renamed Perkins Institute for the Blind. Anne Sullivan and Helen Keller were its most famous students.

235. Joan Goodwin, "Julia Ward Howe," in *Dictionary of Unitarian Universalist Biography.* Goodwin notes that George Ripley, founder of Brook Farm, saw in Julia's work "a product wrung with tears and prayer from the deepest soul of the writer."

236. Wayne Viney, "Dorothea Dix," in *Dictionary of Unitarian Universalist Biography*.

237. Viney, "Dorothea Dix," in *Dictionary of Unitarian Universalist Biography*.

238. Viney, "Dorothea Dix," in *Dictionary of Unitarian Universalist Biography*.

239. Robert Divine, et al, *The American Story, Vol. I, to 1877*, (New York: Pearson Longman, 2007) p.319.

240. Walters, *American Reformers*, pp. 208–10.

241. See Charles Howe, "Mary and Daniel Livermore," in *Dictionary of Unitarian Universalist Biography*. Howe adds that William Ellery Channing's "Moral Argument against Calvinism" was especially convincing to Mary Livermore. See also Howe, "Daniel and Mary Livermore: The Biography of a Marriage," *Proceedings of the Unitarian Universalist Historical Society*, Vol. XIX, Part II (1982–83.)

242. Charles Howe, "Horace Greeley," in *Dictionary of Unitarian Universalist Biography*.

243. Sawyer successfully promoted the establishment of Universalist colleges and seminaries, as will be seen in the chapter on the Theological Schools.

244. Cited in Howe, "Horace Greeley," *Dictionary of Unitarian Universalist Biography*, 2007.

245. This is the same conference for which Emerson turned down an invitation to speak.

246. See Howe, "Greeley," in *Dictionary of Unitarian Universalist Biography*; also George Huntston Williams, *American Universalism*, Fourth Edition (Boston: Skinner House Books and Unitarian Universalist Historical Society, 1971), pp. 32–34.

247. Horace Greeley, "A Prayer for Twenty Millions," *New York Tribune*, August 20, 1862. Found at: http://mac110.assumption.edu/aas/Manu scripts/greeley.html.

248. Howe, "Greeley," in *Dictionary of Unitarian Universalist Biography*.

CHAPTER EIGHT:
Community Ministry in the Era of the Civil War

249. With the first of these compromises had come the infamous Fugitive Slave Law.

250. See Robinson, *Unitarians and Universalists*, pp. 90–91, and Lyttle, *Freedom Moves West*, p. 110.

251. Though Unitarians had disagreed over whether to take an open stand against slavery, they nonetheless joined together in support of the Union once the war began. Collyer supposedly confessed to knowing 500 biblical texts for peace, but after the firing at Fort Sumter, he could only think of one text, on which he preached the following Sunday: "Go sell thy garment and buy a sword." See Lyttle, p. 114.

252. Lyttle, *Freedom Moves West*, pp. 109–11.

253. Lyttle, *Freedom Moves West*, p. 112.

254. Dorothy Boroush, "Biographical Sketch of Julia Ward Howe," in Emerson, ed., *Standing Before Us*, p. 329.

255. See "Thomas Starr King's Statue" at www.aoc.gov/cc/art/nsh/king_t.cfm.

256. Kimberly Geiger, "State Lawmakers Vote to Replace Starr King's Statue with Reagan's," *San Francisco Chronicle*, September 1, 2006.

257. "Thomas Wentworth Higginson: A Representative Life of the 1850s," at www.assumption.edu/ahc/HigginsonDefault.html

258. Of the three Civil War Amendments, the Thirteenth Amendment prohibited slavery in the United States, the Fourteenth guaranteed the rights of citizenship (including due process of law), and the Fifteenth stated that the right to vote shall not be denied on account of race, color, or previous condition of servitude.

259. Margaret Harrelson, "Biographical Sketch on Sallie Holley," in Emerson, ed., *Standing Before Us*, 340.

260. Lyttle, *Freedom Moves West*, p. 105.

261. Material on Clara Barton is taken from Joan Goodwin, "Clara Barton," in *Dictionary of Unitarian Universalist Biography*, and from Janet Bowering, "Biographical Sketch of Clara Barton," in Emerson, ed., *Standing Before Us*, pp. 387–89.

262. See additional material on Barton, including quotes, in *Notable American Women: A Biographical Dictionary, 1607–1950*, ed. Edward T. James and Janet Wilson James (Cambridge: Harvard University Press, 1971), pp. 103–08.

263. This move was inspired by a Swiss banker, Jean Henri Dunant, who had been appalled by the suffering and hunger of wounded soldiers on the battlefield of Solferino in 1859. See James, ed., *Notable American Women*, p. 105.

264. James, ed., *Notable American Women*, p. 106.

265. This quotation is found in Joan Goodwin, "Barton," in *Dictionary of Unitarian Universalist Biography.*

266. Howe, "Mary Livermore," in *Dictionary of Unitarian Universalist Biography.*

267. Robinson, *Unitarians and Universalists*, pp. 130–31.

268. Howe, "Biography of a Marriage," *Proceedings of the Unitarian Universalist Society*, Vol. XIX, 1982–83

269. Rahman, "Frances Ellen Watkins Harper," in Emerson, ed., *Standing Before Us*, pp. 102–05. Beacon Press has reprinted Harper's novels. There is an interesting connection to be made here: Ida B. Wells (Barnett) took the pen name of Iola, perhaps borrowed from Harper's liberated female literary character.

270. Janeen Grohsmeyer, "Frances Harper," in *Dictionary of Unitarian Universalist Biography.*

271. Henry Whitney Bellows, *The Suspense of Faith: An Address to the Alumni of the Divinity School of Harvard University*, July 19, 1859 (New York: C. S. Francis, 1859).

272. Conrad Wright, *The Liberal Christians: Essays on American Unitarian History* (Boston: Beacon Press, 1970), pp. 85, 93–105. Also see David Bumbaugh, *A Narrative History*, 131.

273. See Mark Evans, "Henry Whitney Bellows," in *Dictionary of Unitarian Universalist Biography.*

274. "Jenkin Lloyd Jones," at http://www.harvardsquarelibrary.org.

275. Spencer Lavan, "Jabez Thomas Sunderland," in *Dictionary of Unitarian Universalist Biography.*

276. Lavan, "Sunderland," in *Dictionary of Unitarian Universalist Biography*; see also Robinson, *Unitarians and Universalists*, p. 7.

277. "Jenkin Lloyd Jones," at www.harvardsquarelibrary.org.

278. Lavan, "Sunderland," in *Dictionary of Unitarian Universalist Biography.*

PART III
After the War: From Gilded Age to Social Gospel

CHAPTER NINE:
Mid-Century Continuities: The Theological Schools

279. Robinson, *Unitarians and Universalists*, p. 319.

280. Charles Howe, "Thomas Jefferson Sawyer," in *Dictionary of Unitarian Universalist Biography*, 2007.

281. Howe, "Sawyer," in *Dictionary of Unitarian Universalist Biography*.

282. Charles Howe, "Theological School of St. Lawrence University," in *Dictionary of Unitarian Universalist Biography*, 2007.

283. The Canton Theological School successfully trained Universalist ministers until 1964. Rather than merge with any other Unitarian Universalist theological school, as was being recommended by the newly merged Unitarian Universalist Association, the Canton Board of Trustees voted to close the school. See Howe, "Theological School," in *Dictionary of Unitarian Universalist Biography*.

284. Cited in Howe, "Sawyer," in *Dictionary of Unitarian Universalist Biography*.

285. Ahlstrom, in Williams, ed., *The Harvard Divinity School*, p. 81.

286. Ahlstrom, in Williams, ed., *The Harvard Divinity School*, pp. 90–91.

287. Reynolds, in Williams, ed., *Harvard Divinity School*, p. 180.

288. The two volumes of this work are titled *A History of Unitarianism: Socinianism and Its Antecedents* (1945) and *A History of Unitarianism in Transylvania, England, and America to 1900* (1952).

289. Alan Seaburg, "Earl Morse Wilbur," in *Dictionary of Unitarian Universalist Biography*.

CHAPTER TEN:
Suffrage Pioneers as Lay Community Ministers

290. David Pettee, "Grand and Holy Revolution," p. 18.

291. Russell E. Miller, *The First Century*, pp. 845–48.

292. Nationally, the Alliance of Unitarian and Other Liberal Christian Women was founded in 1890.

293. Pettee, "Grand and Holy Revolution," p. 18.

294. See especially *One Woman One Vote: Rediscovering the Woman Suffrage Movement*, ed. Margery Spruill Wheeler (Troutdale, Oregon: New Sage Press, 1995), pp. 61–79; also see Emerson, ed., *Standing Before Us*, p. 33.

295. Lucy Stone's father had paid for her brothers to attend college, but refused to pay for her.

296. See Elea Kemler, "Biographical Sketch on Lucy Stone," in *Standing Before Us*, pp. 31–34.

297. Goodwin, "Julia Ward Howe," in *Dictionary of Unitarian Universalist Biography*.

298. Goodwin, "Julia Ward Howe," in *Dictionary of Unitarian Universalist Biography*.

299. Julia Ward Howe, *Reminiscences 1819–1899* (Boston: Houghton, Mifflin, 1900), p. 328.

300. Today's Mother's Day celebrates a domestic dependent view of women that may honor the concept of peace for the sake of family harmony, but gives little thought to the politics of world peace as Julia conceived it. Julia's words live on in the current Unitarian Universalist hymnbook, *Singing the Living Tradition,* and are often read on Mother's Day in Reading #573: "Mother's Day Proclamation."

301. Joan Goodwin, "Julia Ward Howe," in *Dictionary of Unitarian Universalist Biography*.

302. No doubt the failure of the family mill resulted from the Panic of 1837, referred to earlier in the discussion of Thomas Whittemore.

303. In 1893, Susan B. Anthony and her sister Mary signed the membership book at a church anniversary celebration. That record book is in the archives at the First Unitarian Church of Rochester, NY.

304. Elizabeth Griffith, *In Her Own Right: The Life of Elizabeth Cady Stanton* (New York: Oxford University Press, 1984), p. 74.

305. See Colleen Hurst, "Biographical Sketch of Susan B. Anthony," in Emerson, ed., *Standing Before Us*, pp. 49–52.

306. Lynn Sherr, ed., *Failure Is Impossible: Susan B. Anthony in Her Own Words* (New York: Times Books Random House), pp. 115–17.

307. Eleanor Flexner, *Century of Struggle: The Woman's Rights Movement in the United States* (New York: Atheneum, 1971), p. 220.

308. Alma Lutz, *Susan B. Anthony: Rebel, Crusader, Humanitarian* (Boston: Beacon Press, 1959), pp. 246–49.

309. Mary Earhart, *Frances Willard* (Chicago, 1944), p. 153, cited in Lutz, p. 323.

310. Paula F. Casey, "Essay on Woman Suffrage," in *American Encyclopedia of Social Movements*, ed. Immanuel Ness (Armonk, New York: Sharpe Reference, 2004). Matilda Joslyn Gage was staunchly opposed to the merger and was horrified at Anthony's efforts to ally with Frances Willard and the WCTU. Like Stanton, Gage had a more sweeping vision of reforms for women. Anthony, being more pragmatic, pushed the vote through when Gage was out of town.

311. In later years, Elizabeth Cady Stanton sought to broaden the goals of the movement beyond suffrage. As part of that effort, she blamed orthodox interpretations of the Bible as the chief cause of societal discrimination against women. She therefore prepared her own version of the Bible, removing or re-writing the passages that presented women in a negative light. *The Woman's Bible* offended even the most ardent suffragists, and Stanton was ostracized from the NAWSA.

312. See Kemler, "Lucy Stone," in Emerson, ed., *Standing Before Us*, p. 34.

313. Boroush, "Julia Ward Howe," in Emerson, ed., *Standing Before Us*, p. 330.

314. Lynn Sherr, ed., *Failure is Impossible*, p. 325.

CHAPTER ELEVEN:
Ordained Women Move Ministry Beyond Congregations

315. Catherine Hitchings, *Universalist and Unitarian Women Ministers* (Unitarian Universalist Historical Society, 1975, 1985), p. 6.

316. Hitchings, *Women Ministers*, p. 6. This quotation is from a letter from Roger F. Etz, General Superintendent of the Universalist Church to the Rev. Ward Brigham, May 23, 1935.

317. Hitchings, *Women Ministers*, p. 6. Letter from Roger F. Etz, to Ward Brigham, May 23, 1935.

318. See JoAnn Macdonald, "Antoinette Brown Blackwell," in *Dictionary of Unitarian Universalist Biography*.

319. McDonald, "Antoinette Brown Blackwell, in *Dictionary of Unitarian Universalist Biography*.

320. Rosalind Rosenberg discusses contemporary feminist intellectual responses to Charles Darwin's gendered theory of evolution (*The*

Descent of Man, 1871) in *Beyond Separate Spheres: Intellectual Roots of Modern Feminism* (New Haven: Yale University Press, 1982), p. 7.

321. See again Rosalind Rosenberg, *Beyond Separate Spheres,*, p. 16.

322. Laurie Carter Noble, "Olympia Brown," in *Dictionary of Unitarian Universalist Biography*.

323. Noble, "Olympia Brown," in *Dictionary of Unitarian Universalist Biography*.

324. It may be argued that this was the second ordination of a woman with full denominational authority. Although Olympia Brown is often cited as the first woman ordained with this authority (1863), a single item in the *Christian Ambassador* reports the ordination of Lydia Ann Jenkins by the Ontario Association of Universalists in Geneva, New York, in 1860. Jenkins and her husband first served as co-ministers of a Universalist society in Clinton, but after two years they became itinerant preachers. The Rev. Jenkins later took a medical degree and operated a homeopathic Hygienic Institute with her husband, thus making her one of the first ordained women community ministers. See Charles Howe, "Lydia Ann Jenkins," in *Dictionary of Unitarian Universalist Biography*.

325. Charles Howe, "Ebenezer Fisher," *Dictionary of Unitarian Universalist Biography*.

326. Noble, "Olympia Brown," in *Dictionary of Unitarian Universalist Biography*.

327. Noble, "Olympia Brown," in *Dictionary of Unitarian Universalist Biography*.

328. Noble, "Olympia Brown," in *Dictionary of Unitarian Universalist Biography*.

329. Mary Ann Porucznik and Glory Southwind, "Biographical Sketch on Augusta Jane Chapin," in Emerson, ed., *Standing Before Us*, pp. 437–40.

330. Porucznik and Southwind, "Chapin," in *Standing Before Us*, pp. 438–39.

331. Charles Howe, *The Larger Faith*, pp. 77–78. The text for each of these speeches is in Emerson, ed., *Standing Before Us*, pp. 447–48.

332. Porucznick and Southwind, p. 439.

333. Dennis Landis, "Celia Burleigh," in *Dictionary of Unitarian Universalist Biography*.

334. This quotation, and much of the material on Burleigh, is taken from the essay by Landis.

335. Dorothy May Emerson, "Biographical Sketch of Florence Ellen

Kollock," in Emerson, ed., *Standing Before Us*, 457–59.

336. Emerson, "Kollock," in Emerson, ed., *Standing Before Us*, p. 459.

337. See Koby Lee, "Biographical Sketch of Celia Parker Woolley," in Emerson, ed., *Standing Before Us*, pp. 492–95.

338. The Chicago Woman's Club, formed in 1876, should not be confused with the Woman's City Club of Chicago, formed in 1910. They were two distinct organizations.

339. June Edwards, "Biographical Sketch on Fannie Barrier Williams," in Emerson, ed., *Standing Before Us*, pp. 275–77.

340. Edwards, "Barrier Williams," in Emerson, ed., *Standing Before Us*, p. 276.

341. See June Edwards, "Fannie Barrier Williams," in *Dictionary of Unitarian Universalist Biography*.

342. See Susan Swan, "Biographical Sketch of Caroline Julia Bartlett Crane," in Emerson, ed., *Standing Before Us*, pp. 127–29.

343. Robinson, *Unitarians and Universalists*, p. 317.

344. See Helene Knox, "Reform in Religion," in Emerson, ed., *Standing Before Us*, pp. 410–11.

345. Celia Parker Woolley, "The Ideal Unitarian Church: From a Paper Read at the Western Unitarian Conference, Chicago, May 16, 1889," in Emerson, ed., *Standing Before Us*, pp. 486–92.

346. Mary Augusta Safford, "Obedience to the Heavenly Vision," (1889–1908), reprinted in *Standing Before Us*, pp. 496–500.

347. Eleanor Elizabeth Gordon, "Our Mission to Save by Culture," *Old and New*, September 1900. See Emerson, ed., *Standing Before Us*, pp. 131–34.

348. Helene Knox, "Reform in Religion," in Emerson, ed., *Standing Before Us*, pp. 405–12.

349. Dorothy Boroush, "Biographical Sketch of Marion Murdoch," in Emerson, ed., *Standing Before Us*, pp. 508–10.

350. See Melissa Ziemer, "Florence Buck," in *Dictionary of Unitarian Universalist Biography*.

351. Ziemer, "Florence Buck," in *Dictionary of Unitarian Universalist Biography*.

352. See Spencer Lavan, "Eliza Sunderland," in *Dictionary of Unitarian Universalist Biography*.

353. Lavan, "Eliza Sunderland," in *Dictionary of Unitarian Universalist Biography*.

354. Lavan, "Eliza Sunderland," in *Dictionary of Unitarian Universalist Biography.*

355. Knox, "Reform in Religion," in Emerson, ed., *Standing Before Us,* pp. 410–11.

356. Celia Parker Woolley, *The Western Slope* (1903), reprinted in Emerson, ed., *Standing Before Us,* p. 494.

CHAPTER TWELVE:
African Americans and Community Ministry

357. Mark Morrison-Reed, *Black Pioneers in a White Denomination* (Boston: Skinner House Books, 1980, 1994), pp. 1, 31–32.

358. Willard C. Frank, Jr., "Joseph Jordan," *Dictionary of Unitarian Universalist Biography.*

359. Willard C. Frank, Jr., "Joseph Jordan," *Dictionary of Unitarian Universalist Biography.*

360. Willard C. Frank, Jr., "Thomas E. Wise," in *Dictionary of Unitarian Universalist Biography.*

361. Frank adds the following note: Sadly, Jordan's young wife and their young son (named Richard Sweetser Jordan) died of tuberculosis within two years of Jordan's death.

362. Frank, "Thomas E. Wise," in *Dictionary of Unitarian Universalist Biography.*

363. Darlene Clark Hine, *Black Women in White: Racial Conflict and Cooperation in the Nursing Profession, 1890–1950* (Bloomington, IN: Indiana University Press, 1989), pp. 26–34; and Louis R. Harlan, "Booker T. Washington and the Politics of Accommodation," in *Black Leaders of the Twentieth Century,* John Hope Franklin and August Meier, eds., (Urbana: University of Illinois Press, 1982) pp. 1–18.

364. Frank, "Thomas E. Wise," in *Dictionary of Unitarian Universalist Biography.*

365. This story comes from an obituary for Annie Bizzell Jordan Willis, which appeared in the 1997 calendar of the Unitarian Universalist Women's Historical Society.

366. Douglas Stange, *Patterns of Anti-Slavery Among American Unitarians, 1831–1860* (Cranbury, NJ: Associated University Presses, Inc.), pp. 226–27.

367. This material on Egbert Ethelred Brown is drawn from a sermon delivered by the Rev. Ann C. Fox at the UU Society of Fairhaven, CT, available at www.uufairhaven.org/Ser2003Jan19.htm.

368. Morrison-Reed, *Black Pioneers*, p. 41.

369. Morrison-Reed, *Black Pioneers*, p. 44.

370. Morrison-Reed, *Black Pioneers*, p. 50.

371. Morrison-Reed, *Black Pioneers*, p. 57.

372. Letter from Secretary Patterson of the Fellowship Committee, February 1928. Quoted in Morrison-Reed, *Black Pioneers*, p. 73.

373. Morrison-Reed, Black Pioneers, p. 77.

374. Morrison-Reed, *Black Pioneers*, pp. 78–79.

375. Morrison-Reed, *Black Pioneers*, pp. 82–83.

376. Morrison-Reed, *Black Pioneers*, p. 86.

377. Morrison-Reed, *Black Pioneers*, p. 92.

378. Morrison-Reed, *Black Pioneers*, p. 95.

CHAPTER THIRTEEN:
Social Gospel: Allies for Racial and Economic Justice

379. The members of the Niagara Movement took their name from the place they met and because of the "mighty current" of protest they hoped to unleash. See www.math.buffalo.edu/~sww/0history/hwny-niagara-movement.html

380. Dorothy Senghas and Catherine Senghas, "Mary White Ovington," in *Dictionary of Unitarian Universalist Biography*.

381. Darlene Clark Hine, William C. Hine, and Stanley Harrold, *The African-American Odyssey* (Upper Saddle River, NJ: Prentice Hall, 2000), pp. 369–70.

382. Senghas and Senghas, "Ovington," in *Dictionary of Unitarian Universalist Biography*.

383. The original mission of the NAACP was to challenge state laws that discriminated against blacks in voting, public accommodations, and education.

384. In the 1892 Homestead Strike, Pennsylvania governor William Stone sent in 8000 state militia to put down the strike. The Pennsylvania militia had been employed routinely to protect strikebreakers and company

property in labor conflicts. See Nell Irvin Painter, *Standing at Armageddon: The United States, 1877–1919* (New York: W. W. Norton, 1987), pp. 110–14.

385. Robinson, *Unitarians and Universalists*, pp. 133–34.

386. Levering Reynolds, Jr., "The Later Years, 1880–1953" in Williams, ed., *Harvard Divinity School*, pp. 180–81.

387. Reynolds, in Williams, ed., *Harvard Divinity School.*

388. Reynolds, in Williams, ed., *Harvard Divinity School*, pp. 180–81.

389. Robinson discusses Peabody's book at length in *The Unitarians and the Universalists*, pp. 135–37.

390. Reynolds, in Williams, *Harvard Divinity School*, p. 182.

391. Jacob Dorn, "The Social Gospel and Socialism: A Comparison of the Thought of Francis Greenwood Peabody, Washington Gladden, and Walter Rauschenbusch," *Church History*, Vol. 62, No. 1 (March, 1993), pp. 82–100.

392. Robinson, *Unitarians and Universalists*, p. 136.

393. Robinson, *Unitarians and Universalists*, p. 137.

394. See Paul Sprecher, "John Haynes Holmes," in *Dictionary of Unitarian Universalist Biography.*

395. Sprecher, "Holmes," in *Dictionary of Unitarian Universalist Biography.*

396. Addams was struggling with the depression of not knowing what to do with her life. This story is told in G. J. Barker-Benfield, "Jane Addams," in *Portraits of American Women: From Settlement to the Present*, ed. G. J. Barker-Benfield and Catherine Clinton (New York: St. Martin's Press, 1991), pp. 339–65.

397. Barker-Benfield, *Portraits*, p. 357. Addams refers here to the demand that women conform to expected societal norms.

398. See Florence Kelley, "I Arrived at Hull House and Discovered the Sweating System," in *Women's America*, fourth edition, ed. Linda Kerber and Jane Sherron DeHart (New York: Oxford University Press, 1995), pp. 295–98. The author of this study, Florence Kelley, worked as chief factory inspector in Illinois until 1896; she returned to New York in 1899 to serve as general secretary of the National Consumers' League until 1932.

399. "Jane Addams," in *Historical Dictionary of Unitarian Universalism* , ed. Mark Harris (Lanham, MD: Scarecrow Press, 1973).

400. Miller, *The Larger Hope: The Second Century*, p. 513.

401. Miller, *The Larger Hope: The Second Century*, p. 513.

402. Emerson, "Florence Ellen Kollock Crooker," in Emerson, ed., *Standing Before Us*, pp. 457–59.

403. Miller, *The Larger Hope: The Second Century*, p. 514.

404. Bethany Union now also serves as the location for the Unitarian Universalist Women's Heritage Society's library of resources on Unitarian, Universalist, and Unitarian Universalist women.

405. Nell Irvin Painter, *Standing at Armageddon: The United States, 1877–1919* (New York: W. W. Norton, 1987), pp. 306–07.

PART IV
Twentieth-Century Challenges in Community Ministry

CHAPTER FOURTEEN:
The Politics of Peace Ministry

406. Sprecher, "John Haynes Holmes," in *Dictionary of Unitarian Universalist Biography*.

407. David B. Parke, "A Wave at Crest: Administration Reform and Depression, 1898–1934," in *A Stream of Light: A Short History of American Unitarianism*, Conrad Wright, ed. (Boston: Skinner House Books, 1975), pp. 102–03.

408. Cynthia Grant Tucker, *Prophetic Sisterhood: Liberal Women Ministers of the Frontier, 1880–1930* (Boston: Beacon Press, 1990), p. 216.

409. Painter, *Standing at Armageddon*, p. 335.

410. Parke, in Wright, ed., *Stream of Light*, pp. 103–04.

411. In a further irony, Holmes put forth a plea in January 1934 to help "stricken Germans" get out of Germany "while there is still time." At the same time, the ACLU presented a request that the AUA petition President Roosevelt to allow more immigrants to enter the U.S. from Germany. The minutes note: "no action was taken."See Parke, in Wright, ed., *Stream of Light*, p. 124.

412. Tucker, *Prophetic Sisterhood*, p. 217.

413. Robinson, *Unitarians and Universalists*, pp. 284–85.

414. Tucker, *Prophetic Sisterhood*, p. 218.

415. This material is taken in part from "Emily Greene Balch—Biography" found atwww.nobelprize.org/peace/laureates/1946/balch-bio.html.

416. Carrie A. Foster, *The Women and the Warriors: The U.S. Section of the Women's International League for Peace and Freedom, 1915–1946* (Syracuse, New York: Syracuse University Press, 1995), pp. 1–4, 34.

417. "Emily Greene Balch," at www.nobelprize.org.

418. Although Emily Balch had also affiliated for part of her life with the Quakers, she never severed her Unitarian connections.

419. Tucker, *Prophetic Sisterhood*, pp. 214–15.

420. Foster, *The Women and the Warriors*, p. 33.

421. Tucker, *Prophetic Sisterhood*, pp. 221–22.

422. Clare B. Fischer, "Aurelia Henry Reinhardt: President of Mills College," available at www.harvardsquarelibrary.org/unitarians/reinhardt.html.

423. Charles Howe, "Clarence Russell Skinner," in Dictionary of UU Biography.

424. It was thought that defense contractors had encouraged U.S. entry into World War I; it was also thought that the deaths of U.S. citizens on ships sunk by German submarines had obligated the U.S. government to respond. Thus, the Neutrality Acts prohibited U.S. companies from selling munitions to nations at war and warned U.S. citizens that if they traveled on ships belonging to belligerent nations, they did so at their own risk.

CHAPTER FIFTEEN:
Ministries of Institutional Leadership

425. Parke, in Wright, ed., *A Stream of Light*, p. 96.

426. Elizabeth Curtiss, "Samuel Atkins Eliot II," in *Dictionary of Unitarian Universalist Biography*.

427. Curtiss, "Samuel Atkins Eliot," in *Dictionary of Unitarian Universalist Biography*.

428. Curtiss, "S. A. Eliot," in *Dictionary of Unitarian Universalist Biography*.

429. Tucker, *Prophetic Sisterhood*, pp. 226–27.

430. Tucker, *Prophetic Sisterhood*, p. 225.

431. Curtiss, "S. A. Eliot,"in *Dictionary of Unitarian Universalist Biography*.

432. One estimate notes that in 1890 there were about 45,000 members; fifty years earlier, there had reportedly been several hundred thousand.See Howe, *The Larger Faith*, p. 76.

433. David E. Bumbaugh, *Unitarian Universalism: A Narrative History* (Chicago: Meadville Lombard Press, 2000), p. 175.

434. Howe, *The Larger Faith*, pp. 61–64.

435. Howe, *The Larger Faith*, pp. 77–79.

436. Howe, *The Larger Faith*, p. 83. Howe suggests that it was perhaps easier to gain support for union on an international level than on a national level.

437. Charles Howe, ed. *The Essential Clarence Skinner: A Brief Introduction to His Life and Writings* (Boston: Skinner House Books, 2005), pp. 2–4.

438. In addition to Francis Greenwood Peabody, the Social Gospel movement derived impetus from Washington Gladden, minister to the First Congregational Church of Columbus, Ohio. Gladden and his followers believed that social reform should come about through personal regeneration. In their efforts to mediate between managers and laborers, Social Gospelers emphasized the "brotherhood of man." After witnessing more violence in strikes, Gladden espoused socialism for the benefit of the masses. Peabody did not go that far. Both Peabody and Gladden held that God should be at the center of the good society. On Gladden, see Painter, *Standing at Armageddon*, pp. 103–04.

439. Howe, *The Essential Skinner*, p. 11.

440. Howe, *Essential Skinner*, p. 94.

441. Charles A. Howe, "Clarence Russell Skinner," in *Dictionary of Unitarian Universalist Biography*.

442. Howe, *Essential Skinner*, pp. 9–10.

443. Nicola Sacco and Bartolomeo Vanzetti were two Italian anarchists who were accused of committing a payroll robbery in South Braintree, Massachusetts, in 1920. Irregularities in their arrest and trial led many to believe their 1927 convictions were due solely to prejudice against them because of their political beliefs. In the 1931 Scottsboro case, nine black youths were convicted in an Alabama court of raping two white women. The Supreme Court overturned their convictions in 1932 because the judge had not assigned an attorney to defend them. Margaret Sanger founded the American Birth Control League and was arrested when she opened in New York City the first public clinic for counseling on contraception.

444. Howe, *The Larger Faith*, p. 97.

445. Howe, *Essential Skinner*, p. 17.

446. Howe, *Essential Skinner*, pp. 28–29.

447. Howe, *Essential Skinner*, p. 17.

448. Howe, "Skinner," in *Dictionary of Unitarian Universalist Biography*.

449. Howe, *The Larger Faith*, pp. 101–03.

450. In 1918, two Unitarian ministers met at the Western Unitarian Conference in Des Moines, Iowa. The Rev. Curtis Reese spoke on "The Religion of Democracy." Afterward, he was approached by the Rev. John Dietrich of Minneapolis, Minnesota, who said, "What you are calling the religion of democracy, I am calling Humanism." See Edwin H. Wilson, *Genesis of the Humanist Manifesto*, Chap. Two: The Background of Religious Humanism, www.infidels.org/library/modern/edwin_wilson/manifesto/ch2.html

    Both ministers were among the original signers of the *Humanist Manifesto*.

451. In 1933, thirty-four men, seventeen of whom were Unitarian ministers and laymen, signed the *Humanist Manifesto*. This document consisted of fifteen statements affirming the primacy of human-centered religion based on "a cooperative effort to promote social well-being."

452. Carol R. Morris, "It Was Noontime Here: Frederick May Eliot and the Unitarian Renaissance, 1934–1961," in Wright, ed., *Stream of Light*, p. 125.

453. At first this group was called the Commission *of* Appraisal.

454. Morris, "It Was Noontime" in Wright, ed., *Stream of Light*, pp. 127–28; Robinson, *Unitarians and Universalists*, p. 166.

455. Edith Fisher Hunter, "Sophia Lyon Fahs: Liberal Religious Educator, 1876–1978" in *Notable American Unitarians*, available at www.harvardsquarelibrary.org/unitarians/fahs.html. Hunter is also the author of *Sophia Lyon Fahs* (Boston: Beacon Press, 1952).

456. Edith Fisher Hunter, "Sophia Lyon Fahs: Liberal Religious Educator, 1876–1978."

457. Hunter, "Sophia Lyon Fahs," at www.harvardsquarelibrary.org/unitarians/fahs.html.

458. Morris, "It was Noontime," in Wright, ed., *Stream of Light*, p. 134. Morris cites David B. Parke's unpublished dissertation "The Historical and Religious Antecedents of the New Beacon Series in Religious Education."

459. Aurelia Isabel Henry Reinhardt, "Worship: Its Fundamental Place in Liberal Religion," from *The Report of the Commission on Appraisal*

(AUA, 1936), as excerpted in Emerson, ed., *Standing Before Us*, pp. 555–63.

460. Reinhardt, "Worship: Its Fundamental Place in Liberal Religion," excerpted in Emerson, ed., *Standing Before Us*, pp. 555–63.

461. Reinhardt, in Emerson, ed., *Standing Before Us*, pp. 565.

462. Cited in Robinson, *Unitarians and Universalists*, p. 162.

463. Morris, "It was Noontime," in Wright, ed., *Stream of Light*, p. 128.

464. Daniel Walker Howe, "At Morning Blest and Golden-Browed," in Wright, ed., *Stream of Light*, p. 35.

465. "Frederick May Eliot," available at www.harvardsquarelibrary.org/unitarians/eliot_f.html.

466. Morris, "It was Noontime," in Wright, ed., *Stream of Light*, pp. 138, 140–41.

467. Howe, *The Larger Faith*, pp. 105–07.

468. Howe, *The Larger Faith*, p. 108.

469. Howe, *The Larger Faith*, p. 108.

470. Howe, *The Larger Faith*, p. 109.

CHAPTER SIXTEEN:
Unitarians and Universalists at Mid-Century

471. Warren R. Ross, "A Precarious Path: The Bold Experiment of the Fellowship Movement," *UU World* November/December 2002.

472. Ross, "A Precarious Path: The Bold Experiment," in UU World, November/December, 2002.

473. The quotation is from the Rev. Dr. John C. Morgan, who succeeded Husbands in the late 1980s as a church growth consultant.

474. Robinson, *Unitarians and Universalists*, p. 156.

475. Morris, "It was Noontime," in Wright, ed., *Stream of Light*, p. 146.

476. Morris, "It was Noontime," in Wright, ed., *Stream of Light*, p. 149.

477. Ross, "Precarious Path."

478. Ross, "Precarious Path."

479. This quote comes from Laile Bartlett's book about the fellowship movement, *Bright Galaxy* (Beacon Press, 1960).

480. This paraphrases the views of Catherine Harris of the Boulder fellowship, in Ross, "Precarious Path."

481. See Morris, "It was Noontime," in Wright, ed., *Stream of Light*, p. 150. She is quoting from Alfred P. Stiernotte, *Frederick May Eliot: An Anthology* (Boston: Beacon Press, 1959).

482. Morris, in Wright, ed., *Stream of Light*, p. 131.

483. Howe, *The Larger Faith*, pp. 111–14, 117.

484. Morris, "It was Noontime," in Wright, ed., *Stream of Light*, p. 151. Also see "Progress of YRUU" in *Resources for Youth and Adults: A Fifteen-Year Review*, at www.uua.org/YRUU/governance/15yr/progress.htm.

485. Orloff Miller, e-mail communication to Patty Franz, February 22, 2001.

486. See "Campus Ministry: Caught between Their Mission and the Church," *LINK*, Fall 1990, cited in Mary Ann Macklin, *A Unitarian Universalist Campus Ministry Manual* (Boston: UUA, Young Adult Ministries Office, 1993), pp. 36–37.

487. Morris, "It was Noontime," in Wright, ed., *Stream of Light*, p. 154.

CHAPTER SEVENTEEN:
New Occasions Teach New Duties

488. Under this act, the creation of the Equal Employment Opportunity Commission provided a federal agency to investigate complaints of racial bias in hiring, compensation, and promotion.

489. Christopher L. Walton, "Selma 65: So Nobly Started," *UU World*, May/June, 2001.

490. Duncan Howlett, *No Greater Love: The James Reeb Story* (New York: Harper and Row, 1966), p. 154.

491. Howlett, *No Greater Love*, p. 157.

492. J. Ronald Engel, "For the Love of the World: The Public Ministry of James Reeb," in *Unitarian Universalism 1989: Selected Essays* (Boston: Unitarian Universalist Ministers' Association, 1989), pp. 117–28.

493. An account of this confrontation is told in "A Civil Rights Martyr Remembered: Rev. Clark Olsen's Memories of the Murder of Jim Reeb in Selma in 1965," *New York Times*, April 8, 2000.

494. Dana McLean Greeley, *25 Beacon Street and other Recollections* (Boston: Beacon Press, 1971), p. 107.

495. King's eulogy opened eloquently with a line from Shakespeare's *Romeo and Juliet* to describe Reeb's "radiant life": "And if he should die, take his body, and cut it into little stars. He will make the face of heaven so fine that all the world will be in love with night." The eulogy can be found at the Princeton Publications website as: "A Witness to Truth: Martin Luther King, Jr.'s Eulogy for PTS Alum James J. Reeb," *inSpire*, Vol. 6, No. 2, Winter 2002, also available at www.ptsem.edu/Publications/inspire.

496. Martin Luther King, Jr., "A Witness to Truth: Martin Luther King, Jr.'s Eulogy for PTS Alum James J. Reeb," *inSpire*, Vol. 6, No. 2, Winter 2002.

497. The words of this hymn are adapted from a poem entitled "The Present Crisis," written by abolitionist James Russell Lowell. Lowell opposed slavery and the Mexican War, by which he feared more land would be acquired for the spread of slavery. The NAACP took the title of its journal, *The Crisis*, from the title of this poem. In the Unitarian Universalist hymnbook *Singing the Living Tradition* (Boston: Beacon Press, 1993), the title line has been altered for gender neutrality, to read "Once to Every Soul and Nation" (#119).

498. Jesse Cavileer, interview with Kathleen Parker, Pittsburgh, PA, May 2004.

499. Linda Deafenbaugh, "The Reverend Jesse R. Cavileer (Dec. 7, 1916–June 4, 2004)" *The Northside Chronicle* (Pittsburgh, PA: Laurel Group Press, July 2004) pp. 6, 15.

500. Cavileer, interview with Parker, May, 2004.

501. Cavileer, interview with Parker, May 2004.

502. Deafenbaugh, "The Reverend Jesse R. Cavileer," *Northside Chronicle*, July 2004.

503. Walter and Martha Brethauer, interview with Kathleen Parker, Pittsburgh, PA, August 2004. The Brethauers are long-time members of the Allegheny Unitarian Universalist Church.

504. Neil Shadle, interview with Kathleen Parker, August 19, 2004.

505. Neil Shadle, "Community Ministry and the True Church of Democracy."

506. The Ministerial Fellowship Committee maintains and upholds professional standards of ministry. It serves an important function in connecting and credentialing the variety of people whose calls to ministry are as geographically dispersed as they are spiritually unique.

507. Howard Matson published his journal of reflections as *A Walk in the Village* (Nybro Press, 1988).

508. Howard Matson, *A Walk in the Village.*

509. The purpose of this act was "to ensure peace in the agricultural fields by guaranteeing justice for all agricultural workers and stability in labor relations." It gave state protection to farm workers to "act together to help themselves, to engage in union organizational activity. . . ." It further prohibited employers from "interfering with these rights." See *Agricultural Labor Relations Act Handbook* (Sacramento, California: Agricultural Labor Relations Board, 1975), p. 1.

510. Rosemary Matson, unpublished notes on the "Unitarian Universalist Migrant Ministry."

511. See Frances Cerra Whittelsey, "Dancing Through Life," *UU World* November/December 2004, pp. 37–41; and John Millspaugh, "Community Ministry Takes Many Forms," *UU World* September/October 2001.

512. Millspaugh, "Community Ministry."

513. Millspaugh, "Community Ministry."

514. Whittelsey, "Dancing Through Life," pp. 38, 40.

515. Whittelsey, "Dancing Through Life," p. 38.

516. "Let It Be a Dance" was published in 1978 and is printed in *Singing the Living Tradition* (# 311).

517. Whittelsey, "Dancing Through Life."

518. Daniel D. Hotchkiss, "Defining Community Ministry," paper prepared for the UUA Department of Ministry, August 1995.

519. In 1976, students at Starr King School convened a class called Specialized Ministry. Clearly interest in the subject had not evaporated.

520. Scotty McLennan, interview with Kathleen Parker, June 15, 2005.

521. Scotty McLennan, "A Vision of Community Ministry," in *The Challenge of Right Relationship*, p. 104.

522. McLennan, "A Vision of Community Ministry," in *The Challenge of Right Relationship*, p. 104.

523. It is worth noting that when McLennan took a new position at Stanford University in 2001, he felt he needed to affirm his Unitarian Universalist connections by being endorsed by an area UU congregation.

524. McLennan, "A Vision of Community Ministry," in *The Challenge of Right Relationship*, p. 103.

CHAPTER EIGHTEEN:
Engaging Social Change in the 1980s

525. Tom Chulak, interview with Kathleen Parker, March 28, 2005.

526. Orloff Miller, interview with Patty Franz, February 22, 2001.

527. Orloff Miller, interview with Kathleen Parker, July 23, 2005.

528. Miller, interview with Franz, 2001.

529. Orloff Miller, interview with Patty Franz and David Pettee, February 23, 2001.

530. Jeremy Taylor, interview with Kathleen Parker, August 11, 2004. In this conversation, Taylor reflected, "I am a UU minister today in part because of the debt I owe to LRY."

531. This project was founded by the Rev. George Johnson, an African American minister who received support from the Rev. Aaron Gilmartin, minister of the Mt. Diablo Unitarian Universalist Church in Walnut Creek, CA. The Mt. Diablo church has long been a strong supporter of racial justice work and community ministry. Jody Shipley, one of the leaders in the community ministry movement, came from this church.

532. Jeremy Taylor, "Social Action, Psycho-Spiritual Growth, and the Community Ministry of Dreams," unpublished essay, 2004.

533. See "Community Ministry: Conscience and Creativity," at http://www.jeremytaylor.com/pages/communityministry.html.

534. Jeremy Taylor, "Social Action, Psycho-Spiritual Growth, and the Community Ministry of Dreams," in *Called to Community: Community Ministry and Unitarian Universalism*, Dorothy May Emerson, ed., (Medford, Mass.: Rainbow Solutions, 2004), p. 70.

535. Taylor, interview with Parker, August 11, 2004.

536. James Zacharias, interviews with Dorothy Emerson, September, 2005. Follow up conversations with Kathleen Parker.

537. David Arksey, untitled notes for a sermon given at First Unitarian Church of Chicago, Illinois, November 1988.

538. David Arksey, "Necrology of Christopher Moore," *UUA Directory*, 1988, pp. 303–04.

539. Wallace P. Rusterholtz, *The First Unitarian Society of Chicago* (First Unitarian Church of Chicago, 1979), pp. 17–18, 25–26.

540. See Moore, "Necrology," and Rusterholtz, p. 26.

541. Chulak, interview withParker, March 28, 2005.

542. Steve Shick, interview with Kathleen Parker, March 26, 2005.

543. Crozer was an American Baptist school. In 1970 it joined with Colgate Rochester to become multi-denominational.

544. Stephen Shick, interview with Kathleen Parker, March 26, 2005.

545. Individual show titles included "Culture and the Bomb" and "Literature and the Bomb." Tapes of these shows are stored in the Peace Collection at the Swarthmore College Library. UUPN archival records are housed there as well.

546. Stephen Shick, interview with Kathleen Parker, July 30, 2005.

547. Shick, interview with Parker, July 30, 2005.

548. Shick, interview with Parker, August 3, 2005.

549. Shick, interview with Parker, August 3, 2005.

550. David Pettee, interview with Kathleen Parker, March 24, 2005.

551. See Sue Guist, *Peace Like a River: A Personal Journey Across America* (Ocean Tree Books, 1991).

552. Morrison-Reed, *Black Pioneers*, p. 189.

553. Mark Morrison-Reed, interview with Kathleen Parker, March 14, 2007.

554. These events are described in Morrison-Reed, *Black Pioneers*, pp. 189–92.

555. Leslie Westbrook, interview with Kathleen Parker, June 29, 2005.

556. Mark Morrison-Reed, *Black Pioneers*, p. 192.

557. Betty Reid, quoted in Morrison-Reed, *Black Pioneers*, p. 190.

558. Chulak, interview with Parker, March 28, 2005.

559. Chulak, interview with Parker, March 28, 2005.

560. See "UrbanUU: History of the Urban Ministry Efforts of the UUA from 1971-1998," at http://archive.uua.org/urbanuu/history.html.

561. The Urban Concerns and Ministry Committee was a committee of the UUA Board, formed in 1981 as the Urban Concerns Advisory Committee. The Urban Church Coalition, on the other hand, was an independent affiliate organization of the UUA. The two groups worked hand in hand to promote greater awareness of urban concerns within the UU movement.

562. This plan brought Rebecca Parker, Dan Aldridge, Tim Malone, and Chester McCall, among others, into dual fellowship.

563. Morrison-Reed, interview with Kathleen Parker, March 14, 2007.

564. Morrison-Reed, interview with Parker, 2007.

565. Sanford D. Horwitt, "Alinsky: Now More than Ever," *The Progress Report: Champion of the Nonsocialist Left*, Saul Alinsky and the Industrial Areas Foundation, at http://www.progress.org/alinsky.htm.

566. Chulak, interview with Parker, March 28, 2005.

567. Shick, interview with Parker, March 26, 2005.

568. Chulak, interview with Parker, March 28, 2005.

569. Rosemary Matson, *Unitarian Universalist Women and Religion Movement: The Beginnings, 1977–1981—A Memoir* (Pacific Central District Women and Religion Committee, 1997, 2001).

570. This story is told in greater detail in Rosemary Matson, *Unitarian Universalist Women and Religion Movement*.

571. Drafted and debated over a period of three years, the de-gendered and non-Theistic Seven Principles that emerged were voted on and approved at GA in 1984 and 1985. Upon final approval, the room was filled with "loud applause, sighs of relief, tears, and a few shrugs of 'wait and see.'" Warren R. Ross, *The Premise and the Promise: The Story of the Unitarian Universalist Association* (Boston: Skinner House Books, 2001), pp. 94–99.

572. David Pohl, Director of Ministry, reported on November 10, 1986 that women now made up twenty percent of all Unitarian Universalist ministers. Address given at the Community Focus Ministries Convocation, Boston, November 8–11, 1986.

573. See again, Rosemary Matson, *Unitarian Universalist Women and Religion Movement*.

574. See Jeremiah 7:18. [The word came to Jeremiah from the Lord, saying] "The children gather wood, and the fathers kindle the fire, and the women knead their dough, to make cakes for the queen of heaven, and to pour out drink offerings unto other gods, that they may provoke me to anger."

575. Shirley Ann Ranck, *Cakes for the Queen of Heaven* (Boston: UUA, 1986). Again, this process is described in Matson.

576. Shirley Ann Ranck, "The Unbroken Circle: A Short History of 'Cakes for the Queen of Heaven,'" unpublished paper, Carlsbad, California, 1987.

577. This later curriculum was funded and published by the Unitarian Universalist Women's Federation.

578. Here was a Unitarian Universalist counseling ministry patterned after the counseling ministry of James Zacharias in Seattle. The New Jersey

ministry was hampered in its development because its lead minister did not have the training to obtain a counseling license in the state of New Jersey, making it impossible for the counselors associated with the ministry to obtain third-party payments.

579. Deborah Pope-Lance, interview with Kathleen Parker, March 23, 2005.

580. Pope-Lance, interview with Parker, March 23, 2005.

581. Pope-Lance, interview with Parker, March 23, 2005.

582. Pope-Lance, interview with Parker, March 23, 2005.

PART V
Community Ministry Gains Formal Standing

CHAPTER NINETEEN:
Founding the Society for the Larger Ministry

583. Credit must go primarily to Dorothy Emerson, and also to Robert Rafford, for much of the research that made possible this account of organizational development.

584. Robert Rafford, interview with Kathleen Parker, June 21, 2005. The first vote to add religious education ministry barely passed.

585. Jody Shipley, cover letter to paper on community ministry, submitted to the Commission on Appraisal, August 25, 1986.

586. Shipley's cover letter to that paper, dated August 25, 1986, mentions having had "many conversations with students and fellowshipped ministers interested in Community Ministry." Shipley had the impression at the time that nothing came of her paper. No doubt her paper contributed to the long conversation that led the Commission on Appraisal to report in 1997 on "Interdependence: Renewing Congregational Polity," which addressed community ministry issues.

587. Elizabeth Ellis-Hagler, interview with Dorothy Emerson, August 20, 2005.

588. The Convocation had been conceived by Tom Chulak. Roberta Mitchell and Elizabeth Ellis-Hagler, both ministers at large with the Benevolent Fraternity, wrote the grant proposal.

589. David Pohl, "Community Focused Ministries," address to the Convocation on Community Focus Ministries November 10, 1986.

590. Pohl, "Community Focus Ministries."

591. Pohl, "Community Focus Ministries."

592. Shick, interview with Parker, March 26, 2005.

593. *Newsletter of the Community Focused Ministers* (Berkeley, California), January 1987.

594. *Newsletter of the Community Focused Ministers*, January 1987.

595. Beside Cole, the Steering Committee included Jody Shipley, Susan Starr, Jane Boyajian, Stephen Shick, John Frazier, and Thom Payne.

596. The UUA Board later voted on and approved the affiliate status of CFM.

597. Robert Rafford, interview with Kathleen Parker, September 24, 2005.

598. Rafford, interview with Parker, September 24, 2005.

599. Roberta K. Mitchell, letter to the Unitarian Universalist Denominational Grants Panel, August 31, 1987.

600. This statement is quoted from a Bay Area Ministries Brochure, representing the co-ministry of Jody Shipley and her partner, Marilyn Gentile, A.C.S.W., a counselor to the Gay and Lesbian Program at the University of California at Berkeley Counseling Center. Gentile also served on the UUA Women and Religion Committee, ran a private therapy practice, and taught Pastoral Counseling at Starr King School for the Ministry.

601. Members of the Planning Committee included David Gilmartin, Til Evans, Marilyn Gentile, Susan Starr, and Jody Shipley, chair.

602. Report on the Conference of the Society for the Larger Ministry, November 6–8, 1987, Berkeley, CA.

603. The Holmes-Weatherly Award is one of the major awards given out at GA.

604. Spencer Lavan, interview with Kathleen Parker, August 6, 2004.

605. Carol Graywing, tape recording of SLM history reflections, SLM conference, Point Bonita, CA, December 1993.

606. Carolyn McDade, interview with Kathleen Parker, August 30, 2005.

607. Bylaws of the Society for the Larger Ministry, 1994.

608. Jody Shipley, "Reflection on the Theological Sustenance for Good Practice in Community Ministry," unpublished paper, 1987.

609. Neil Gerdes, interview with Kathleen Parker, August 3, 2004.

610. Carolyn McDade, "Spirit of Life," *Singing the Living Tradition* (Boston: Beacon Press, 1993), #123.

611. At present, this song is signed by whole congregations, including the First Unitarian Church of Pittsburgh.

612. The original signers of the Proclamation were Robert Rafford, Neil Gerdes, Orloff Miller, Melvin Hoover, James Zacharias, David Dalrimple, Roberta King Mitchell, Elinor Berke, Susi Pangerl, Linda Hart, Karuna Alan Kistler, Shermie Schafer, Judy Morris, Jody Shipley, Carolyn McDade, Karla Hansen, Cheng Imm Tan, Joseph Chancey, Richard Rodes, Lila Forest, Douglas Strong, Catherine Cogan, Thomas Payne, Stephen Shick, Spencer Lavan, Lillie McGauran, Neil Shadle, John Weston, Stephanie Nichols, Thomas Chulak, John Godbey, Carolyn Mitchell, Susan Grubb, Florence Gelo, Thomas Wakely, Ben Tousley, and Penny Hackett-Evans.

613. David Arksey, unpublished notes for a sermon given at First Unitarian Church, Chicago, Illinois, November 1988.

614. Jody Shipley, unpublished notes for a sermon given at First Unitarian Church, Chicago, Illinois, November 1988.

615. This language is found in Shipley's grant proposal to the UUA Grants Panel for the 1989 conference.

616. Shadle, interview with Parker, August 19, 2004.

617. Charles Howe, interview with Kathleen Parker, September 1, 2005.

618. The text of the bylaws change and the rationale for it was printed in the May 1990 issue of *Crossroads*, SLM's newsletter.

619. Shipley's Bay Area Ministries brochure, produced before the formation of SLM, featured the story of a North Carolina UU prison chaplain, John Frazier, that pointedly highlighted the need for a community ministry credential. Nearly shot in a prisoner intervention, Frazier lamented, "I thought I was going to die right there, and if I had died, who in my denomination would even know I was there or why?" The story is also told by Jody Shipley in "Worth Living For," unpublished sermon, 1987.

620. This article appeared as "Outside Church Walls," by Neil Chethik, *UU World* September/October 1994. It featured the work of Cheng Imm Tan, Donald Robinson, Barbara Jo Sorensen, and David Pettee.

621. *Crossroads,* May 1991.

622. The amended bylaw (Article XI, Section C-11.1) reads in part: "Fellowship may be for the purposes of parish, religious education, and/or community ministry as determined by action of the Ministerial Fellowship Committee."

623. David Pohl, "To Respond, to Engage, to Celebrate, to Challenge,"

sermon at General Assembly sponsored by SLM, Hollywood, Florida, June 1991.

CHAPTER TWENTY:
Community Ministry Since 1991

624. Barbara Child, "The Society for the Larger Ministry: A History of Impassioned Vision Brought to Life," in *Community Ministry: An Opportunity for Renewal and Change—A Report on Research and Reflection by the Starr King Community Ministry Project,* Starr King School for the Ministry, 1995.

625. This was accomplished by amending Article VII, Section 7.6 of the UUA bylaws.

626. Gerdes, interview with Parker, August 2004.

627. Ralph Mero, interview with Kathleen Parker, March 25, 2005.

628. Scott Giles, interview with Kathleen Parker, August 2005.

629. See the website for the Rev. Dr. Scott Giles, www.counselingministries.com.

630. Michelle Bentley, interview with Kathleen Parker, July 12, 2005.

631. Alice Walker says the term "Womanist" may be applied to a black feminist or feminist of color; one who appreciates and prefers women's culture, women's emotional flexibility, and women's strength; one who is committed to the survival and wholeness of an entire people, male and female; and one who is traditionally universalist (with a small "u") as in "'Mama, why are we brown, pink, and yellow, and our cousins are white, beige, and black?' Answer: 'Well, you know the colored race is just like a flower garden, with every flower represented.'" See *In Search of our Mothers' Gardens: Womanist Prose by Alice Walker* (New York: Harcourt Brace Jovanovich, 1967, 1983), p. xi.

632. Michelle Bentley, interview with Kathleen Parker, July 12, 2005.

633. Michelle Bentley, interview with Kathleen Parker, July 12, 2005.

634. Michelle Bentley, interview with Kathleen Parker, July 12, 2005.

635. "UrbanUU: History of the Urban Ministry Efforts of the UUA."

636. The text of this resolution is available at www.uua.org/actions/racialjustice/97uua.html.

637. "The Journey Toward Wholeness Transformation Committee: Vision,

Charge, and History," compiled by Susan Suchocki Brown, member of JTWTC, June 2003.

638. "Continuing the Journey," Report and Recommendations to the 2001 General Assembly from the Journey Toward Wholeness Transformation Committee, Susan Suchocki Brown, Chair (Boston: JTWTC/UUA, 2001).

639. The name Jubilee comes from the ancient Hebrew concept of Jubilee, by which slaves were to be freed and debts were to be forgiven every seventh year.

640. Faithful Fools was founded and is run by the Rev. Dr. Kay Jorgenson and Sister Carmen Barsody, OST. See Faithful Fools Street Ministry: Our Mission, at http://www.faithfulfools.org/.

641. Kurt Kuhwald, interview with Kathleen Parker, October 12, 2005.

642. Tom Chulak, "Reflections on Being White." This paper was delivered to the Greenfield Group (original date unknown). It is one of several resources available to congregations participating in anti-racism and anti-oppression programs.See UUA Anti-Oppression/Anti-Racism: Many Paths, One Journey at www25.uua.org/msd/RE_documents/ UUA%20Anti-opp%20%20Anti-race.pdf.

643. Paula Cole Jones, interview with Kathleen Parker, October 13, 2005.

644. Cole Jones, interview with Parker, October 13, 2005.

645. Frances Barnes, interview with Kathleen Parker, October 7, 2005.

646. These ministerial roles in this period fit within the expanded definition of parish ministry used by the MFC from 1982 to 1991. The official community ministry track was approved by the General Assembly in 1991.

647. Chulak was at that time the New Congregations Program Director and Urban Extension Consultant for the UUA.

648. Tom Chulak, "Community Focused Ministry and the Future of the Unitarian Universalist Association," sermon delivered at the first Conference on Community-Focused Ministry, Roxbury, Massachusetts, November 13, 1986.

649. See Dorothy Emerson's essay "Anti-Racism as Spiritual Practice" in *Everyday Spiritual Practice: Simple Pathways for Enriching Your Life,* ed. Scott Alexander (Boston: Skinner House, 1999).

650. Dorothy May Emerson, interview with Kathleen Parker, September 8, 2005.

651. Dorothy May Emerson, interview with Kathleen Parker, June 17, 2005.

652. Emerson, interview with Parker, June 17, 2005.

653. Dorothy May Emerson, "The Microcredit Revolution," *UU World* March/April 2005, pp. 33–38.

654. Emerson, "Microcredit Revolution," pp. 33–38.

655. Carl Scovel of King's Chapel, for example, opposed the idea that several churches could collectively ordain a minister. Others of the nearly 60 UUUM member congregations simply did not know Tan, or Peter Thoms, who was ordained with her.

656. Neil Chethik, "Outside Church Walls," *UU World* September/October 1994, p. 19.

657. Cheng Imm Tan, "Building Inclusive Cities and What That Demands of Us," sermon delivered at the UUA Continental Conference on Urban Ministries, March 11, 2001, as reported by Deborah Weiner, "Urban Church Conference Participants Celebrate Sunday Worship at Peoples Church in Chicago." See www.uua.org/urbanuu/urbanministriescon ference/sunworship.html.

658. Tan, as reported by Weiner.

659. Chethik, "Outside Church Walls," p. 19.

660. Tan explains that this program was a response to 1996 cutbacks specifically targeting food stamps to legal immigrants.

661. Cheng Imm Tan, sermon delivered at the UUA Continental Conference on Urban Ministries, March 11, 2001, Chicago, Illinois.Reported by Deborah Weiner, "Urban Church Conference Participants Celebrate Sunday Worship at Peoples Church in Chicago." Found at: www.uua. org./urbanuu/urbanministriesconference/sunworship.html

662. Cheng Imm Tan, interview with Kathleen Parker, July 11, 2005.

663. Maddie Sifantus, interview with Kathleen Parker, March 16, 2005.

664. Maddie Sifantus, letter to Kathleen Parker, March 8, 2005.

665. Jose Ballester, interview with Dorothy Emerson, August 10, 2005.

666. Ballester, interview with Emerson, August 10, 2005.

667. Jade Angelica, interview with Kathleen Parker, August 5, 2005.

668. See http://www.uua.org/actions/peace/85march.html.

669. David Pettee, interview with Kathleen Parker, March 24, 2005.

670. Neil Chethik, "Outside Church Walls," *UU World*, September/October, 1994, p. 21.

671. Chethik, "Outside Church Walls," p. 21; Pettee, interview with Parker, March 24, 2005. A note of interest: the First Unitarian Church of San

Francisco is the same church previously served by the Rev. Thomas Starr King and the Rev. Howard Matson.

672. For this course, Pettee developed an overview of community ministry history and collected a number of documents, especially those pertinent to Joseph Tuckerman and William Ellery Channing.

673. Pettee, interview with Parker, July 8, 2005.

674. The chief exceptions to this pattern are found in the ordination of ministers by the Benevolent Fraternity in the 1830s; Charles Barnard and Frederick T. Gray became ministers-at-large to the Benevolent Fraternity in 1834. Also, throughout the nineteenth century, the AUA recognized the ministerial standing of presidents of Harvard Divinity School who had previously served as Unitarian ministers.

675. Ralph Mero, interview with Kathleen Parker, March 25, 2005

676. Scotty McLennan, interview with Parker, June 15, 2005.

677. Neil Gerdes, interview with Kathleen Parker, August 3, 2004.

678. Mero, interview with Parker, 2005; Angelica, interview with Parker, 2005.

679. Neil Shadle, interview with Kathleen Parker, August 19, 2004.

680. Hotchkiss, "Defining Community Ministry."

681. Hotchkiss, "Defining Community Ministry."

682. "Changes in MFC Rules Passed by UUA Board," in *Crossroads, Newsletter of the Society for the Larger Ministry,* Vol. 5, No. 1, February 1992.

683. Westbrook, it will be recalled, served as UUA staff person on the Women and Religion Committee from 1978 to 1981. Ordained to parish ministry in 1973, she was credentialed in community ministry in 1991.

684. Leslie Westbrook, interview with Kathleen Parker, June 29, 2005.

685. Chethik, "Outside Church Walls," p. 19.

686. Mero, interview with Parker, March 25, 2005.

687. Jody Shipley, Report on the Conference of the Society for the Larger Ministry, Berkeley, California, November 6-8, 1987. Meg Whitiker-Greene, interview with Kathleen Parker, September 13, 2005.

688. Patty Franz, interview with Kathleen Parker, June 19, 2005.

689. Leslie Westbrook, interview with Kathleen Parker, March 24, 2005.

690. David Pettee, interview with Kathleen Parker, July 8, 2005.

691. Hotchkiss, "Defining Community Ministry."

CHAPTER TWENTY-ONE:
The Revival of Campus Ministry

692. Mary Ann Macklin, *A Unitarian Universalist Campus Ministry Manual* (Unitarian Universalist Association: Young Adult Ministries Office, 1993), p. 36.

693. Joseph Santos-Lyons, interview with Kathleen Parker, September 6, 2005.

694. Tom Chulak, interview with Kathleen Parker, August 25, 2005.

695. Donna DiSciullo, interview with Kathleen Parker, September 15, 2005.

696. DiSciullo, interview with Parker, September 15, 2005.

697. Santos-Lyons. interview with Kathleen Parker, September 6, 2005.

698. Santos-Lyons. interview with Kathleen Parker, September 6, 2005

699. Santos-Lyons, interview with Parker, September 6, 2005.

700. Devon Wood, interview with Kathleen Parker, September 19, 2005. Wood reports that at Pitt, if you are not on the Council, you have no credibility as a religious presence on campus.

701. Wood, interview with Parker, September 19, 2005.

702. The bequest was a gift from Herbert A. and Dorothea Simon. Herbert Simon was a professor of economics and psychology in the Department of Social and Decision Sciences at Carnegie Mellon University, where he had made hundreds of connections with students. He received the Nobel Prize for his work in economics in 1978. He died at age 84 in February 2001.

703. Wood, interview with Parker, September 19, 2005.

704. See Donald E. Skinner, "UU Young Adult Population Grows in Number and Voice," *UU World* November/December 2003, pp. 57–58.

705. Wood, interview with Parker, September 19, 2005.

706. Wood, interview with Parker, September 19, 2005.

707. Wood, interview with Parker, September 19, 2005.

708. The Clara Barton student, Kierstin Homblette, completed the internship and is now serving in the Peace Corps.

709. Macklin, *Campus Ministry Manual*, p. 7.

710. Wood, interview with Parker, September 19, 2005.

711. Campus Ministry Advisory Committee, "A Call to Work—A Statement on Campus Ministry 2002 and Beyond" (UUA, 2002).

CHAPTER TWENTY-TWO:
The Community Ministry Summit:
A Framework for the Future

712. The several conference locations, set up as a way to reduce travel costs, attest to the logistical challenges of maintaining SLM as an organization.

713. The James Reeb Memorial Lecture became a tradition at GA, sponsored by SLM from 1989 to 1995.

714. Child, "The Society for the Larger Ministry," in *Community Ministry: An Opportunity for Renewal and Change*, pp. 15–16.

715. According to Sue Adams of the Unitarian Universalist Funding Program, the grant from the Fund for Unitarian Universalism was for a total of $8000, of which $2000 was a matching grant. It appears that at least part of the grant was used to fund the development of a book on community ministry; see the Starr King Community Ministry Project report *Community Ministry: An Opportunity for Renewal and Change*. No final report on the UUA grant was submitted. Sue Adams, interview with Dorothy Emerson, July 20, 2005.

716. Although the UUA Board agreed to the Consultation, it was held "at no cost to the UUA" and was supported by an additional grant SLM received for this purpose. In addition, the UUMA contributed funds to cover their participation.

717. Groups represented at the consultation included: SLM, the UUA Board and Staff, the Ministerial Fellowship Committee, the Commission on Appraisal, the UU theological schools, the UUMA, African American and Latino/a UU ministers, and the UUSC.

718. "Recommendations from the Consultation on Community Ministry to the Board of Trustees of the Unitarian Universalist Association," March 1–3, 1996.

719. This history is described in "A Draft Proposal to Redesign Fellowship for Unitarian Universalist Ministry," March 2004, reviewed and amended April 2004.

720. Funding for this book derived from the grant to support a community ministry staff person at the UUSC. Though the book was not published, it has served as an important resource for the present book.

721. Dorothy Emerson, interview with Kathleen Parker, August 18, 2005.

722. Stephen Shick, interview with Kathleen Parker, August 3, 2005.

723. Patty Franz, interview with Kathleen Parker, 2005.

724. Those meeting to revive SLM included Steve Schick, Judy Morris, Linnea Pearson, Jody Shipley, and Marilyn Gentile, according to a promotional flyer, 2000.

725. Jody Shipley, "Under the Golden Arches," *Crossroads: Society for the Larger Ministry*, November 24, 1999.

726. The Community Ministry Focus Group would function like the focus group already in place for ministers of religious education. Because it came out of the UUMA, the CMFG did not include lay ministers. The initial Steering Committee included Roger Brewin, Dorothy Emerson, Anita Farber-Robertson, Ann Galloway-Edge, Jeanne Lloyd, Bonnie Meyer, Suzanne Owens-Pike, Deborah Pope-Lance, and Jody Shipley.

727. Jeanne Lloyd from SLM, Dorothy Emerson from CMFG, and Margie McCue from UUCMC were joined by Maddie Sifantus from both SLM and UUCMC in forming the Planning Committee. Dorothy Emerson wrote the grant proposal to the Fund for Unitarian Universalism. SLM was the fiscal agent. Nancy Bowen served as the facilitator, beginning in March 2003, working with the Planning Committee and continuing after the Summit to facilitate the Coalition.

728. David Hubner, interview with Kathleen Parker, July 21, 2005.

729. The initial grant for the present book had been received from the Fund for Unitarian Universalism just prior to the Summit. Dorothy Emerson wrote the proposal. SLM had agreed to serve as the fiscal agent.

730. Jeanne Lloyd, email to Kathleen Parker, Dorothy Emerson, Maddie Sifantus, David Pettee, and Ralph Mero, June 30, 2005.

731. David Pettee, interview with Kathleen Parker, July 8, 2005.

732. See the SCM Annual Report, FYE June 30, 2005, available at www.uuscm.org.

733. Jeanne Lloyd, interview with Kathleen Parker, March 22, 2005.

734. At GA 2005, Nadine Swahnberg was given the SCM Community Minister of the Year for her work on the Code, and Tom Kirkman, an attorney and SCM board member, was given the Lay Community Minister of the Year award for helping SCM incorporate.

735. Pettee, interview with Parker, July 8, 2005.

736. See http://www.uua.org/aboutus/governance/officers/president/sinkfordwilliam/index.shtml for a biographical sketch of the current UUA president, Bill Sinkford.

737. Lloyd, email to Parker et al, June 2005.

738. David Hubner, interview with Kathleen Parker, July 21, 2005.

739. David Pettee, interview with Kathleen Parker, July 7, 2005.

740. Wayne Arneson, interview with Kathleen Parker, July 13, 2005.

741. Hubner, interview with Parker, 2005.

Conclusion

742. Chulak, interview with Parker, August 2005.

743. This congregation is in a neighborhood that is 62 percent African American. In 2002, the congregation was 98 percent white; now, 37 percent of its members are people of color, and the congregation is 50 percent larger. The Rev. Crestwell has recorded this story in a book, *The Charge of the Chalice: The Davies Memorial Unitarian Universalist Church Growth and Diversity Story*.

744. This project, known as "UU Sankofa: People of Color Archive" is being funded by a grant from the UUFP, obtained via a proposal written by Michelle Bentley. The archive will be housed at the Meadville Lombard library.

Index

Abraham Lincoln Center, 164
Adams, James Luther, 2, 6, 7, 11, 189, 191, 244
Addams, Jane, 137, 160, 165–66, 168, 176
Alinsky, Saul David, 233
  and Industrial Areas Foundation, 233
American Anti-Slavery Society, 92, 104
American Civil Liberties Union, 169
American Congress of Liberal Religious Societies, 184
American Unitarian Association (AUA), 33, 37, 62, 111, 145, 153–57, 163, 169, 177, 181, 190, 192, 197–200, 202, 203
Angelica, Jade, 266–67
  and *The Moral Emergency: Breaking the Cycle of Child Sexual Abuse*, 266
  and *We are Not Alone: A Guidebook for Helping . . . Victims of Sexual Abuse*, 266
Anti-racism:
  Davies, A. Powell Memorial Church, 293
  Dialogue on Race and Ethnicity, (ADORE), 293
  Journey Toward Wholeness Transformation Committee (JTWTC), 257, 258, 293

Jubilee Working Group, 258
JUUST Change Consultancy, 293
Racial and Cultural Diversity Task Force, 257
Racial/Cultural Diversity Resolution of Immediate Witness, 256
"Toward an Anti-Racist UUA" Resolution, 257
UUA Task Force on Anti-Racist Multi-Cultural Congregations, 260
Anthony, Susan B., 51, 54, 83, 127–30, 131, 136, 168
Anti-war movement, 227
Arianism (Arian view), 25
Arksey, David, 223–24, 248, 252
Arminian(ism), 19, 24, 41

Balch, Emily Greene, 3, 169, 173, 175–77
Ballester, Jose, 265–66
Ballou, Adin, 73–76, 92, 98
  and Christian Non-resistance, 75
Ballou, Hosea, 30, 41–43, 83, 118
Barnes, Frances, 259
Barton, Clarissa, 106–08
Bellows, Henry Whitney, 73, 102, 110–11, 117
Benevolent Fraternity of [Unitarian Universalist] Churches, 38, 63, 217, 243, 260, 262, 292
Bentley, Michelle, 3, 254, 255, 259, 287

Berry Street Conference, 33
Berry Street Lecture, 83
Betsworth, Roger, 6
Black and White Action (BAWA), 231
Black Empowerment, 230–32
  Black Affairs Council (BAC), 231
  Black Concerns Working Group, 258
  Black Unitarian Universalist Caucus (BUUC), 231
Blackwell, Alice Stone, 129
Blackwell, Antoinette Brown, 128, 134–35, 136
Boston Athenaeum, 31
Boston Vigilance Committee, 85
Bowen, Nancy, 284
Boyajian, Jane, 243
British and Foreign Unitarian Association, 154
Brook Farm Institute for Education and Agriculture, 77–79
Brown, Egbert Ethelred, 153–57, 182
Brown, John, 50, 89, 93, 103, 109
Brown, Olympia, 135–37, 146
Buck, Florence, 144–45
Buckminster, Joseph Stevens, 30–31, 39
Burleigh, Celia, 138–39, 146
Burns, Anthony, 86–88

"Cakes for the Queen of Heaven," 236 (*see* Women and Religion Committee)
Cambridge Platform, 15
Campus (and Young Adult) Ministry: Bridging Ceremony, 273
  Campus Ministry Advisory Council, 274
  Continental UU Young Adult Network (CUUYAN), 273, 276–77
  UU Campus Ministry Manual, 273
  UUA Campus Ministry Advisory Council, 276
  UUA Continental Youth Council, 274

UUA Office for Young Adult and Campus Ministry, 275
UUA Statement on Campus Ministry (2002), 277
UUA Young Adult Ministries Office, 273
Young Adult and Campus Ministry Pittsburgh, 275
Young Adult Network, 274
Youth Network, 274
Canton Theological School (at St. Lawrence University), 118, 139, 195
Cavileer, Jesse, 209–11
Center Cities Advisory Committee, 217, 232
Channing, William Ellery, 30–39, 92, 96, 119, 292
  and Berry Street Conference, 33
  on self-culture, 81–82
  on Unitarian Christianity, 32
  and Wednesday Evening Association, 34
Channing-Murray Clubs, 201–02
Chapin, Augusta Jane, 137–38, 139
Chauncy, Charles, 18–20, 24
Chavez, Cesar, 213–14
Chicago Children's Choir, 224–25
Chicago Theological Seminary, 252
Child, Lydia Maria, 3, 34, 51, 91–94, 150
  and Harriet Brent Jacobs, 92
Chulak, Tom (Thomas), 219, 226–27, 230, 232, 233, 248, 255, 258, 260, 271–72, 291
Church, Forrest, 10
Church of the Larger Fellowship, 194, 197, 264
Christian Ambassador, 118
Christian Register, 62, 174, 193
Citizens for a Sane Nuclear Energy Policy (SANE), 228
Civil Rights Movement, 205, 218, 232

and Civil Rights Act of 1964, 205
and Voting Rights Act of 1965,
207–08
Clarke, James Freeman, 51, 54, 57,
61–62, 63, 103, 110, 117
Coffin, Paul, 22–23
Cole, David, 244
College Centers Program, 202
Collyer, Robert, 60, 64– 65, 103, 105,
224
Commission on Appraisal
(1935–1936), 189–92
Commission on Appraisal (1986), 243
Commission on Appraisal (1989), 249
COA Report: "Our Professional
Ministry," 249
Commission on Appraisal (1997), 281
Community Church of New York
(*see* John Haynes Holmes)
Community Focused Ministers, 244,
245
*Community Ministry: An Opportuni-
ty for Renewal and Change*, 281
Community Ministry Focus Group,
283, 286–87, 288
Community Ministry Summit
(2003), 239, 279, 284, 285, 287,
289
Community Ministry Coalition, 284,
285
Community Ministry Code of Pro-
fessional Practice, 286
Consultation on Community Min-
istry (1996), 280
Convocation on Community Focused
Ministries (1986), 243, 262
Cooley, Teresa, 272
Cotton, John, 16
Crane, Caroline Bartlett, 143, 173,
177–78
Crane Theological School, 117, 143,
185–86
Crestwell, John T., Jr., 293

Crooker, Florence Ellen Kollock (*see*
Kollock)
Cummins, Robert, 189, 194, 201

Darwin, Charles, 135
De Lange, Mordecai, 59, 60–61, 63,
111
Dial, the, 78
DiSciullo, Donna, 272
and Bridging Ceremony, 273
Divinity School Address, 47–48, 55
Dix, Dorothea Lynde, 84, 96–98,
105–06
Douglass, Frederick, 128
Dred Scott v. Sanford, 101
Dubois, W. E. B., 152, 153, 160
Dunster, Henry, 17

Eliot, Charles, 120, 162
Eliot, Frederick May, 2, 156, 189–93,
199, 200, 201
and Committee of Fourteen, 193
Eliot, John, 16–17
and praying towns, 16 –17
Eliot, Samuel Atkins, 120, 154, 163,
181–83, 188
Eliot, William Greenleaf, 59– 60, 63,
102, 111, 189
Ellis-Hagler, Elizabeth, 262
Emancipation Proclamation, 103
Emerson, Dorothy May, 259– 62
and Friends of the Mystic River, 260
and *Glorious Women: Award-
Winning Sermons About
Women*, 261
and Rainbow Solutions, 261
and *Standing Before Us: Unitarian
Universalist Women and Social
Reform*, 261
and UU Women's Heritage
Society, 260–61
Emerson, Ralph Waldo, 3, 39, 45–50,
76

and Divinity School Address, 47
and Self-Reliance, 47–48
and Slavery, 49
and political parties, 49
"Empowerment: One Denomination's Quest for Racial Justice," 1967–1982", 232
Engel, J. Ronald, 206, 211
Espionage Act (1917), 174
Everyday Church, The, 139–40, 166, 293
Extra Parochial Clergy, 242, 243, 244, 245

Fahs, Sophia Lyon, 3, 189–90, 199
and New Beacon Series, 190, 199
Faithful Fools, 258
Federal Council of Churches in Christ, 195
Fellowship Movement, 197–200
Fisher, Ebenezer, 118–19, 135
Five Smooth Stones, 6–8
Fourier, Charles, 77
Frederick Douglas Center, 142, 175
Free Church Fellowship, 188
Free Religious Association, 111
Fugitive Slave Law, 3, 35, 43, 49, 82, 85–86, 92, 95, 104, 292
Fuller, Margaret, 51–54, 76, 99, 237

Gandhi, Mohandas, 75
Garrison, William Lloyd, 34, 82, 92, 95, 128
and The Liberator, 104
Gautama Buddha, 9–10
Gay, Ebenezer, 18, 24
Gerdes, Neil, 247, 252, 268
Gilbert, Richard S., 5, 10, 11, 171
Gilded Age, 115, 161
Giles, Scott, 253
Gilmartin, David, 279
Gordon, Eleanor, 144
Great Black Migration, 150

Great March for Global Nuclear Disarmament, 229–30, 267 (see also UUPN)
Greeley, Horace, 93, 98–100, 117
Guist, Sue, 230

Harbinger, 78
Harper, Frances Watkins, 94–95, 109, 130, 141
Harvard Divinity School, 39, 46, 57–58, 119–20, 163, 234
Herndon, David, 275
Higginson, Thomas Wentworth, 3, 85–87, 89, 93, 104, 125, 150
Holley, Sallie, 95, 104–05, 128
Holmes, John Haynes, 3, 157, 160, 163–165, 168, 169, 173–75, 186
and Community Church of NY, 164
Holmes-Weatherly Award, 246
Hopedale, 74–76, 78–79
Hosmer, George, 62
Hotchkiss, Daniel, 216, 269, 270
Howe, Charles, 117, 184, 187, 249
Howe, Julia Ward, 95–103, 108, 126, 131
and Battle Hymn of Republic, 103
and Mother's Peace Day, 127
Howe, Samuel Gridley, 95–96, 103, 108, 127
Hubner, David, 284, 285, 288, 289
Huidekoper, Frederick, 60, 61–63
Huidekoper, Harm Jan, 55, 61
Hull House, 142, 165–66
Humanist Manifesto II, (and Humanist) 10, 188, 200, 201
Humiliati, 200
Husbands, Munroe, 197–99

Industrial Areas Foundation, see Alinsky, Saul David
Industrial Workers of the World (IWW), 174

Inquiry into the Foundation, Evidences, and Truths of Religion, 26
Institute for the Church in Urban and Industrial Society, 233
International Congress of Religious Liberals (1905), 184–85, 193
International Congress of Women (1915), 168 176
International Council of Unitarians and Universalists, 221
Iowa Sisterhood, 143–44, 147

Jackson, Jimmy Lee, 205, 209
Jesus, sayings in Nazareth, 9
  feeding large crowds, 9
Jones, Jenkin Lloyd, 111–12, 141, 160, 164–66, 168, 173, 175
  and Jenkin Lloyd Jones Lecture, 232
Jones, Paula Cole, 259
Jordan, Joseph, 150
Jordan, Joseph Fletcher, 152

King, Martin Luther Jr., 75, 206, 208–09
King, Thomas Starr, 60, 65–66, 102–04
Kirkland, John Thornton, 30
Kollock, Florence Ellen (Crooker), 139–140, 167
Kuhwald, Kurt, 258, 285

Latino/a Unitarian Universalist Networking Association (LUUNA), 257
Lavan, Spencer, 226, 246, 294
Liberal Religious Educators Association, 274
Liberal Religious Youth, 201–02, 221, 231, 287
  Also: Young People's Religious Union, 201
  American Unitarian Youth, 201

Universalist Youth Fellowship, 201
Young People's Christian Union, 201
Liuzzo, Viola Gregg, 209
Livermore, Mary, 3, 98, 103, 108–09, 126, 135, 139
  and Northwest Sanitary Fair, 103
Lloyd, Jeanne, 285–86, 288
Lombard College, 137
  L. University, 138
Longview, Lucille Shuck, 234
Lothrop, Samuel Kirkland, 119

Macklin, Mary Ann, 273, 277
  and A Unitarian Universalist Campus Ministry Manual, 273
Mann, Horace, 63, 97
Mann, Rowena Morse, 182–83
Marin Institute for Projective Dream Work, 238
Marshall, George, 5, 9
Massachusetts Association of Universal Restorationists, 74
Masten, Ric, 214–16
Matson, Howard, 212–14, 216, 219
  and UU Migrant Ministry, 212
Matson, Rosemary, 212, 214
Mather, Cotton, 20
May, Samuel Joseph, 34, 82, 89, 128, 138, 150
  and Prudence Crandall, 82
Mayhew, Jonathan, 18, 24
  and Seven Sermons, 19
McDade, Carolyn, 246, 248
McLennan, Scotty (William L.), 217–18, 243, 268
Mero, Ralph, 252, 253, 268–269, 270, 287
  and Compassion in Dying, 253
Meadville Theological School, 59, 61–62, 144–45, 153, 154, 211, 219–21, 223, 226, 246, 247, 252, 253, 254, 294

Miller, Orloff, 3, 202, 206–207
"Mind the Gap" Youth, Campus, and Young Adult Sunday, 274
Ministerial Fellowship Committee (MFC), 212, 216, 218, 221, 224, 232, 243, 251, 252, 267, 270, 279, 280, 281, 288
Ministers Convocation and debate on tracks (2002), 283
Mitchell, Roberta King, 245, 249
Mohammad (and Muslims), 10, 207
Moore, Christopher, 224–226
and Chicago Children's Choir, 224–26
Morris, Judy, 247
Morrison-Reed, Mark, 149, 230, 231, 232
Morse, Jedidiah, 29
Murdoch, Marion, 144–45
Murray, John, 20, 22, 24, 27, 41, 83, 85

National Assoc. for the Advancement of Colored People (NAACP), 143, 159–61, 163, 168, 292
National Assoc. of Colored Women, 109, 142
National Conf. of Unitarian Churches, 110–11
Neutrality Acts, 180
New England Non-resistance Society, 84
Niagara Movement, 159–60
Nichols, Stephanie, 230
Nobel Peace Prize, 168, 177

Olsen, Clark, 206–07
Olson, Beverly, 272,
Ovington, Mary White, 159–61, 165, 168

Pacific Unitarian School, 120–21
Parker, Theodore, 3, 56, 76, 87–89, 93, 110, 174, 150

Payne, Thom, 244
Peabody, Ephraim, 55, 60, 62–63
Peabody, Francis Greenwood, 3, 119–120, 161–63
Perin, George L., 167–68
and Bethany Home for Young Women, 168
and Franklin Square House, 167
Pettee, David, 230, 267–68, 270, 286, 287, 289
Picket, Eugene, 227, 271
Pohl, David 243, 250
Pope-Lance, Deborah, 236–37
Powers, Carol, 230
Priestley, Joseph, 19
Prophets, Isaiah, Amos, 8–9

Rafford, Robert, 241, 245
Ranck, Shirley, 236
Reeb, James, 3, 206–09, 219, 231
Reeves, Gene, 254
Reinhardt, Aurelia Henry, 173, 178–79, 190–91
Restorationist Universalism, 53, 83, 84, 98, 119
Rich, Caleb, 21, 24
Ripley, George, 74, 76–78
and Associationism, 77
and Fourierism, 77
Robinson, David, 19, 30, 31, 48, 76, 117, 161, 163, 192, 198
Rush, Benjamin, 23–24, 85, 86, 150

Safford, Mary, 144
Sanitary Commission, U.S., 102–04, 123, 127, 292
Santos-Lyons, Joseph, 274
Sawyer, Thomas Jefferson, 99, 117–19
Seaburg, Carl, 252
Second Great Awakening, 81
Secret Six, 87
Sedition Act (1918), 174

Shadle, Neil, 3, 16, 89, 211–12, 219, 246, 249, 250, 254, 259, 269, 279
and James Reeb Memorial Lecture, 279
Shick, Steve, 228–29, 233–34, 244, 249, 251, 252, 253, 265, 279, 280
Shinn, Quillen Hamilton, 60, 66–69, 151, 265
Shipley, Jody, 242, 246, 247, 248, 249, 264, 270, 279, 281, 283, 284
and Community Ministry Council (1996), 281
and *Guidelines for Affiliation . . .* , 282
and UU Community Ministry Center, 282
Sifantus, Maddie, 263–65, 281, 285
and Golden Tones, 263–65
Sinkford, Bill, 287
Skinner, Clarence Russell, 173, 179, 185–87, 194, 200, 201
Social Darwinism, 161, 163
Social Gospel Movement, 3, 11, 120, 145, 161, 164–65, 171, 185, 188
Socinian View, 26
Society for Community Ministries (SCM), 285
Society for the Larger Ministry, 237, 241, 245, 247, 250, 251, 267, 270, 279, 280, 281, 283, 285
SLM *Crossroads*, 270, 282
SLM Proclamation, 247, 248, 287
SLM Task Force on Fellowshipping, 280
SLM Task Force on Ministerial Fellowship, 249
Sorenson, Barbara Jo, 279
Southworth, Rev. Franklin, 153
Spear, Charles, 83–84, 89
Spear, John Murray, 83–85, 89
Specialized Minister, 212, 213, 214, 243
Spiritualism, 85

Standing Before Us: Unitarian Universalist Women and Social Reform, 261
Stanton, Elizabeth Cady, 51, 83, 128–30, 136, 137
and *The Woman's Bible*, 130, 137
Starr King School for Religious Leadership (Ministry), 222
Starr King School for the Ministry, 242, 267, 287
St. Lawrence University, 67, 118, 135, 137, 139
Strong, Douglas Morgan, 248
Stone, Lucy, 125–26, 128, 129–130, 131, 134, 136
Student Religious Liberals, 202–03
Sunderland, Eliza Jane Read, 145–46
Sunderland, Jabez T., 112–13, 146
Supernatural Rationalism, 18, 25

Tan, Cheng Imm, 251, 252, 262, 263
and Asian Women's Task Force Against Domestic Violence, 263
and Gund Kwok, 263
and New Bostonians, 263
and Ricesticks and Tea, 263, 292
Taylor, Jeremy, 221–22
Tholuck, Frederick A. G., 161–62
Tino, Michael, 275
Toynbee Hall, 139, 165, 167
Trachtenberg, Alan, 6
Transcendentalism, Transcendentalist Club, 4, 47, 50, 52, 56, 68, 99, 110, 141, 183
Tuckerman, Joseph, 30, 34–39, 63, 292
and Ministry-at-Large, 37
and Society for Seamen, 36
Tufts College [University], 117–18, 294

Ultra-Universalism, 42, 43, 54
Unitarian Service Committee, 192–93

Unity (periodical), 111–12, 175
Unitarian Universalist Association (UUA), 203, 212, 215, 286
UUA Social Action Clearing House, 235
Unitarian Universalist Ministers' Association, 222
Unitarian Universalist Peace Network (UUPN), 227, 229
   The Great March for Global Nuclear Disarmament, 229–30, 267
Unitarian Universalist Service Committee (UUSC), 227, 233, 265, 280
   and Promise the Children, 233
   and Just Works, 233
Universalist Church of America, 194, 195, 203
Universalist General Convention, 67, 68, 117, 151, 184, 194
Universalist Leader, 138
Universalist Quarterly, 118
Universalist Washington Avowal, 195
Urban Church Coalition, 217, 232, 233, 243, 256
   and Industrial Areas Foundation, 233
   and Jenkin Lloyd Jones Lecture, 232
   "Restoring Our Theology of Hope," 256
Urban Church Profile (1994), 257
UUA Commission on Community Ministry, 280
UUA Commission on Race and Religion, 230
   and Emergency Conference of Unitarian Universalist Response to the Black Rebellion, 230
UUA Department of Ministry, 253, 266, 269
UUA Ministerial and Professional Leadership Staff Group, 284, 288
UUA Office of Advocacy and Witness, 277

UUA Statement of Principles and Purposes (1985), 232
UUA Task Force on Community Ministry, 250
UU Community Ministry Center, 283, 285
UU Professional Leadership Coordinating Council (2005), 288
UU Urban Concerns and Ministry Committee, 232, 257, 287
UU Urban Ministry, 262, 263, 292
   Renewal House, 262, 292
   Ricesticks and Tea, 263, 292
   United Souls, 292
UU Legal Ministry, 260
UU Women's Federation, 277
   and Clara Barton Internship, 277
UU Women's Heritage Society, 260–61
UUMA Task Force on Categories, 281
UUMA Committee on Categories, 283

Villard, Oswald Garrison, 160

Ware, Henry Jr., 30, 39–41, 46, 119
Ware, Henry Sr., 25–27, 29
Ware Lecture, 169, 179
Washington, Booker T., 151, 159, 160
Washington University, 59
Wells (Barnett), Ida B., 109, 160
Westbrook, Leslie, 231, 235–36, 270
Western Messenger, 55, 63
Western Unitarian Conference, 61, 110–11, 112, 124, 141
Westminster Confession, 25
Weston, John, 250, 287
Wheelock, Eleazar, 17
   and Dartmouth College, 18
Whittemore, Thomas, 30, 41–43, 63, 118, 150
Wilbur, Earl Morse, 120–21
Williams, Fannie Barrier, 141–43

Willis, Annie B. Jordan, 152–53
and Jordan Neighborhood House, 152
Winchester Profession, 41, 67, 74, 184
and Liberty Clause, 184
Wise, Thomas E., 151
Woman Suffrage:
AWSA, 124–25, 128–29, 137
History of Woman's Suffrage, 129
National Assoc. of Colored Women, 109, 142
National Woman's Party, 136
National Women's Rights Convention, 99, 135
New England Woman's Suffrage Assoc., 126
NAWSA, 130, 168
NWSA, 124, 128–29, 136
Woman's Journal, The, 126
Woman's Centenary Aid Assoc., 123–24, 151
Women's Christian Temperance Union (WCTU), 129
Woman's Peace Party, 168, 176
Women and Religion Committee, 235
and "Beyond this Time: A Conference on Women and Religion", 235
and "Cakes for the Queen of Heaven," 236
and "Rise up and Call her Name," 236
and Women and Religion Convocation on Feminist Theology, 235–36
Women and Religion Resolution, 234, 235
and Affirmative Action for Women Ministers Committee, 235, 236
Women's International League for Peace and Freedom, 137, 169, 176
Wood, Devon, 275–77

Woolley, Celia Parker, 141–43, 144, 147, 168, 175
World Congress of Representative Women, 140, 142, 146, 147
World Parliament of Religions, 112, 127, 138, 142, 146, 147, 175, 184
Women's Committee of, 138
Wright, Conrad, 19, 26, 40

Zacharias, Jim, 222–23

Printed in the United States
214626BV00001B/154/A

9 780979 558900